MW00718575

Taming the River

Taming the River

Negotiating the Academic, Financial, and Social Currents in Selective Colleges and Universities

Camille Z. Charles

Mary J. Fischer

Margarita A. Mooney

Douglas S. Massey

with assistance from

Gniesha Dinwiddie

Brooke Cunningham

PRINCETON UNIVERSITY PRESS *Princeton and Oxford*

Published by Princeton University Press, 41 William Street, Princeton, New Jersey 08540

In the United Kingdom: Princeton University Press, 6 Oxford Street, Woodstock, Oxfordshire OX20 1TW

Library of Congress Cataloging-in-Publication Data

Taming the river : negotiating the academic, financial, and social currents in selective colleges and universities / Camille Z. Charles . . . [et al.].

p. cm.

Includes bibliographical references and index.

ISBN 978-0-691-13964-7 (hardcover : alk. paper) 1. College students—United States—Social conditions. 2. Minorities—Education (Higher)—United States. 3. Academic achievement—United States. I. Charles, Camille Zubrinsky, 1965–

LC208.8.T36 2009

378.1′980973—dc22 2008031874

British Library Cataloging-in-Publication Data is available

This book has been composed in Minion and Myriad

Printed on acid-free paper. ∞

press.princeton.edu

Printed in the United States of America

10 9 8 7 6 5 4 3 2 1

Contents

List of Tables and Figures

Tables

Figures

Acknowledgments

The authors would like to thank the Andrew W. Mellon Foundation for its generous support of the National Longitudinal Survey of Freshmen, and particularly William Bowen and Harriet Zuckerman for their continuing interest in and support for the project. We would also like to thank Mitchell Stevens, Kimberly Torres, Rachel Brunn, Nicholas Ehrmann, and two anonymous reviewers for their helpful comments and suggestions on an earlier draft.

Taming the River

1 Entering the Current

A contentious debate has raged over race-conscious admissions policies at selective U.S. colleges and universities since the end of the civil rights era. After decades of exclusion, the nation's elite colleges and universities, beginning in the 1970s, undertook a series of "affirmative actions" designed to ensure the inclusion of formerly underrepresented minorities within bastions of academic privilege. Overnight, college admissions officials sought to transform prestigious campuses from citadels of whiteness into diverse reflections of an increasingly multiracial society. Owing to their historical exclusion from selective institutions of higher education, minority group members generally lacked the family connections that would entitle them to special consideration as "legacy" students. At the same time, owing to the ongoing segregation and stratification of American education, Latinos and African Americans often lacked the academic preparation necessary to succeed in a very competitive admissions process. Paradoxically they also lacked athletic experience, not in football or basketball, but in elite sports such as swimming, tennis, golf, lacrosse, squash, fencing, and water polo that together account for a large share of athletic recruitments at selective institutions.

Inevitably, therefore, efforts by college administrators to incorporate underrepresented minorities somehow had to take race and ethnicity into account, quickly leading to charges of "reverse racism" and "affirmative discrimination" (see Lokos 1971; Glazer 1976). Over the ensuing decades the fight over race-sensitive admissions was enjoined on a variety of fronts—political, legal, administrative, and academic. As with many contentious public issues, a salient feature of the debate on affirmative action was a lack of reliable information about its implementation and effects. To remedy this situation, William G. Bowen and Derek Bok, in the mid-1990s launched the College and Beyond Survey, which surveyed the 1979 and 1989 cohorts of freshmen from a set of selective colleges and universities, seeking to learn about their college experiences and subsequent achievements.

These data, summarized in *The Shape of the River* (1998), documented the positive consequences of affirmative action for minority students, their communities, and for American society generally in the years following the students' college graduation. The authors argued that instead of abandoning the social experiment, Americans should seek to know more about "the shape of the river" (borrowing a phrase from Mark Twain) and should consider the multiple "downstream" benefits to society as minority students' lives unfolded over many years, weighing these against whatever short-term costs might be incurred by taking race and ethnicity into account during college admissions.

As is often the case with social science research, *The Shape of the River* raised as many questions as it answered, for it also uncovered significant differentials between racial and ethnic groups in their academic achievement during college. Among those admitted to selective institutions in the 1989 cohort, for example, 96% of Asians ultimately graduated, compared with 94% of whites, 90% of Latinos, but just 79% of African Americans. The groups also evinced substantial gaps in grade point average and time taken to graduate. More distressingly, these intergroup differentials persisted after controlling for the usual background variables, such as academic ability (SAT scores) and socioeconomic status (parental education and income).

Sorting out which factors contributed to academic success at selective institutions was impossible using the *College and Beyond Survey*, given that it interviewed students long after their college years had ended. In order to examine the determinants of academic achievement directly, a new prospective study known as the National Longitudinal Survey of Freshmen (NLSF) was launched. Large, representative samples of white, Asian, Latino, and black freshmen entering twenty-eight selective colleges and universities in the fall of 1999 were surveyed and reinterviewed in 2000, 2001, 2002, and 2003, essentially following the cohort of freshmen entering

Bowen and Bok's sample of schools as they became sophomores, juniors, and, ultimately for most, graduating seniors.

The baseline survey—a personal interview lasting up to two hours—gathered detailed information about students' lives up to the point of their arrival on campus and compiled comprehensive data on their attitudes, expectations, and values. The first book analyzing these data sought to document background differences between groups and to determine their effects on academic achievement during the very first term of college. Continuing Bowen and Bok's metaphor, Massey et al. (2003) called their book *The Source of the River*, for it documented individual and group characteristics with respect to family, neighborhood, school, and peer settings—that is, the social origins or "source" of the "river" of students entering elite schools during 1999. After describing intergroup differences along a variety of social and economic dimensions, the authors estimated statistical models to determine their effect on initial academic performance during the first term in college.

The current volume picks up where *The Source of the River* left off. Rather than dwelling on where the students came from, we build on this knowledge to move forward and examine the social and academic experiences of students during the first two years of college. Recent research suggests that most of the improvements in substantive knowledge and academic skill that take place in college transpire in the first two years (Osterlind 1996, 1997), especially in math and science (Flowers et al. 2001). Choices made as freshmen and sophomores—about which courses to take, which majors to select, which professors to seek out, and how much time to devote to academic pursuits—thus have strong effects in constraining or enhancing later academic possibilities (Pascarella and Terenzini 2005).

In a very real way, therefore, the first two years of college constitute the foundation upon which future academic and intellectual achievements will ultimately be built. Continuing the river metaphor begun by Bowen and Bok (1998), we now turn to consider the experiences of students as they wade into the crosscutting currents of college life and begin the long process of *taming the river* of higher education. Before examining the nature of these crosscurrents and the degree to which students are successful in taming them, however, we recap what we have learned—substantively and theoretically—about student origins and their influence on academic achievement from *The Source of the River*.

Substantive Lessons from *The Source*

The NLSF baseline survey offered the first in-depth look at the characteristics not only of blacks, Latinos, and Asians entering America's prestigious institutions of higher education but also of European-origin whites. The process of admission to elite institutions of higher education has never been strictly "meritocratic" and certainly not "scientific" in any meaningful sense of the word. Gaining admission to an elite school has always depended on a complicated alchemy that blends academic qualifications, athletic abilities, geographical location, gender considerations, family connections, and personal interests, not to mention more random chance than most students and college admissions offices would care to admit (Shulman and Bowen 2001; Steinberg 2002.

Among the various "nonacademic" admissions criteria routinely considered in college admissions, race and ethnicity have received by far the greatest attention and the lion's share of the public criticism (see Curry 1996). Minority affirmative action, however, is just one of *three* large preferential admissions programs common at America's selective colleges and universities (Massey and Mooney 2007). In addition to underrepresented minorities, elite schools also give extra consideration to athletes (Shulman and Bowen 2001) and the children of alumni (Karabel 2005). Indeed, statistical analyses show that being an athlete or the child of an alumnus greatly increases the odds of admission to a selective college or university, controlling for a variety of personal and academic variables (Espenshade, Chung, and Walling 2004). In practice, moreover, both athletic and "legacy" recruitment enhance the already advantaged position of affluent whites in the competition for scarce entry slots (Golden 2006; Schmidt 2007), leading some to call for colleges to pay greater attention to social class in the admissions process (Bowen et al. 2005).

Consistent with these findings, *The Source of the River* documented stark differences in socioeconomic background across racial and ethnic groups. Whatever the particular alchemy prevailing in college admissions during 1999, the selection criteria then in force produced socially and economically homogeneous cohorts of white freshmen but diverse cohorts of black and Latino freshmen. Although Asians were slightly more diverse than their white counterparts, their backgrounds were much closer to those of whites than to those of other minority groups. The typical white or Asian student grew up in an intact family and attended a resource-rich suburban or private school; both parents were college graduates; most fathers held an advanced degree and worked at a professional or managerial job; a large plurality of mothers also held advanced degrees, and most also worked in a white-collar occupation, thus yielding a family income high enough to enable ownership of a valuable home.

In contrast to this relatively clear portrait of homogeneous socioeconomic privilege among white and Asian students, it was virtually impossible to generalize about the socioeconomic status or demographic background of Latino and black students. They were just as likely to be the children of well-heeled, highly educated suburban professionals as to be the offspring of single, inner-city welfare mothers who never finished high school. The most salient feature about black and Latino freshmen was their social, economic, and demographic diversity. They came from all walks of life and all socioeconomic backgrounds.

Prior research has documented a sharp divergence in child-rearing practices along the lines of both class (Kohn 1985; Lareau 2000) and race (Lareau 2003). Whereas middle-class white parents generally adopt a strategy of "concerted cultivation" in raising and educating their children, lower-class and minority parents tend to stand back more passively and simply facilitate "the accomplishment of natural growth" (Lareau 2003: 2–3). Thus, middle- and upper-class parents are very directly involved in scheduling their children's time, participating in their educational decisions, interacting with teachers and counselors, and promoting a sense of autonomy and, ultimately, entitlement among their children. In contrast, working-class and poor parents assume a more passive role in their children's development, deferring to educational authorities, promoting obedience at home and school, and leaving children to interact among themselves rather than organizing their lives, all of which tend to produce a "sense of constraint" rather than entitlement among less-advantaged children.

Consistent with Lareau's work, *The Source of the River* showed that students in different racial and ethnic groups experienced very different styles of child rearing while growing up. Whites generally reported a supportive, companionate style of child rearing, as one would expect given their high average class standing. Parents were involved in their lives, knew their friends, took an active role in developing their educational skills, and were reluctant to make use of punishment, shame, or guilt to secure compliant behavior. Instead they used reasoning and explanation to encourage autonomy, independence, and self-regulation. In contrast, black parents were much less involved in cultivating their children's educational skills and monitoring their social relationships, and they relied more heavily on a regime of reward and punishment combined with strict limits on behavior, though without much reliance on guilt or shame. Asian parents were the least companionate and in terms of discipline the strictest of all groups. In addition to relying heavily on punishment to secure compliant behavior, they were also the most likely to employ guilt and shame as a strategy in child raising, and they were largely uninvolved in cultivating their children's educational or social skills. As parents, Latinos were a mixed bag—generally more authoritarian and less companionate than white parents, and less involved in their children's education or social relations, but relatively unlikely to rely on shame and guilt as tools in child rearing.

American culture historically has employed a "one-drop rule" to define race, labeling all people with any discernable African ancestry as "black" (Sweet 2005) and thus rendering race what sociologists call a "master status," a categorization that trumps others and renders diversity within the black population largely invisible to white Americans (Hughes 1945). Nonetheless, recent work has underscored the growing diversity of America's black population (Kasinitz 1992; Spencer 1997; Waters 1999; Rockquemore and Bunsma 2002), especially on college campuses (Smith and Moore 2000; Charles, Torres, and Brunn 2007; Massey et al. 2007). Apart from documenting the heterogeneity of African Americans with respect to socioeconomic status and family background, *The Source of the River* revealed diversity along three additional dimensions, the first of which was gender. Specifically, on the campuses of elite colleges and universities, black males were hugely underrepresented relative to black females. Whereas white, Asian, and Latino freshmen evinced a rough parity between male and female students, black women outnumbered black men by a margin of two to one, with obvious implications for dating, mating, and gender dynamics, issues that we will explore later in this volume.

In addition, we found that immigrants and the children of immigrants were hugely overrepresented among black freshmen at elite institutions. Whereas first- and second-generation immigrants constituted only around 13% of 18–19-year-old African Americans in 1999, they comprised a quarter of all black freshmen entering elite institutions that year (Massey et al. 2007). Although large fractions of Asian and Latino freshmen were also of immigrant origin, in these groups the high percentage of immigrants and their children accurately reflected conditions in the general population.

Whereas 97% of Asians and 73% of Latinos in the NLSF were first- or second-generation immigrants, their respective shares in the population of 18–19-year-olds were 91% and 66% (Massey et al. 2007).

Finally, *The Source of the River* reported that biracial children were substantially overrepresented among African American freshmen. Whereas only around 4% of blacks identify themselves as multiracial nationwide (Spencer 1997), 17% of black freshmen in the NLSF did so, suggesting that a rather large share of black freshmen at selective schools had at least one nonblack parent. Black diversity with respect to class background, when combined with an overrepresentation of foreign and multiracial origins, virtually guarantees a lengthy conversation among African American students on campus about what it means to be "black" and what the "true" components of a black identity really are (Torres and Charles 2004; Charles, Torres, and Brunn 2008; Torres 2008). For collegiate African Americans, especially, racial identity is more problematic and contentious than it used to be.

Within the United States, blacks and to a lesser extent Latinos remain segregated from whites and Asians in schools (Orfield 2001) and neighborhoods (Charles 2003). It is not surprising, therefore, that virtually all white and Asian students interviewed in the NLSF came of age in white-dominant settings that contained very few African Americans or Latinos. Most Asian and white freshmen experienced little interracial contact before college, and their arrival on campus was their first opportunity to meet and interact with blacks and Latinos on a sustained, equal-status, face-to-face basis. The same was true for a significant subset of blacks and Latinos who grew up living in racially isolated neighborhoods and attended segregated, inner-city schools. They also had little experience with other-race peers prior to their arrival on campus. But another subset of blacks and Latinos grew up in integrated neighborhoods and attended racially diverse schools that afforded considerable opportunities for interracial contact and experience.

In terms of the quality of the students' residential and educational environments, the sample divided clearly into two basic categories. On the one hand were whites and Asians, along with African Americans and Latinos who grew up in integrated settings. They generally experienced high-quality schools filled with resources and well-developed infrastructures, located in peaceful neighborhoods within which disorder and violence were rare. On the other hand were blacks and Latinos who grew up under conditions of high segregation. For them, the quality of instruction was significantly lower, resources were less plentiful, infrastructures more deteriorated, and daily life in hallways and on the streets was characterized by remarkably high rates of exposure to social disorder and violence.

These contrasting backgrounds yielded different levels of preparation for college life. Perhaps the best prepared were blacks and Latinos who grew up under conditions of integration. Not only were they well prepared academically and possessed of a high degree of self-confidence and self-efficacy; they were also unique among freshmen in having considerable interracial and interethnic experience. By virtue of their upbringing within integrated schools and neighborhoods, they were comfortable in multiracial settings within which they were not a majority and which required interacting with people of diverse backgrounds.

While less prepared socially for the diversity of college life, whites and Asians were highly prepared on most other dimensions. On average, they were the most prepared academically and financially to assume the challenge of an elite college education. Moreover, although their prior experience with blacks and Latinos may have been limited, the campus environment they entered was overwhelmingly white and possessed of an academic culture with which they were quite familiar. The main difference between Asians and whites was that Asians displayed lower levels of self-esteem, self-confidence, and self-efficacy—indeed they were the lowest of all groups on these three psychological dimensions.

At the other extreme of the continuum of self-perception were blacks and Latinos who grew up under conditions of high segregation, who not only evinced high degrees of self-esteem, self-confidence, and self-efficacy, but also a high degree of racial pride and in-group solidarity. As already noted, however, they also perceived themselves as being at the greatest social distance from whites and were least prepared academically in terms of their own self-assessment as well as objective indicators such as high school grades, advanced placement courses, and SAT scores.

Theoretical Lessons from *The Source*

Although *The Source of the River* considered the effect of these background differences on grade performance only during the first term of the freshman year, significant differences had already emerged between groups.

Although grades across all racial and ethnic categories generally fell into the B range and few reported failing a course, intergroup differences in grade point average (GPA) were nonetheless significant. Whereas whites and Asians evinced very similar GPAs of 3.31 and 3.28, respectively, Latinos lagged behind at 3.05, and blacks trailed at 2.95. These performance differentials were most strongly and consistently predicted by indicators of academic preparation (which were, as already mentioned, strongly influenced by segregation), followed by parental education and, to a lesser extent, self-confidence and sensitivity to peer influence.

The analyses performed in *Source* endeavored to test several leading theories of minority underachievement. The theory of *capital deficiency* argues that differences in performance reflect differences in access to various forms of capital while growing up—financial, social, cultural, and, of course, human capital, the label economists have given to skills and education (Jencks 1972). This hypothesis received strong support in that differences in parental education, income, and wealth translated directly into different levels of preparation along a variety of dimensions, and differences in preparation, in turn, translated directly into differences in academic performance. Parental education also had a strong direct effect on college GPA (with preparation and other key variables held constant), underscoring the important role played by parents in shaping the educational trajectories of their children long after they have left home (Cameron and Heckman 1999).

The theory of *stereotype threat* argues that blacks are very well aware of negative societal stereotypes about their group's intellectual ability, and that this awareness transforms any academic evaluation into a psychologically threatening event: if blacks do their best and still come up short, they confirm the stereotype of black intellectual inferiority, not only to themselves but to everyone else. To compensate, they disinvest in academics as a domain of self-evaluation by studying less and generally making less of a scholastic effort (Steele 1998, 1999). If they do not succeed, rather than confirming that the stereotype might be true, they can attribute the failure to their self-conscious lack of effort. *The Source of the River* uncovered considerable evidence for this hypothesis, finding that minority students who doubted their own ability and were sensitive to the views of others earned significantly lower grades than other students.

Another prominent explanation for black underachievement is the *theory of oppositional culture*, which argues that black students view educational success to be a component of "white" identity and reject it as a betrayal of racial authenticity. This conceptualization of racial identity is strongly reinforced by peer culture, so that even those who are well positioned to do well in school are reluctant to perform well for fear of being accused of "acting white" by their peers (Ogbu 1977). The NLSF data offered no evidence that this mechanism had anything to do with the grade performance of African Americans at selective colleges or universities, however. Both in high school and as college students black respondents reported having peers that strongly supported and valued educational success; and indicators developed to assess susceptibility to negative peer pressure among blacks and Latinos had no significant effect in predicting college grades.

Finally, results were supportive of broader *structural theories of stratification*, which argue that social and economic features of society that are beyond individual or family control put members of some groups in a position to gain access to and excel in selective schools while leaving others without the resources they need to achieve success (Bowles and Gintis 1976; McDonough 1997; Rothstein 2004). In *The Source of the River*, the feature of American social structure that seemed to carry the most weight in accounting for intergroup differences in academic performance was racial-ethnic segregation—which as already noted is still a pervasive feature of American schools and neighborhoods (see Iceland, Weinberg, and Steinmetz 2002; Kozol 2005). Black and Latino students who grew up under conditions of school and neighborhood segregation experienced lower-quality educations and were exposed to higher levels of disorder and violence than those who came of age within integrated schools and neighborhoods, giving the students from segregated backgrounds personal characteristics that left them with less ability to excel in the highly competitive milieu of selective academia.

Beyond *The Source* and into the Stream

To sum up what we have learned so far: prior work with the National Longitudinal Survey of Freshmen has documented very clear differences in early grade performance between whites, African Americans, Latinos, and Asians. These differentials, which emerged during the first term of college study, were strongly associated with preexisting differences in social and academic preparation that themselves reflected differential access to various forms of capital—financial, human, social, and cultural—between blacks and Latinos, on the one hand, and Asians and whites, on the other. The differential access to education-related capital was, in turn, structured by the ongoing segregation of American society, which isolates blacks and Latinos in disadvantaged settings characterized by a paucity of resources. We found no evidence that segregation contributed to the formation of an oppositional culture that undermined grade performance. We did find, however, that America's historical legacy of racism—and specifically the stereotyping of African Americans as intellectually inferior—lowered the grades of minority students by raising the level of threat implicit in the academic evaluations that are an inevitable part of college life.

Despite the seeming clarity of these findings, the analyses done to date are substantively and theoretically limited because they took no account of developments in the students' lives on campus. *The Source of the River* focused entirely on precollege characteristics and determined their influence on grades earned during the first academic term. Although controlling for preexisting differences mitigated intergroup differences in grade performance, it did not eliminate them; nor did knowing the importance of students' backgrounds provide any insight into *how* differences in grade performance came about within the collegiate context. In addition to these substantive limitations, moreover, the reliance on first-term GPA as the sole academic outcome did not permit the consideration of important theories of college achievement that focus on what students do and how they are incorporated into the academic milieu.

The most prominent of these theories is the model of student integration developed by Vincent Tinto (1993). He focused on the process of dropping out and argued that leaving college is much like the process of exiting other human communities—departure generally reflects the absence of effective integration and the social supports it provides. Although Tinto focused on dropping out, we generalize his analysis here by noting that even though school departure may be signaled by a discrete act such as failing to enroll for the next academic term or not graduating, in reality it is as much a process as an event. In most cases the final action is preceded by the accumulation of a variety of signs of social and academic disengagement. In the academic realm, these signs include earning low grades, failing multiple classes, dropping too many courses, and ultimately failing to accumulate course credits in a reasonable time. In the social realm, the signs include a lack of friends or study partners, nonparticipation in campus groups or organizations, and a sense of alienation and estrangement from other students, faculty, and the campus community generally. As these manifestations of disengagement accumulate, satisfaction with social and academic life on campus declines and leads ultimately to the expression of a radical outcome: expulsion, transfer, delayed graduation, or the decision to abandon higher education altogether.

In other words, according to Tinto, college students who earn low grades, fail to accumulate credits, and drop out are those who are insufficiently attached, socially and academically, to the college or university they have chosen to attend:

> An institution's capacity to retain students is directly related to its ability to reach out and make contact with students and integrate them into the social and intellectual fabric of institutional life. It hinges on the establishment of a healthy, caring educational environment which enables all individuals, not just some, to find a niche in one or more of the many social and intellectual communities of the institution. (1993: 204–5)

Figure 1.1 offers a schematic of our interpretation of Tinto's theory of social and economic integration in college. As indicated on the left side of the diagram, each student enters college with a certain educational background and family background that jointly determine his or her academic skills and abilities. These skills and abilities, along with the student's educational and family background, combine to determine overall aspirations, both in terms of academic goals and overall commitment to the institution. Goals and commitment, in turn, condition a student's experience on campus with respect to academic performance, interactions with faculty and staff members, peer group interactions, and participation in extracurricular activities. These specific campus experiences yield more or less academic and social integration within the particular educational institution, and students who are more integrated are more likely to make additional social and academic investments, which reinforces the foregoing cycle to promote further integration and continued investments in social and academic activities, resulting in higher grades, more courses completed, greater academic and social satisfaction, and ultimately progress toward college graduation.

Whereas *The Source of the River* focused on precollege experiences and the arrows depicted on the left-hand side of figure 1.1, here we focus on the pathways depicted to the right of the figure, seeking to measure aspirations, experiences, and integration during the first two years of higher education

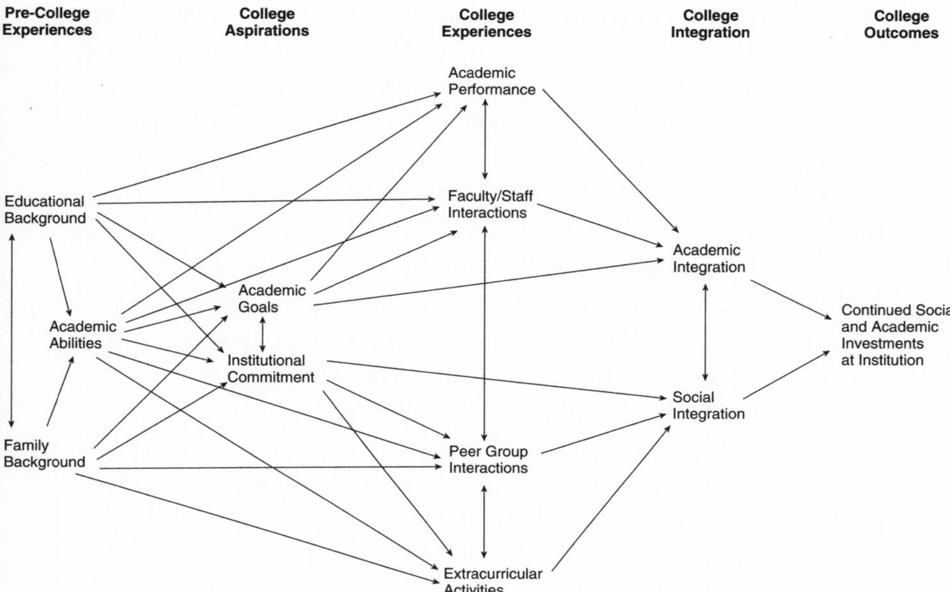

Figure 1.1
Schematic representation of Tinto's model of social and academic progress within college

and to use these measures to predict educational outcomes such as grade performance. In designing later waves of the NLSF, therefore, we self-consciously sought to develop survey instruments that would enable us to measure the constructs and concepts depicted in figure 1.1. The data analyzed in this book come mainly from follow-up surveys conducted among NLSF respondents during the spring of their freshmen and sophomore years (i.e., calendar years 2000 and 2001). In contrast to the baseline survey, the follow-ups were administered via telephone and were much shorter, usually lasting only around forty minutes.

In order to avoid building selection bias into the out-year samples, we attempted to follow and reinterview all students from the baseline survey, including dropouts (those who had left school with no plans to return), "stopouts" (those currently not enrolled but planning to return), and transfers (those who had reenrolled at another institution). In *The Source of the River*, we described in considerable detail the nature and characteristics of the sample, and we included a list of the institutions invited to participate in the NLSF, along with the names and characteristics of those schools that ultimately joined the study and detailed profiles of the respondents along a variety of social and economic dimensions. Rather than repeat this information, we invite readers to consult the book, whose appendix also contains a copy of the baseline questionnaire (which is also available publicly on the project website).

Table 1.1 shows response rates achieved in the two follow-up surveys. The freshman follow-up occurred only a few months after the baseline, of course, and completion rates are therefore very high, ranging narrowly from 93.7% among whites to 96.0% for blacks, with an overall average of 95%. The sophomore year follow-up, of course, occurred an average of twelve months after the second wave, and the response rates are correspondingly lower but still quite high by the standards of contemporary survey research. The overall response rate on sophomore follow-up was roughly 89%, with a range of 87.8% for whites to 89.3% for Asians. Completion rates are always computed relative to the baseline, not the prior wave. Thus, during all rounds of the survey, interviewers endeavored to reinterview all respondents in the original baseline survey whether or not they had completed the prior wave, unless they had explicitly requested not to be contacted again.

The high response rates reflect the selected nature of the sample—all respondents were by definition smart, well educated, and verbally adept—as well as the salience of the questions being asked to the respondents themselves. Being new arrivals at institutions they had worked long and hard to enter, most were eager to talk about their experiences. A facsimile

Table 1.1
Sampling information on first three waves of the National Longitudinal Survey of Freshmen, 1999–2001

Wave and Outcome	Total	White	Asian	Latino	Black
Baseline Survey					
Completed	85.8%	83.0%	85.8%	85.5%	88.9%
Refused	14.2%	17.0%	14.2%	14.5%	11.1%
Number Selected	4,573	1,202	1,118	1,071	1,182
Freshman Follow-up					
Completed	95.0%	93.7%	95.9%	94.3%	96.0%
Refused	5.0%	6.3%	4.1%	5.7%	4.0%
Number in Baseline	3,924	998	959	916	1,051
Sophomore Follow-up					
Completed	88.6%	87.8%	89.3%	88.4%	88.7%
Refused	11.4%	12.2%	10.7%	11.6%	11.3%
Number in Baseline	3,924	998	959	916	1,051

of the freshman follow-up survey instrument is included in appendix A, and the sophomore instrument is included in appendix B. The freshman survey begins by asking students to list the courses they have taken and are taking and the grades they received or expect. It goes on to ask whether the respondent has declared a major and, if so, which one. The short section on courses and majors is followed by a block of questions about living arrangements at college, including the kind of housing, number of roommates, bedroom and bathroom arrangements, the quality of the study environment, the costs of room and board, and the number of visits to parents during the academic term.

In order to discover how students allocate their time among the many competing demands of college life, the survey compiles an hour-by-hour account of their most recent Tuesday beginning from the time they awakened until the hour they went to bed. This systematic time budget is followed by a module that asks students to consider a typical Monday through Friday and to estimate the number of hours spent in different activities, and then to do the same for a typical weekend. Students then answer a battery of questions about academic-related behaviors on campus, inside and outside the classroom, as well as a series of questions about the frequency with which they have experienced various personal and family problems that could interfere with their studies.

Financial pressures on the student are assessed by asking respondents to estimate the total cost of their first year of college and then to allocate that cost to various potential sources of revenue, such as parents, other relatives, grants, loans, and paid work. Those who report working for pay are asked to identify the specific job, the number of hours worked per week, and the wages earned per hour. At the end of the financial module, students are asked about their use of credit cards and to whom the bills are sent and, apart from birthday or holiday gifts, to report on the receipt of cash remittances from parents or other family members during the school year, as well the sending of any money to parents or other relatives.

In order to get at the shaping and content of students' aspirations, we ask a series of questions about their academic preparation, scholastic goals, perceptions of academic progress, ratings of problems encountered so far, and the degree of effort they are putting into different classes and college in general. We also ask about the nature and extent of their motivation to attend college and to do well academically and specifically inquire about how these compare to the views of their parents, friends, and acquaintances with respect to academic achievement. Social integration on campus is assessed in a variety of ways. One series of questions asks about prejudice and racism on campus as well as the racial-ethnic background of professors, students, and people in their personal networks. Given that the students are almost all single and 18–20 years old, we also ask about dating, romantic experience, and sexual relationships, including those with members of other racial and ethnic groups.

The sophomore survey instrument is very similar, except that it begins by determining whether the respondent is still enrolled at the same school or a different one and, for those who have left the original institution, the reason for their departure. For those still enrolled in school, as before, the questionnaire determines which courses have been taken, those currently being taken, and the grades earned or expected and majors chosen. In addition to asking about declared majors, however, the sophomore follow-up also asks students to name the highest degree they expect to attain, the number of colleges to which they applied, the degree to which they think they made the right college choice, the importance of college graduation to them and their families, and their satisfaction with their social life and intellectual development on campus, along with their overall evaluation of the college experience so far.

Information about living arrangements, time allocation, academic behaviors, the costs of college, and the meeting of these costs is solicited using the same modules as before. In addition to offering perceptions of progress, ratings of problems, and the degree of effort they put into their studies, sophomores are also asked about their participation in different kinds of social organizations on and off campus. Respondents are also to list and describe their six strongest personal connections, how close they feel to them, and the degree to which they draw on them for different kinds of support. After asking about romantic relationships, perceptions of prejudice, and various interfering problems, the questionnaire ends by compiling specific tracking information to facilitate relocation of respondents on later survey waves.

Looking Downriver

The transition from high school to a selective college or university is bound to be stressful for entering students, regardless of race or ethnicity.

In coming to an elite campus, students move from an academic environment where they were one of a small coterie of "stars" to one where *all* their fellow students were presumably high school "stars" in one way or another. At the same time, they exchange an environment where expectations about students were variable and where they may not have been fully challenged intellectually to one where expectations are universally high and where the academic standards are among the most rigorous to be found anywhere in the world. Finally, in going off to college students make a great social leap, moving out of parental households and into new social settings where they assume responsibility for day-to-day decisions. All students are subject to these pressures to a greater or lesser extent, and in the first part of the volume we explore whether and how these common sources of anxiety differ across groups.

We begin in chapter 2 with academics, the central reason for most students' presence on campus. We examine the content and characteristics of the courses selected by students during their first two years of college, the majors they choose, the academic difficulties they experience, the efforts they put into schoolwork, their scholastic aspirations, and the influence of these decisions, efforts, and aspirations on the grades that they ultimately earn as freshmen and sophomores. In terms of the model depicted in figure 1.1, this chapter focuses on the components and determinants of academic integration.

In chapter 3 we take a step back to consider academic decisions and behaviors in light of the broader social context of college. We begin by documenting the living situations of freshmen in different groups and how those situations change from the freshman to the sophomore year. In doing so, we measure the frequency of various distractions to studying that might be encountered in different living environments—dormitories versus apartments versus fraternities or sororities. These locations are, of course, filled with fellow students who constitute the respondents' reference group, and to assess the nature of the peer environment, we present data on the academic, social, and community behaviors valued by students with whom the respondents frequently interact. We also analyze respondents' degree of involvement in various academic, social, and community activities and then move on to a detailed assessment of time use on a typical weekday and weekend. This chapter thus focuses on social integration and uses time budget data as a concrete way of measuring the relative importance of academic versus social pursuits in their daily lives. We conclude our analysis of social life by measuring how the living situations, distractions, peer values, participation patterns, and time constraints combine to influence academic performance during the first two years of college.

Attending a selective academic institution—especially one that is private—obviously entails a serious commitment of financial resources, and the socioeconomic differences between groups documented earlier naturally imply that the financial pressures involved in attending college will fall unevenly on members of different racial and ethnic groups. In order to understand these pressures and their effects, in chapter 4 we undertake a detailed analysis of the cost of higher education, how it is financed from different sources, and the pressures that different kinds of support packages impose on students. Whereas 38% of white and 34% of Asian freshmen said their families were paying the full cost of an elite education, only 10% of blacks and 17% of Latinos said their families were doing so. We conclude this chapter with an in-depth analysis of the pressures and stresses that result from a reliance on student loans, consumer credit, and work rather than grants or family funds and conclude by determining how these stresses influence grade achievement.

Navigating a very competitive academic environment, adjusting to new living situations on campus, and putting together the money to finance a college education are pressures that all students face regardless of race or ethnicity. Although the relative burdens of academic, social, and financial adjustment to college may fall disproportionately on minority students, these are nonetheless stresses that all students face and thus constitute a broadly shared experience, even if the experience is more intense for the average black or Latino student. However, Latinos and African Americans face other pressures on campus that arise explicitly from being minority group members.

For African Americans and Latinos, and to a much lesser extent Asians, minority status means there are social undercurrents to be navigated—largely unspoken but nonetheless important ideas and expectations about the nature of race and ethnicity, the qualities and characteristics of different groups, and the norms of interaction between them. Chapter 5 thus looks at social integration on campus from the viewpoint of minority group members. Ideas and preconceptions about race and ethnicity come to bear in the expression of intergroup social relationships such as friendship and especially dating, and in this chapter we undertake a detailed analysis of patterns of intergroup friendships, including romantic relationships and dating. Our analysis highlights the unique position of black women, who must not only deal with the social reality of race, but within their group manage the social fallout from a sex ratio that militates against finding same-race partners.

Whereas race and ethnicity may be social undercurrents that influence students in subtle ways that are difficult to observe, race also influences the lives of students in ways that are more concrete and direct, and this is the subject of chapter 6. Given the ongoing reality of segregation in the United States, it is inevitable that the social networks of black and Latino students extend back into racially isolated inner-city neighborhoods. Because these neighborhoods are also characterized by high rates of social disorder and violence, negative events are very likely to happen to people to whom the students are socially connected, causing them to devote greater amounts of time, emotional energy, and resources to personal and family issues compared with other students, investments that detract from their studies and undermine academic achievement in a variety of concrete ways that we document using data from the NLSF.

Although less concrete than residential segregation, the influence of stereotype threat is no less real in the lives of minority students. In *The Source of the River* we showed that certain subsets of minority students who doubted their abilities, believed negative stereotypes about their group, and were sensitive to the opinions of others tended to earn lower grades and experience higher failure rates than other students, which we took as supportive of the hypothesis of stereotype threat. In chapter 7, we build on this earlier work to specify a more elaborate model of how stereotype threat operates to sabotage the performance of minority students. Estimates of this model provide further, and more detailed, evidence showing that stereotype threat indeed operates in powerful ways to undermine the grade performance of black and Latino students.

The last topic related to race and ethnicity that we consider is the contentious issue of affirmative action—the use of race-conscious criteria in college admissions and recruiting to bolster minority enrollments. In chapter 8, we develop indicators of the degree to which different institutions have employed race-conscious criteria in admissions and estimate the likelihood that particular minority students might be beneficiaries of such criteria. We then use these two indicators to test a variety of hypotheses developed by critics of affirmative action (see Sowell 2004; Thernstrom and Thernstrom 1999). Although we find little support for the idea that affirmative action produces a mismatch between the abilities of minority studies and the demands of academic institutions they attend, we do find that the use of affirmative action by colleges and universities may inadvertently create social stigma and exacerbate psychological performance burdens for minority students, causing them to underperform.

Finally, in the last chapter we employ key variables from all the foregoing chapters to estimate a series of comprehensive models to determine how each variable independently affects not only grade achievement but also course failing, school leaving, the accumulation of credits, and student satisfaction. Our results suggest the existence of two very different and largely independent components that underlie academic success during the first two years of higher education.

The first is retention—staying in school and progressing from year to year. The second is achievement—earning high grades and avoiding course failures. Remaining in school is more a social than an academic process and is determined by how well students are integrated into campus society generally, not how well they are doing scholastically or the specific academic decisions they might have made. Grade achievement, in contrast, is determined much more by academic factors such as degree of scholastic preparation, the choice of major, the selection of courses in terms of ease or difficulty, interaction with faculty, and educational aspirations. Although social factors have some effect in determining outcomes within courses, they generally play a detracting role: too much time spent on recreation, living off campus in fraternities or sororities or with family members, and relying on peers for academic assistance generally reduce student GPAs.

The major exceptions to the predominance of academic factors in determining course outcomes are those social factors related to membership in a minority group. Social undercurrents relating to race and ethnicity influence the likelihood of failing a course, specific sequelae associated with segregation affect grades earned, and social-psychological influences deriving from stereotype threat and affirmative action affect both outcomes. Once these minority-specific effects are incorporated into models predicting grade point average and the likelihood of leaving school, along with the academic and social factors that are common to all students, intergroup differences in performance disappear.

On the one hand, the fact that minority performance differentials can be eliminated by the application of theoretically specified statistical controls offers hope that by addressing the specific problems and issues we have identified, faculty and administrators at selective schools may be able to devise workable strategies to mitigate the academic underperformance of black and Latino students. On the other hand, the facts that so many factors are involved and that the unadjusted gaps remain so large suggest that we still have a long way to go.

2 Staying Afloat Academically

The Source of the River examined the divergent backgrounds of students attending selective colleges and universities—the source of the "river" of students flowing into the nation's elite institutions of higher education. Even after controlling for background differences, however, the book's authors were not able to eliminate intergroup differentials in grade performance. As they noted at the closing of their book, "these preexisting circumstances explain some, but by no means all, of the observed differentials in achievement among whites, blacks, Asians, and Latinos." The authors went on to argue that subsequent research needed to focus on how "campus-based actions, in turn, produce different academic outcomes" (Massey et al. 2003: 207). In this chapter we begin our analysis of these "campus-based actions," focusing particularly on courses taken, majors chosen, difficulties experienced, efforts expended, aspirations held, and the effect of the foregoing on grades earned during the first two years of college.

Curricular decisions are a logical place to begin. In their exhaustive review of the research literature on higher education, Pascarella and Terenzini concluded that "what is learned during college is differentially influenced by the pattern of courses taken, even when student ability is controlled" (2005: 89). As one would expect, then, students acquire greater knowledge and more skills in subject areas where they take more courses (Jones and Ratcliff 1991; Pike 1992; Ratcliff and Jones 1993). As a result, choices made by 18–19-year-old college students about which courses to take and which majors to pursue will have a lasting influence on their later skills and abilities, areas of competence and expertise, and ultimately their choice of careers.

All knowledge is necessarily path-dependent, building and expanding on what has already been learned to shape potential areas of competence years later. If a student takes no math or science courses in college, it will be difficult later on to become not just a scientist or mathematician but also a physician, dentist, engineer, architect, statistician, actuary, or veterinarian. Students who take few quantitative courses during the first two years of college may even regress in their facility with mathematics by graduation (Wolfle 1983). Consequently, decisions made by freshmen and sophomores will push them toward or away from certain occupations and thus channel them along specific earnings pathways and career trajectories. If members of different racial and ethnic groups make systematically different choices about majors and courses, then these early decisions carry a nontrivial potential to explain differential patterns of income and occupational attainment later in life.

The selection of courses is probably the most important determinant of later career paths, for research shows that the choice of a major has little effect on what is learned, outside of material from the major itself (Angoff and Johnson 1990; Lehman and Nisbett 1990; Astin 1992; Anaya 1996; Pascarella and Terenzini 2005). Thus, if a student wishes to major in English but takes numerous science and math courses, he or she will master the science and math material as well as any science or math major and could just as easily decide later to attend medical school as enter a doctoral program in comparative literature. Just because one majors in the humanities does not mean that one will not acquire a strong background in math and the sciences.

In addition to course selection, the acquisition of knowledge and skills is also influenced by the degree of effort students put into their studies. As one would expect, the greater the effort put forth, the more students learn (Kuh et al. 1991, 2005; Astin 1992; Pascarella and Terenzini 2005). This conclusion holds whether one considers self-reported learning gains (Arnold et al. 1993; Davis and Murrell 1993; Pike 1991; Watson and Kuh 1996) or gains assessed using objective indicators of achievement (Johnstone, Ashbaugh, and Warfield 2002). As a result, intergroup variations in academic effort also have significant potential for explaining ethnic and racial differences in grade performance and other indicators of academic achievement.

Finally, academic goals and aspirations have an obvious bearing on college achievement. In general, those who aspire to more years of education and to acquiring more and higher degrees are more likely not only to accumulate additional years of schooling and more credentials but also to earn higher grades along the way (Sewell and Hauser 1980; Hauser, Tsai, and Sewell 1983; Tinto 1993; Kao and Tienda 1998). Despite the seemingly obvious connection between aspirations and outcomes, however, research consistently shows that despite having very high academic aspirations, black students are less likely than others to translate these ambitions into actual educational achievements (Portes and Wilson 1976; Kerckhoff and Campbell 1977), a paradox that Morgan (2005) attributes to different expectations about the *likelihood* of achieving success in school. Given perceptions of ongoing discrimination and stratification in the realm of education, and the limited educational success achieved by most people in their families, schools, neighborhoods, and social networks, minority students all too often conclude that realizing their educational aspirations is not very realistic and thus not worth expending a great deal of time and effort in pursuing. Thanks to data collected in the NLSF, we are here able to assess the independent role of aspirations in academic achievement while controlling for time and effort devoted to academic endeavors.

Navigating the Curriculum

As students wade into the academic current of higher education, the first important decisions they make are which courses to take. As noted in the prior chapter, in order to study course selection the NLSF questionnaire compiled a complete list of courses taken and grades received during each term of the freshman and sophomore years. Table 2.1 combines data across the two academic years to show the distribution of courses taken by students in different racial and ethnic groups. Course selections are organized by disciplinary division and department and, given the different number of students in each group and variation in response rates across years of the survey, we standardized the tabulation by assuming a fixed cohort of students going through two years of college with no attrition. Specifically, the columns show the number of courses that would be accumulated in different academic divisions and departments if 1,000 whites, 1,000 Asians, 1,000 Latinos, and 1,000 blacks went through their freshman and sophomore

Table 2.1
Number of courses taken during freshman and sophomore year (standardized cohort of 1,000 students)

Division and Department	Whites	Asians	Latinos	Blacks
Humanities				
Art and Art History	541	459	505	291
Classics	84	52	42	51
Comparative Literature	55	57	102	99
English	1567	1414	1536	1589
Foreign Language	1685	1517	1805	1714
Spanish	593	337	918	807
Other	1092	1180	887	990
History	827	584	811	751
Music	782	823	655	657
Philosophy	519	426	446	406
Religion	357	249	288	248
Rhetoric	22	18	16	21
Theater and Media Arts	298	160	306	278
Other Humanities	768	357	893	801
Total	*7,505*	*6,296*	*7,605*	*6,989*
Ratio to Whites	*1.00*	*0.84*	*0.99*	*0.93*
Sciences, Math, and Engineering				
Biology	825	1,033	750	770
Chemistry	1,102	1,607	1,065	1,078
Computer Science	474	672	416	357
Ecology	92	57	77	65
Engineering	620	646	484	365
Geology	113	58	78	66
Mathematics or Statistics	1,675	1,842	1,651	1,733
Operations Research	28	54	27	24
Physics	651	797	539	404
Zoology	26	25	9	12
Other Sciences	427	440	369	370
Total	*6,033*	*7,231*	*5,465*	*5,244*
Ratio to Whites	*1.00*	*1.20*	*0.91*	*0.87*
Social and Behavioral Sciences				
Anthropology	429	337	417	347
Criminal Justice	7	6	5	4
Economics	794	1,094	734	715
International Relations	30	44	49	35
Political Science	732	556	711	593
Psychology	868	742	911	904
Sociology	429	371	465	594
Urban Studies	18	8	21	24
Other Social Sciences	63	85	71	121
Total	*3,485*	*3,356*	*3,496*	*3,230*
Ratio to Whites	*1.00*	*0.96*	*1.00*	*0.98*

(continued)

Table 2.1 *(continued)*

Division and Department	Whites	Asians	Latinos	Blacks
Professions				
Architecture	106	61	126	34
Business and Finance	493	701	527	412
Communications	232	212	227	258
Education	151	95	140	213
Journalism	46	29	40	34
Legal Studies	21	24	39	17
Total	*1,049*	*1,122*	*1,099*	*968*
Ratio to Whites	*1.00*	*1.07*	*1.05*	*0.92*
Health and Physical Education				
Allied Health Systems	2	1	1	5
Health	25	38	33	68
Nutrition	11	24	25	17
Physical Education	386	343	412	609
Total	*424*	*406*	*472*	*699*
Ratio to Whites	*1.00*	*0.96*	*1.11*	*1.65*
Ethnic, Area, and Gender Studies				
African or Afro-American Studies	47	34	56	599
American Studies	33	32	48	34
Asian-Mideast Studies	110	408	71	87
Latin American or Latino Studies	27	6	88	25
Other Ethnic or Area Studies	14	14	47	25
Women's Studies	90	57	95	103
Total	*321*	*551*	*405*	*873*
Ratio to Whites	*1.00*	*1.72*	*1.26*	*2.72*
Military Studies				
ROTC	2	7	11	11
Military Science	8	24	6	22
Total	*10*	*31*	*17*	*33*
Ratio to Whites	*1.00*	*3.10*	*1.70*	*3.30*
Miscellaneous Courses				
Agriculture	19	1	10	3
Applied Studies	15	8	5	13
Comprehensive	0	1	9	9
Core Curriculum	40	31	75	53
Experimental Curriculum	9	13	21	15
Freshman Seminar	67	48	49	84
Honors Seminar	20	17	5	3
Interdisciplinary Studies	55	48	47	51
Total	*164*	*167*	*221*	*231*
Ratio to Whites	*1.00*	*1.02*	*1.35*	*1.41*
Total Courses Taken	19,159	19,327	18,647	18,586
Ratio to Whites	1.00	1.01	0.97	0.97
Courses per Student per Year	9.58	9.66	9.32	9.29

years with no one dropping out. Variations in observed frequencies thus reflect the real choices made by students and are not artifacts of group size or differential attrition.

During the first two years, of course, students are primarily focused on meeting general requirements and exploring their emerging interests rather than majoring in specific subjects. We thus expect to observe rough similarity in the distribution of courses across groups, and this is basically what we find. Within each group, humanities was the largest disciplinary division with roughly 6,300 to 7,600 courses taken, followed by the sciences, mathematics, and engineering at 5,200 to 7,200 courses taken in each category; social and behavioral sciences at 3,200 to 3,500 courses taken; the professions at 1,000 to 1,100 courses taken; health and physical education at 400 to 700 courses taken; ethnic, area, and gender studies at 300 to 800 courses taken; and military studies at just 10 to 33 courses taken. A residual miscellaneous category had between 160 and 220 courses per group.

With respect to the largest subject division, humanities, among all groups the most frequent courses taken were in English, foreign languages, history, music, and art, in that order. Nonetheless, there were certain differences between groups in the frequency of course selection, with Asians displaying a relatively greater propensity toward music courses and an avoidance of history courses. Latinos, perhaps not surprisingly, evinced an attraction to Spanish-language courses, and whites were notable for taking a relatively large number of philosophy courses. The bottom of the panel shows the total number of humanities courses taken by each group, and the ratio of this number to that displayed by whites. Statistical tests indicate that the number of humanities courses taken varies significantly across groups ($F = 16.1, p < .001$) and that the numbers reported by both Asians and blacks are significantly below those of whites ($t = -5.3$ and $t = -3.2$, both $p < .001$) whereas the numbers reported by Hispanics and whites are statistically identical ($t = 0.89, p > .10$).

Compared with other groups, Asians exhibit a very clear disinclination to take humanities courses. Whereas the ratio of humanities courses taken by Latinos to humanities courses taken by whites was virtually unity at 0.99, and that for blacks was close at 0.93, the ratio for Asians stood at just 0.84. In other words, although whites and Latinos took nearly the same number of humanities courses during their freshman and sophomore years and blacks took only 7% fewer, Asians were 16% less likely to take a humanities course over their first two years of college.

This relative deficit of Asians in the humanities was effectively counterbalanced by a surfeit of courses taken in the sciences, math, and engineering. Whereas Asians recorded a total 7,231 such courses taken over the first two years of college, the figure for whites was only 6,033, yielding a ratio of 1.20, meaning that on average Asians took 20% more science, math, and engineering courses than whites, a difference that is highly significant statistically. In contrast, Latino and black students took far fewer such courses than whites. The relative number of math, science, and engineering courses taken by Latinos was 0.91 compared with whites, and the ratio for African Americans was 0.87. Nonetheless, within each group the top five sciences-math-engineering disciplines were the same: math, followed by chemistry, biology, and more distantly physics and computer science; but within each of those five disciplines Asians always accumulated the largest number of course credits.

After humanities and sciences-math-engineering, the next largest division was the social and behavioral sciences. In contrast to marked intergroup differentials in enrollment evinced in humanities and math-science-engineering, all groups took roughly the same number of social sciences courses, with ratios to whites being 0.96 for Asians, 0.98 for blacks, and 1.0 for Latinos. Underlying this divisional homogeneity, however, are differences in the distribution of courses across specific fields of social science. Whites were most attracted by psychology, followed by economics, political science, and then anthropology and sociology in equal numbers. In contrast, Asians preferred economics, followed by psychology, political science, sociology, and anthropology. Among Latinos the ranking of social sciences was almost the same as for whites—psychology, economics, political science, sociology, and anthropology—but for blacks the ranking was psychology, economics, sociology, political science, and anthropology.

The panel of table 2.1 pertaining to the professions probably understates the number of people in professional or preprofessional tracks, as many students who are prelaw, premed, or prebusiness take many, if not most, of their courses in regular academic departments. Among the professional courses listed here, the least susceptible to this kind of understatement is probably business, which as a field offers a relatively abundant selection of courses to undergraduates. It is thus not surprising that business and finance lead the pack among professional courses taken in all groups, followed by communications, education, and architecture.

Asians display by far the greatest proclivity toward professional courses, and blacks the least. Among the professions, African Americans show a relatively strong attraction to communications and education, whereas whites and Latinos stand out for their commitment to architecture and education. As already noted, Asians display the greatest attraction to the professions, with a ratio of professional courses relative to whites of 1.07, followed by Latinos at 1.05. African Americans were below whites at 0.92.

Although relatively few members of any group took courses in health and physical education, the unusual proclivity of African Americans toward these courses clearly stands out. Whereas whites took only 424 courses under this rubric, African Americans took 699, yielding a ratio to whites of 1.65, substantially higher than the Latino ratio of 1.11 and considerably greater than the Asian ratio of 0.96. The high rate of health-related course taking among blacks stems not from differences in registration for courses in nutrition or allied health systems but from large numbers in health and physical education. To some extent, this difference may reflect the fact that health and physical education courses are required in the only historically black institution in our sample, Howard University, whereas such requirements are rare elsewhere in academia.

African Americans also display a markedly greater propensity toward ethnic studies, area studies, and gender studies as well, led by a strong attraction to African and African American studies. Whereas blacks reported taking 599 courses under this category, the number was just 56 for Latinos, 34 for Asians, and 47 for whites. The attraction to own-group courses was much stronger for blacks than for Asians or Latinos. Although Asians reported taking a relatively large number of courses in Asian–Middle Eastern studies, 408, the number of Latin American or Latino studies courses taken by Latinos was just 88. African Americans also displayed a strong attraction toward women's studies, an attraction shared by whites and Latinos but not so much by Asians. Overall, African Americans were 2.72 times more likely to take an ethnic, area, or gender studies course than whites, and Asians were 1.72 times more likely, compared with a figure of 1.26 for Latinos.

Although members of all groups reported taking tiny numbers of courses in military studies, Asians and African Americans stood out from the others. Whereas black students reported taking 33 ROTC or military science courses and Asians reported 31, the number for Latinos was only

17 and for whites 10. Given the mixed bag and unclear content of courses listed under the miscellaneous rubric, it is difficult to interpret group differentials in this category, except to note that Latinos and blacks took relatively more such courses than whites or Asians.

In the end, however, students within all groups took roughly the same number of courses during the freshman and sophomore years, with Latinos and blacks averaging around 9.3 courses per student per year compared with 9.6 to 9.7 for whites and Asians. Although not large, these differences are statistically significant. Thus minority students had fallen slightly behind the average number of credits accumulated during the first half of college. Table 2.2 sheds further light on intergroup differentials in course selection by listing the ten most popular courses taken by whites, Asians, Latinos, and blacks as freshmen and sophomores.

As can be seen, the four top courses are remarkably similar across all groups in each year. Among freshmen, math and English always rank close together as number one and number two, followed more distantly by chemistry and a non-Spanish foreign language, though the ranking of the latter two does vary slightly by group. Among whites and blacks, foreign-language courses precede chemistry in popularity, while among Asians and Latinos chemistry is more popular. In general, 64% to 71% of all freshman took a math class, 62% to 66% took an English class, 28% to 34% took a non-Spanish foreign language, and 27% to 31% of whites, Latinos, and blacks took chemistry, while Asians are a clear outlier with 42% taking chemistry. Courses ranked six to ten are generally quite similar for whites and Latinos, except for the higher ranking of economics among whites and Spanish among Latinos. The basic set of courses is essentially the same, however. The percentage of students in both groups taking psychology, history, economics, biology, Spanish, and philosophy ranges from 19% to 18%.

Among Asians and blacks, however, several anomalies appear in the lower half of the popularity distribution. Courses that appear in the top ten only for the group in question are marked with a footnote. Alone among the four groups, Asians chose physics and computer science courses to be among their ten most popular, with 21% of all Asians taking physics and 19% taking computer science. For their part, African Americans were unique in selecting physical education to be among the ten most popular freshman courses, with a 19% frequency. In other words, almost a fifth of all black students represented in the NLSF took a physical education course as freshmen.

Table 2.2
Ten most popular classes taken during students' freshman and sophomore years

Rank	Freshman Courses	Percent	Sophomore Courses	Percent
Whites				
1	Math	64.5	Math	33.0
2	English	61.5	English	29.2
3	Other Foreign Language	34.0	History	26.6
4	Chemistry	29.8	Other Foreign Language	25.0
5	Psychology	26.6	Psychology	24.7
6	History	24.1	Economics	24.1
7	Economics	23.7	Biology	22.7
8	Biology	21.0	Political Science	20.1
9	Spanish	20.7	Chemistry	18.4
10	Philosophy	19.2	Philosophy[a]	18.0
Asians				
1	Math	71.1	Math	37.4
2	English	62.6	Economics	31.8
3	Chemistry	42.3	Other Foreign Language	29.4
4	Other Foreign Language	36.0	Biology	36.8
5	Economics	31.3	Chemistry	26.2
6	Biology	26.4	English	24.3
7	Psychology	23.2	Psychology	22.0
8	Physics[a]	21.1	Physics[a]	21.1
9	History	21.0	History	20.2
10	Computer Science[a]	19.0	Computer Science[a]	17.9
Latinos				
1	Math	63.8	Math	32.5
2	English	61.7	English	29.0
3	Chemistry	30.9	History	25.7
4	Other Foreign Language	28.4	Psychology	25.0
5	Spanish	27.8	Economics	23.6
6	Psychology	26.8	Spanish	22.8
7	History	26.0	Other Foreign Language	20.6
8	Biology	21.2	Biology	18.6
9	Economics	20.4	Political Science	18.6
10	Philosophy	18.8	Chemistry	16.5
Blacks				
1	Math	69.3	Math	35.8
2	English	66.5	English	27.5
3	Other Foreign Language	32.2	Psychology	26.6
4	Chemistry	27.4	History	25.6
5	Spanish	25.5	Economics	25.5
6	Psychology	25.1	Other Foreign Language	23.8
7	Biology	21.4	Spanish	20.4
8	History	21.1	Sociology	19.8
9	Economics	20.2	Physical Education[a]	19.1
10	Physical Education[a]	19.4	Sociology[a]	18.6

(continued)

Table 2.2 *(continued)*

Rank	Freshman Courses	Percent	Sophomore Courses	Percent
Average Percentage in Top Ten				
	Whites	32.5	Whites	24.2
	Asians	35.4	Asians	26.7
	Latinos	32.6	Latinos	23.3
	Blacks	32.9	Blacks	24.3

[a]Unique entry on top ten list for that group in that year.

By the sophomore year, course taking diverges across groups as students shift from completing core requirements to focusing on personal interests and exploring possible majors. Thus, instead of 64% to 71% taking the most popular courses, the range among sophomores is 33% to 37%. Nonetheless, very few new course classifications appear on the list of top ten sophomore courses; and with the exception of Asians, the rank orderings are also quite similar across groups. Among Asians, economics and biology move up in popularity and English moves down compared with the freshman year. As before, only Asians place physics and computer science among the top ten, and whites are anomalous in their continued preference for philosophy. Among blacks, physical education moves up to the ninth most popular course, sociology moves into the tenth spot, and chemistry disappears from the list entirely (plummeting from fourth place in freshman year).

In sum, although courses selected by freshmen and sophomores are generally constrained by the need to meet distributional requirements, certain differences in preferences are discernible in the portfolios of courses taken by members each group. Figure 2.1 summarizes these differences by graphing the number of courses taken by Asians, Latinos, and African Americans in each academic division relative to whites. If a bar reaches the solid horizontal line, it indicates the same proclivity as whites toward courses in that category. As can be seen, Asians display a tendency to avoid the humanities, a strong attraction to sciences-math-engineering, and an even stronger proclivity toward area-ethnic-gender studies. Blacks, in contrast, display a modest tendency to avoid the humanities, a stronger tendency to avoid sciences-math-engineering and the professions, and, relative to other groups, a rather pronounced attraction to health–physical education and to ethnic-area-gender studies.

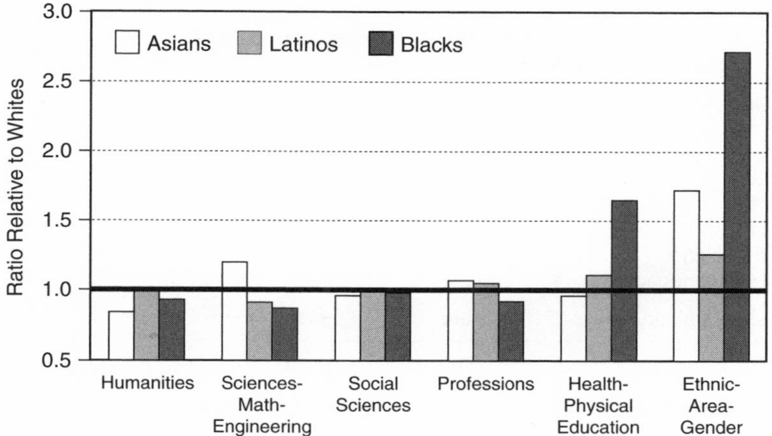

Figure 2.1.
Ratios of courses taken by minority students to courses taken by white students in various subject areas

Difficult Passages

Differences in course selections carry important implications for grades earned because grading standards and grade distributions vary between programs and across departments. It does not take a great deal of imagination to appreciate that the distribution of grades in a physical education class is likely to be quite different from that in a physics class, and that the self-selection of students into different courses of study is likely to yield very different class compositions and grade distributions. Some courses—particularly those in math and the sciences—tend to be "hard" for most students while others, such as those in health or general studies, tend to be "easy."

We cannot, of course, observe directly how easy or hard a course is. We can, however, indirectly assess the relative difficulty of courses in two ways: subjectively by asking students how easy or hard they *perceived* courses to be, and objectively by determining the grades they actually *earned* in various classes. Grades earned, of course, reflect not only the difficulty of the material being presented but also students' efforts, preparation, and abilities. Nonetheless breaking courses down by average grades earned is likely to reflect in some manner the relative difficulty of the subject, however imperfectly.

Table 2.3
Difficulty of different subjects (on a 0–10 scale) as perceived by students during freshman year of college

Degree of Difficulty	Whites	Asians	Latinos	Blacks
English	5.04	5.10	4.91	4.17
History	4.81	4.72	4.73	3.94
Math	6.20	5.97	6.30	6.26
Science	5.96	6.04	6.12	6.21
Social Science	4.48	4.55	4.45	3.96
Foreign Language	4.94	4.63	4.15	4.50
Overall Difficulty	5.86	5.72	5.78	5.65

The NLSF survey administered in the spring of the freshman year asked students to state how difficult they found various kinds of courses on a 0 to 10 scale, where 0 meant the course was extremely easy and 10 meant it was extremely hard. Average ratings assigned by the four groups to various courses of study are reported in table 2.3. Whereas the average difficulty rating assigned to courses was quite similar across students, black students generally found their classes to be somewhat easier, with an average difficulty rating of 5.65, and white students experienced their courses to be relatively harder, with a difficulty score of 5.86. Asians and Latinos were in between with scores of 5.72 and 5.78, respectively. In statistical terms, these ratings are significantly different from one another ($F = 3.98, p < .01$).

There was a great deal of consensus between groups concerning the relative *ordering* of courses with respect to difficulty. All agreed that math and science courses were the hardest, with difficulty ratings in the range of 6.0 to 6.3 (no statistically significant differences). These were generally followed by English and then foreign-language courses, with history and social science courses being viewed as easiest. Whereas African Americans rated math and the sciences to be as difficult as other students, they perceived English, history, social sciences, and foreign languages to be much easier, accounting for their lower overall difficulty rating. Not surprisingly, Latinos found foreign-language courses to be relatively easy, as most of them concentrated in Spanish, the language spoken at home by many of their parents.

To arrive at an "objective" evaluation of course difficulty, we computed the grade point average for each course reported by students in the NLSF and inspected the distribution of grades. We discovered natural break points in the distribution of GPAs at 3.05 and 3.40. Students taking courses with average GPAs above 3.40 received a preponderance of A's and B's with few

Table 2.4
Courses with average grade points above 3.4 and below 3.05

Threshold and Course		Total Courses Taken	Mean GPA Earned
High-Grading Courses (GPA > 3.40)			
1	Honors Courses	12	3.73
2	Applied Studies	9	3.71
3	Physical Education	361	3.65
4	Music and Dance	547	3.64
5	Urban Studies	18	3.64
6	Core Curricular Studies	51	3.62
7	Military Science	21	3.61
8	Human Development	37	3.51
9	Interdisciplinary Studies	50	3.55
10	Education	157	3.55
11	American Studies	49	3.55
12	Asian–Mideast Studies	243	3.54
13	Theater/Radio/Television/Film	281	3.54
14	Learning Assistance	2	3.50
15	Health	49	3.49
16	Freshman Seminar	86	3.47
17	African American Studies	246	3.45
18	Women's Studies	126	3.44
19	Writing and Composition	145	3.43
20	Foreign Language	1,312	3.42
22	Air Force ROTC	6	3.42
22	Ethnic Studies	35	3.40
Low-Grading Courses (GPA < 3.05)			
1	Physics	754	3.04
2	Science Unspecified	512	3.04
3	Zoology	20	3.04
4	Finance	43	3.03
5	Economics	1,027	3.00
6	Accounting	157	2.97
7	Agricultural Sciences	7	2.97
8	Biology	948	2.96
9	Mathematics and Statistics	2,376	2.94
10	Chemistry	1,234	2.91
11	Geography	67	2.91

grades of C or lower, whereas those taking courses with average GPAs of 3.05 or less received few A's, many B's, a substantial number of C's and D's, and even a few F's. Courses above and below these cut points are shown in table 2.4.

Although the number of courses in which high grades were the norm substantially exceeds the number of courses in which low grades were routinely given, the number of students who took each of the former is generally less than the number taking the latter. Whereas high-grading courses constitute 30% of the courses named by students, they comprised only 18% of total course enrollment. Conversely, whereas the low-grading courses constitute only 15% of those named by students, they constituted 23% of total enrollment. The only high-grading courses that attracted over 500 registrants were non-Spanish foreign-language courses and courses in music and dance, but among those courses that consistently gave low grades, six had enrollments in excess of 500.

Consistent with their subjective ratings, courses in which students routinely performed poorly are overwhelmingly in the sciences and quantitative disciplines such as mathematics, statistics, finance, and economics. Courses in which high grades were commonly earned include numerous "general" courses not tied to a particular discipline, such as applied studies, core curricular studies, American studies, military studies, urban studies, interdisciplinary studies, Asian–Middle Eastern studies, freshman seminars, African American studies, women's studies, and ethnic studies. In addition, high grades characterized courses in physical education, human development, and health, as well as artistic "performance courses" in music, dance, writing, and composition.

In general, the data in table 2.4 suggest that "easy" courses are those that are general, nonquantitative, and lack a strong disciplinary foundation, whereas "hard" courses are those associated with specific, usually quantitative disciplines characterized by a high degree of consensus, common methodologies, and an accepted corpus of knowledge. Table 2.5 shows the distribution of courses taken by whites, Asians, Latinos, and blacks according to the grading standards employed. Whether one considers the percentage of students taking "easy," "hard," or medium-difficulty courses,

Table 2.5
Distribution of course taken by freshmen and sophomores according to standards of grading

Category of Grading	Whites	Asians	Latinos	Blacks
High-Grading "Easy" Courses	15.4%	16.2%	14.0%	19.8%
Medium-Grading Courses	52.7%	46.5%	55.3%	50.5%
Low-Grading "Hard" Courses	31.9%	37.3%	30.7%	29.7%
Mean High-Grade Courses Taken	2.4	2.5	2.1	2.9
Mean Low-Grade Courses Taken	4.1	5.2	3.9	3.9

intergroup differences are all highly significant statistically (with F-tests consistently yielding p values under .001).

As can be seen, whites and Latinos are concentrated in courses that offer medium GPAs—those ranging from 3.05 to 3.40. Some 55% of Latinos and 53% of whites ended up in such courses, with 15% to 16% in high-grading courses and 31% to 32% in low-grading courses. In contrast, 37% percent of the courses taken by Asians were "hard" courses in which low grades were routinely given and only 47% were in the medium category, leaving only 16% in "easy" courses. At the other extreme, 20% of the black distribution was in "easy" courses, with 50% in the medium category and only 30% in the "hard" category. In terms of absolute numbers, the average black student took 2.9 "easy" courses compared with figures of 2.4 for whites, 2.5 for Asians, and 2.1 for Latinos. At the same time, the average African American and Latino took 3.9 "hard" courses, compared with 4.1 for whites and 5.2 for Asians. Given these distributional differences, subsequent analyses of grades earned by respondents will endeavor to control for the relative number of courses taken in each category, thereby obtaining a measure of grade performance that controls, however imperfectly, for the relative difficulty of courses taken.

Efforts and Aspirations

As noted earlier, the grade earned in any course reflects not only the relative difficulty of the material but also the effort expended by students to master it and whatever concrete actions are taken to facilitate that mastery. In the spring of their freshman year, students were asked to estimate the degree of effort they put into various kinds of classes on a 0 to 10 scale, where 0 was no effort at all and 10 indicated the greatest possible effort. Average ratings assigned to various courses of study are shown by group in the top panel of table 2.6. As can be seen, degree of academic effort clearly varies by course among all groups; and, quite remarkably, the degree of effort seems to bear only a minimal correspondence to the perceived difficulty of courses. Thus, the greatest effort was put into relatively "easy" courses such as English (with effort ratings of 6.0 or above) whereas the least effort was put into relatively "hard" courses in the sciences (with effort ratings of 3.7 or lower).

If anything, effort and difficulty seem to be inversely related, as illustrated by figure 2.2, which orders the courses by degree of difficulty and

Table 2.6
Degree of effort and frequency of various academic behaviors exhibited by freshmen on a 0–10 scale

Academic Behavior	Whites	Asians	Latinos	Blacks
Degree of Effort				
English	6.52	6.04	6.49	6.54
History	4.60	5.20	4.42	4.31
Math	4.50	4.22	4.30	4.06
Science	3.41	3.45	3.68	3.57
Social Science	3.82	3.91	3.90	3.73
Foreign Language	4.88	4.47	4.20	4.13
Institutional Help				
Writing Instruction	0.98	1.09	1.42	1.89
Reading Instruction	0.30	0.49	0.60	0.79
Math Instruction	0.58	0.81	1.01	1.49
Test Taking	0.36	0.58	0.68	1.11
Study Skills	0.42	0.66	0.91	1.42
Visit Adviser	2.65	2.73	3.24	3.79
Go to Tutor	0.78	1.08	1.46	2.28
Professorial Help				
Ask Professors in Class	4.02	3.56	4.15	4.74
Raise Hand in Class	2.86	2.71	2.99	3.76
Approach Prof after Class	3.92	3.92	4.11	4.76
Meet Prof to Understand	3.28	3.50	3.61	4.39
Meet Prof Other Matters	1.58	1.62	1.83	1.91
Peer Help				
Study with Others	4.19	4.63	4.49	4.51
Organize Study Groups	2.67	3.05	3.08	3.30
Get Help from Friends	3.74	4.27	4.17	4.55
Use of Library and Laboratory				
Study in Library	3.90	4.47	4.32	4.26
Research in Library	2.86	3.18	3.47	3.72
Work in Computer Lab	2.66	3.53	3.52	4.03
Use Internet for Schoolwork	5.85	6.16	6.40	6.80

plots the two sets of ratings. Whereas difficulty and effort seem to correspond in foreign language, history, and social science courses, there are rather large discrepancies for math, science, and English courses. Relatively less effort was put into the two most difficult courses of study (math and science) whereas relatively greater effort was put into English, which was perceived as being much easier. The reasons for this apparent disconnect are not immediately clear, but it may be that effort is governed at least partly by factors other than course difficulty (e.g., interest, aptitude, teacher quality, etc.), a question to which we will return later in the chapter.

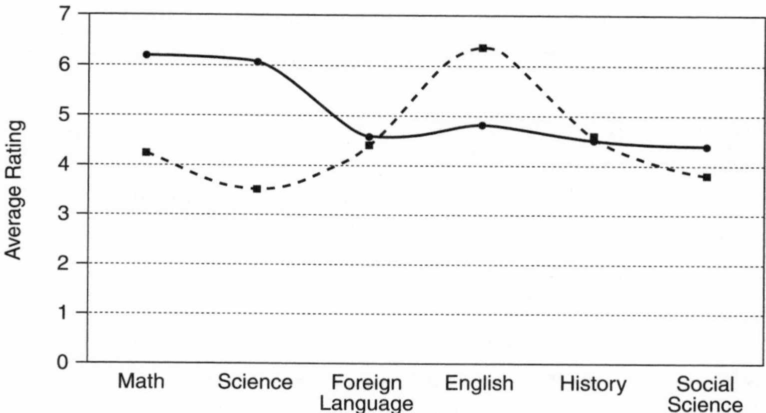

Figure 2.2.
Average difficulty and effort ratings assigned by freshmen to different courses of study

All groups reported the same level of effort in science and math courses (F-tests not significant), with effort ratings ranging narrowly from 4.1 to 4.5 for math and 3.4 to 3.6 for science. Although intergroup differences in effort ratings are statistically significant in English, history, social science, and foreign-language courses, these differences generally reflect the lower ratings offered by Asians, and in substantive terms the differences are not very large. Moreover, the rank ordering of courses with respect to effort is more or less the same across groups. Thus there do not appear to be pronounced intergroup differences in self-assessed academic effort.

The remaining sections in table 2.6 present the frequency with which students reported engaging in specific learning-related behaviors as freshmen, again on a scale of 0 (never) to 10 (always). The second panel, for example, assesses the degree to which the different groups availed themselves of various educational services provided by the college or university, such as getting special instruction in reading, writing, or math; visiting an adviser or tutor; or signing up for training in study skills or test taking. Across all groups, these services were used rather infrequently. The most commonly used service was academic advising, but the greatest frequency rating for visiting an adviser was only 3.8. None of the other frequency ratings exceeded 2.3.

Despite the relatively low frequency with which students in all groups sought institutional assistance as freshmen, within each category there is a very clear rank ordering that is quite significant statistically ($F > 20.0$, $p < .001$). Black students made the most frequent use of institutional services, followed by Latinos, Asians, and then whites. For example, when asked to rate the frequency with which they went to a tutor for help, whites assigned an average frequency rating of just 0.8, compared with 1.1 for Asians, 1.5 for Latinos, and 2.3 for blacks. Thus, even though the frequency with which students sought assistance was low for all groups, the rate of service usage was nonetheless higher for underrepresented minorities, especially African Americans.

The third panel in the table shows the frequency with which students sought out their professors in and out of the classroom—by raising their hands in class, asking a question in class, approaching a professor after class, or meeting a professor outside class—all obvious indications of academic integration. In this category of behavior, the frequency ratings are generally higher. When asked to describe how often they asked questions of professors in class, for example, whites offered an average rating of 4.0; Asians estimated their frequency at 3.6; Latinos put theirs as 4.2; and African Americans were greatest at 4.7 ($F = 33.4$, $p < .001$). Across all behaviors, whites and Asians generally display similar frequency ratings that are both on the low side, whereas Latinos are higher and African Americans the highest.

All groups display relatively similar propensities to study with peers. Although the differences are statistically significant, they are generally small in substantive terms. Whites rated their frequency of study with peers at an average of 4.2, compared with 4.6 for Asians and 4.5 for both Latinos and blacks (see next to bottom panel in table 2.6). Again, however, we observe an upward progression from white to Asian to Latino to black. The same progression prevails with respect to use of basic facilities such as the library and laboratory: whites reported least frequent use and blacks most frequent use, with Asians and Latinos in between but with the former closer to whites and the latter closer to blacks (both F-tests significant at $p < .001$).

In sum, although groups do not seem to exhibit very large differences with respect to overall efforts and actions, consistent intergroup differences do emerge in terms of the propensity to engage in specific learning-related behaviors on campus. Using the items shown table 2.6 and others available from the survey, we created a set of summary scales for degree of academic effort, institutional help, professorial help, peer help, and use of library and laboratory facilities (summarized in appendix C). The scale of overall

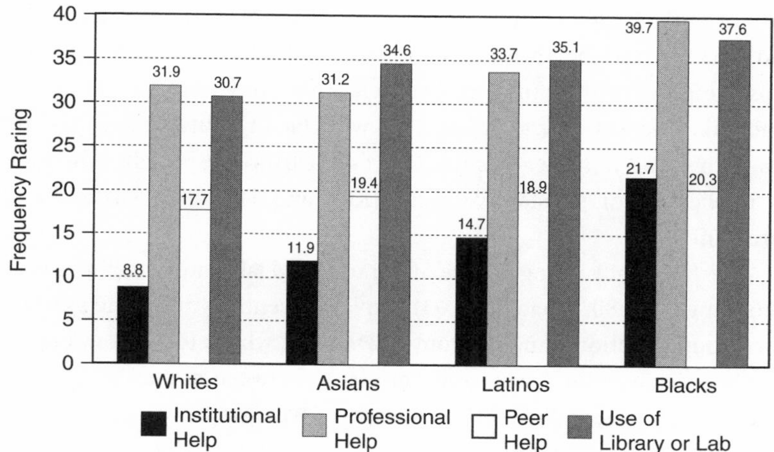

Figure 2.3.
Percentages of students who sought different kinds of academic assistance, by racial-ethnic group

effort contains eight items—the six shown in table 2.6 plus two additional ratings of overall effort from the freshman and sophomore years. The eight item scores were added together to yield a an overall effort scale ranging from 0 to 80, with a mean of 66.2, a standard deviation of 16.9, and a Cronbach's alpha reliability coefficient of .82. As already noted, there is relatively little variation across groups in terms of perceived effort, so we did not include it in graphical presentations. The average perceived effort score for whites and blacks is roughly 67, compared with a value of 66 for Hispanics and 64 for Asians.

There is greater variation with respect to the other indexes, however, and the pattern of intergroup differences is summarized by figure 2.3, which plots average scale scores for each racial-ethnic group. In terms of institutional help (mean 14.4, range 0 to 120, reliability .86), blacks earned an average score of 21.7, compared with 14.7 for Latinos, 11.9 for Asians, and just 8.8 for whites ($F = 116.1$, $p < 001$). Thus white students made least use of institutional services, at just 40% of the rate reported by African Americans.

We find a similar pattern with respect to the seeking of faculty assistance. The average score for seeking professorial help (mean 34.2, range 0 to 100, reliability .86) is 31.9 for whites and 31.2 for Asians, but 33.7 for

Latinos and 39.7 for African Americans ($F = 46.8$, $p < .001$). Thus whites and Asians made the fewest demands on faculty time and African Americans the most, with Latinos in between. These differences carry concrete academic implications, as interacting with faculty outside the classroom has been found to have a positive effect on learning, especially when it has an intellectual or substantive focus (Kuh and Hu 2001; Pascarella and Terenzini 2005).

The frequency rating for use of libraries and laboratory facilities (mean 34.6, range 0 to 80, reliability 0.63) displays essentially the same pattern of intergroup variation, ranging from 30.7 among whites to 37.6 among African Americans, with Asians and Latinos in between at 34.6 and 35.1, respectively ($F = 38.7$, $p < .001$). Differences with respect to the seeking of peer help are more muted, though once again statistically significant. The average frequency rating of the index (overall mean 19.0, range 0 to 60, reliability.77) stands at 17.7 for whites, 19.4 for Asians, 18.9 for Latinos, and 20.3 for African Americans ($F = 19.2$, $p < .001$). Thus whites and blacks always anchor opposite ends of the spectrum in seeking academic assistance from outside agents.

In summary, although all groups reported that they put similar efforts into their studies, black and Latino students were significantly more disposed to take concrete actions to avail themselves of institutional services, faculty support, peer assistance, and basic facilities such as laboratories and libraries. Paradoxically, we also find a bit of a disconnect between the difficulty students reported in different subjects and the efforts they expended. Though math and the sciences were rated as hardest, they received relatively low effort ratings; and whereas English was rated as less difficult, it received the highest effort rating, which we took to indicate the relevance of other factors besides difficulty in determining student effort.

One potential factor affecting the effort that students put into courses is educational aspirations—whether students simply wish to graduate with a bachelor's degree and get on with their lives, or whether they hope to attend a graduate or professional school and earn a higher degree. If the goal is the former, then perhaps putting in maximal effort to attain high grades does not represent a good use of a student's time. If the student seeks some kind of postgraduate training, however, good grades are essential, and a high degree of effort is in order. To discern educational aspirations, we asked sophomores to tell us the highest degree they expected to earn, and answers to this question are summarized in table 2.7.

Table 2.7
Efforts and expectations that students expressed as sophomores (percent)

Efforts and Expectations	Whites	Asians	Latinos	Blacks
Highest Degree Expected				
Less than Bachelor's	0.4	0.5	0.1	0.4
Bachelor's Degree	28.6	29.5	28.3	27.4
Master's or Equivalent	42.1	35.9	37.9	39.7
Doctorate or Equivalent	27.2	32.1	32.5	31.1
Don't Know	0.0	0.0	0.0	0.1
Refused	1.9	2.0	1.3	1.2

A majority of students in all groups expected to seek education beyond the bachelor's degree. Only 27% of blacks, 28% of Latinos, 29% of whites, and 30% of Asians said they planned to earn only a four-year degree. Among whites, the largest share, 42%, expected to earn a master's degree or equivalent, and 27% said they planed to go on for a doctorate or equivalent. Among other groups, the relative number expecting to go on for a doctorate was significantly higher (t-tests <0.05), with roughly a third (32% of Asians, 33% of Latinos, and 31% of African Americans) saying they planned to earn a Ph.D. or equivalent. Likewise 36% of Asians, 38% of Latinos, and 40% of blacks expected to earn a master's. Obviously, then, students in all groups had very high aspirations and, if anything, those of Asians, Latinos, and blacks exceeded those of whites.

Major Decisions

By the end of the sophomore year, most students had selected a major, with the percentage ranging from 71% of Latinos to 78% of whites. Majors declared by the spring of the sophomore year are listed in table 2.8, again classified by academic division and field, and standardized to a cohort of 1,000 students. Among the sciences, biology is the most common major and the only one to rise into double digits, with 63 majors for Asians, 50 for blacks, 47 for whites, and 39 for Latinos. In all, a total of 124 Asians had declared a science major by the sophomore year, compared with 114 whites, 85 blacks, and just 71 Latinos ($F = 9.0$, $p < .001$). Expressed as a ratio of white science majors, the figure of 1.09 for Asians reconfirms the proclivity toward science already noted in their course selections, and the

Table 2.8
Majors declared by spring term of sophomore year (standardized cohort of 1,000)

Division and Field	Whites	Asians	Latinos	Blacks
Biological and Physical Sciences				
Biochemistry	2	4	1	0
Biological Bases of Behavior	6	1	3	1
Biology	47	63	39	50
Botany	5	0	3	3
Materials Science	2	9	0	3
Mechanical Science	5	2	4	2
Physics	7	7	3	3
Neuroscience	7	12	4	4
Zoology	8	4	3	3
Other Science	25	22	11	13
Total	*114*	*124*	*71*	*85*
Ratio to Whites	*1.00*	*1.09*	*0.62*	*0.75*
Math, Computer Science, and Engineering				
Actuarial Science	1	1	0	2
Aerospace Engineering	2	1	3	4
Bioengineering	3	4	0	2
Chemical Engineering	12	5	1	9
Civil Engineering	7	1	5	3
Computer Science	36	63	42	37
Electrical Engineering	20	26	16	9
Engineering	21	45	24	23
Mathematics	15	11	4	13
Total	*117*	*157*	*95*	*102*
Ratio to Whites	*1.00*	*1.34*	*0.81*	*0.87*
Social and Behavioral Sciences				
Anthropology	10	9	10	10
Criminal Justice	3	0	5	2
Economics	43	50	37	24
Geography	2	4	0	2
International Relations	18	28	38	15
Political Science	46	34	61	65
Psychology	52	24	47	77
Sociology	22	17	15	39
Urban Studies	1	2	4	7
Total	*197*	*178*	*217*	*241*
Ratio to Whites	*1.00*	*0.90*	*1.10*	*1.22*
Humanities				
Art or Art History	18	17	22	9
English	53	28	37	34
Foreign Language	13	8	32	10
History	42	11	27	30
Music or Dance	15	12	9	9
Philosophy	6	4	4	4

Table 2.8 *(continued)*

Division and Field	Whites	Asians	Latinos	Blacks
Religion	6	5	8	4
Total	*153*	*85*	*139*	*100*
Ratio to Whites	*1.00*	*0.56*	*0.91*	*0.65*
Professions				
Architecture	10	13	19	5
Business	60	69	59	61
Communications	28	12	19	22
Education	13	17	13	13
Journalism	12	13	14	12
Radio/TV/Film/Drama	16	5	19	18
Total	*128*	*129*	*143*	*131*
Ratio to Whites	*1.00*	*1.01*	*1.12*	*1.02*
Health and Sports				
Nursing	9	5	10	3
Premed	1	6	3	4
Health or Health Policy	1	14	0	7
Pharmacology	1	5	0	2
Physical Therapy	1	1	6	2
Sports Science	9	4	8	16
Total	*22*	*35*	*27*	*34*
Ratio to Whites	*1.00*	*1.59*	*1.23*	*1.55*
Interdisciplinary Majors				
African American Studies	1	1	0	15
Environmental Studies	12	7	6	2
Other	6	0	3	5
Total	*19*	*8*	*9*	*22*
Ratio to Whites	*1.00*	*0.42*	*0.47*	*1.16*
No Major Declared	224	262	288	264
Ratio to Whites	*1.00*	*1.17*	*1.29*	*1.18*

corresponding figures of 0.62 and 0.75 for Latinos and blacks underscores the general impression of their avoidance of science.

In terms of majors, though, the pattern of black and Latino avoidance of science is not as marked with respect to math, computer science, and engineering; but the attraction of Asians is more accentuated. Whereas 157 Asians declared a major in this category, only 117 whites did so, giving Asians a relative prevalence ratio of 1.34, compared with figures of 0.87 for blacks and 0.81 for Latinos ($F = 8.8$, $p < .001$). For all groups, computer science is the most popular major in this category, followed by general engineering and electrical engineering. Whites and Latinos were more likely than either blacks or Asians to select a humanities major ($F = 8.8$, $p < .001$).

The relative equality between groups in selecting social science courses gives way to more variety in the choice of social science majors. The strongest proclivity toward a social science major is exhibited by blacks, 241 of whom selected a major in this category compared with 197 whites, yielding a ratio of 1.22. For Latinos the ratio is 1.10, and for Asians it is 0.90. Thus, Latinos were around 10% more likely than whites to major in the social sciences. and Asians were 10% less likely, with African Americans being the standout at 22% more likely ($F = 4.0$, $p < .01$). Among social science disciplines, the most popular majors for African Americans are psychology, political science, sociology, and economics, whereas among Asians the ordering is economics, political science, psychology, and sociology. For whites the ranking is psychology, political science, and economics, and among Latinos political science, psychology, economics, and sociology. Asians and Latinos also display unusually high concentrations in international relations.

Whites, Asians, and blacks display roughly equal propensities toward professional majors, with ratios of 1.00 to 1.02. Latinos are slightly higher with a ratio of 1.12, owing mainly to a strong representation in architecture and radio-TV-film-drama, but in general the differences were not significant ($F = 0.3$, $p = .820$). For all groups, the most popular professional major was business, usually followed by communications and radio-TV-film-drama. In the category of health and sports, meanwhile, blacks and Asians have roughly the same number of majors, although they are concentrated in very different subfields, with 14 Asians specializing in health or health policy and 16 African Americans in sports science. Latinos and Asians display a more pronounced tendency to major in nursing.

Table 2.9 compares racial/ethnic groups by ranking the broad categories of major separately for each group. As can be seen, for all groups the number one category of major is still, by the end of the sophomore year, "no major declared," and the next most popular category is social and behavioral sciences. Beyond second place, the preference rankings of the various groups begin to diverge. For whites, humanities is the third most popular area for a major, whereas among Asians and African Americans it is fifth and among Latinos fourth. The professions stand at the fourth position for whites and Asians, and this category is third for Latinos and blacks. Math–computer science–engineering comes in at fifth place for

Table 2.9
Rank of division for majors selected by students by the spring term of their sophomore year

General Division of Major	*Rank of Division for:* Whites	Asians	Latinos	Blacks
No Major Declared	1	1	1	1
Social and Behavioral Sciences	2	2	2	2
Humanities	3	5	4	5
Professions	4	4	3	3
Math–Computer Science–Engineering	5	3	5	4
Biological and Physical Sciences	6	5	6	6
Health and Sports	7	7	7	7
Interdisciplinary	8	8	8	8

whites and Latinos and fourth place for blacks, with Asians being the standout by boosting it to third place. Biological and physical sciences are the sixth most popular area for a major among whites, Latinos, and blacks and the fifth most popular among Asians. The seventh and eight positions are the same across all groups: health and sports followed by interdisciplinary studies.

The notable finding with respect to the broad divisions of declared major is thus Asians' strong preference for mathematics, computer science, and engineering compared with other groups. The distinctiveness of Asians' choice of major is further revealed in table 2.10, which shows the top ten major subjects rather than broad divisions. For Asians, business is first in popularity, followed by biology and computer science in a tie for second/third, engineering in fourth, economics in fifth, political science and psychology in a tie for sixth/seventh, international relations in eighth, English in ninth, and electrical engineering in tenth position. Thus, only one of the top ten Asian major subjects is in the humanities. All the rest are natural sciences, engineering, the quantitative social sciences, or business.

In contrast, the very top major among whites, English, is in the humanities, and history stands at number seven. Three of the most popular majors are social sciences (psychology is second, political science fifth, and economics sixth), and two are in the professions (business is third and communications ninth). No engineering discipline appears in the top ten white majors, though computer science ranks eighth; and the only science apart from the residual "other" category is biology, which is in fourth place.

Table 2.10
Rank of field for majors selected by students by the spring term of their sophomore year

	Rank of Field for			
Field of Major	Whites	Asians	Latinos	Blacks
Top Ten Majors for Whites				
English	1	9	7.5	7
Psychology	2	6.5	3	1
Business	3	1	2	3
Biology	4	2.5	5	4
Political Science	5	6.5	1	2
Economics	6	5	7.5	9
History	7	*	10	8
Computer Science	8	2.5	4	6
Communications	9	*	*	*
Other Sciences	10	*	*	*
Additional Top Ten Majors for Others				
Engineering	*	4	*	10
Electrical Engineering	*	10	*	*
International Relations	*	8	6	*
Foreign Language	*	*	9	*
Sociology	*	*	*	5

*Not applicable.

Latinos display a proclivity toward majors in social science disciplines, including political science (first in preference), psychology (third), international relations (sixth), economics (tied for seventh/eighth), and the related professional field of business (second). The humanities have three entries in the top ten but fairly low on the list, with English tied for seventh/eighth, foreign languages in ninth (including Spanish), and history in tenth place. The only sciences are computer science (fourth) and biology (fifth). Engineering subjects do not appear at all on their list of most popular major subjects.

Blacks display an even stronger attraction to social science majors, with psychology ranking first, political science second, sociology fifth, economics ninth, and the related profession of business in third place. In contrast to these five social science–related courses, just two are in the humanities (English in seventh place and history in eighth), and three are in the sciences or engineering (biology in fourth place, computer science in sixth, and general engineering in tenth).

Predicting the Selection of Courses

The data analyzed so far reveal clear differences among groups in the propensity to take different sorts of courses—science versus humanities, math and engineering versus social science, easy versus hard. Here we consider the degree to which intergroup differences in course taking are attributable to differences in social and economic background, or whether they reflect something about groups per se—their values, cultural orientations, historical experiences, or position in society. *The Source of the River* clearly documented intergroup differences with respect to demographic background, parental education, economic status, academic preparation, and social preparation, and showed that specific variables under each heading were important in determining grade performance.

Here we use the same set of background variables to predict course selection, along with dummy variables measuring group membership. We control for demographic background using dummy variables for gender (1 if male, 0 otherwise), foreign origins (1 if a parent was born abroad, 0 otherwise), and family status (1 if the respondent grew up in a two-parent family, 0 otherwise), and by counting the number of siblings under 18 in the respondent's household. Parental education is measured using a series of dummy variables indicating the number of degrees held by parents, with no college degree serving as the reference category. Parental socioeconomic status is measured using the value of the home owned by the respondent's custodial parent, coded as 0 if no home was owned, along with dummy variables for household income greater than $100,000 (1 if yes, 0 otherwise) and whether or not the respondent's family had ever been on welfare (1 if yes, 0 otherwise). Academic preparation is measured by the number of advanced placement courses taken in high school, the cumulative GPA earned in high school, and the respondent's self-assessed preparation on a 0 to 10 scale. Finally, social and psychological preparation for college is measured using scales of self-esteem and self-efficacy developed by Rosenberg and Simmons (1971) and scales of social distance from whites and sensitivity to peer influence developed by Massey et al. (2003), both of which are described in detail in appendix B of *The Source of the River*.

Table 2.11 presents a series of equations estimated using ordinary least squares to predict the number of courses taken by students in different subject categories: humanities, math and sciences, social sciences, professional

Table 2.11
OLS equations estimating determinants of number of courses taken in different subjects in freshman and sophomore years

Independent Variable	Humanities	Math & Sciences	Social & Behavioral Sciences	Professional Studies	Area, Ethnic, & Gender Studies	Health & Physical Education
Group						
White	—	—	—	—	—	—
Asian	−1.323***	1.397***	−0.182	0.223**	0.115†	−0.018
Latino	−0.228	0.038	−0.025	0.018	−0.023	0.012
Black	−0.535**	0.081	−0.129	−0.088	0.309***	0.131
Demographic Background						
Male	−0.828***	1.312***	−0.456***	0.066	−0.269***	−0.118†
Foreign-Born Parent	−0.333	0.467	0.008	0.021	0.003	0.081
Two-Parent Family	−0.405†	0.499*	−0.168	0.111	−0.045	0.085**
Siblings under 18	−0.038	0.134	−0.132*	−0.037	0.020	0.013
Education of Parents						
No College Degrees	—	—	—	—	—	—
One College Degree	0.279	−0.361	0.125	0.036	0.026	−0.062
Two College Degrees	0.252	−0.041	0.244	0.126	−0.115	−0.107
One Advanced Degree	0.434†	−0.075	0.103	0.003	−0.067	0.166***
Two Advanced Degrees	0.891**	−0.388	0.255†	−0.307†	−0.060	−0.188***

Economic Status						
Home Value (000)	0.000	0.000	0.000	0.000	0.000	0.000
Ever on Welfare	0.046	−0.173	−0.162	−0.134	0.064	0.088
Income > $100,000	−0.317†	0.057	0.060	0.036	−0.011	0.080†
Academic Preparation						
AP Courses Taken	0.033	0.100†	0.139***	−0.103†	0.016	−0.026
High School GPA	−0.497	2.050***	−0.342	−0.339	0.072	−0.120
Self-rated Preparation	0.071†	−0.082**	0.031*	0.034*	−0.003	0.005
Social Preparation						
Self-efficacy	0.026	−0.006	−0.002	−0.008	0.003	−0.004
Self-esteem	−0.029	0.002	0.035	0.011	0.001	0.004
Susceptibility to Peer Influence	0.089***	−0.015	0.003	−0.034**	0.002	−0.004
Social Distance from Whites	−0.028	−0.025	0.017	−0.017*	0.031***	0.002
Intercept	8.712***	−2.042	3.198**	2.743*	0.152	1.033**
R^2	0.051***	0.081***	0.032***	0.038***	0.075***	0.026***
Number of Cases	2,839	2,839	2,839	2,839	2,445	2,839

†$p < .10$ *$p < .05$ **$p < .01$ ***$p < .001$

studies, area-ethnic-gender studies, and health and physical education. In these regression equations, if the dummy variable for a group proves to be insignificant, it means that its members are no more or less likely than whites to take courses in the category under consideration, once background factors are controlled. However, if a group's indicator remains significant despite the application of statistical controls, it suggests that something else about the group in question accounts for its distinctive pattern of course selection. In order to conserve space we show only coefficient estimates and not the associated standard errors; the statistical significance of effects is indicated by asterisks.

The first column in the table shows the effect of different variables on the number of humanities courses taken during the freshman and sophomore years. It strongly confirms the pattern of Asian avoidance noted in the descriptive tabulations. Even controlling for a host of background factors, Asians are much less likely to enroll in humanities courses than whites. Once background differences are held constant statistically, whites, Latinos, and blacks are found to display identical tendencies to take humanities courses; but not Asians.

Male students also take significantly fewer courses in the humanities once background factors are controlled. Aside from gender, other factors that appear to be relevant in predicting humanities course taking are parental education, susceptibility to peer influence, and to a lesser extent income and self-rated preparation. Susceptibility to peers is measured using a seven-item rating scale that varies from 0 to 18 and has a reliability of 0.59 (see appendix B in *Source*). Other things equal, those students who report themselves as being more sensitive to what their friends and associates think about them tend to enroll in more humanities courses. Likewise, the greater the number of degrees held by a respondent's parents, the more humanities courses he or she takes.

Looking across the remaining columns in the table we see that Asians stand out in the selection of other kinds of courses as well. Compared with the other groups, they are significantly more likely to take math and science courses, more likely to take courses in one of the professions, and to a lesser extent are also more likely to take courses in area-gender-ethnic studies (mainly courses in East Asian studies). The only other group-specific coefficients to attain significance across this set of regressions pertain to African Americans. Like Asian students, black students are less likely than whites and Latinos to take courses in the humanities and much more likely to take courses in area-gender-ethnic studies, reflecting the concentration in African and African American and women's studies noted earlier. However, the apparent attraction of black students to health and physical education courses disappears once background factors are controlled, suggesting that black students take more physical education and health courses not because they value them per se as African Americans but because they come from less-advantaged family backgrounds, and in particular have less-educated parents. Students who grow up in families with less human capital generally gravitate toward such nonacademic courses (see Massey et al. 2003).

Among the equations in the table, the only other consistent effect is that of gender. Other things equal, males tend to avoid courses in the humanities, social sciences, and area-ethnic-gender studies but are attracted to math and science courses. Thus, consistent with studies by Jacobs (1986, 1999), we find significant gender segregation across college courses. Academic preparation also plays some role in determining the number of courses taken in the social and the natural sciences. Students who entered college with more advanced placement courses and higher grades generally enrolled in more math and science courses; and more advanced placement courses also predicted enrollment in social science courses. Interestingly, self-rated preparation for college (on a 0 to 10 scale) was *negatively* related to the number of courses taken in math and science. Students who felt less prepared academically seem to take more courses in science and math, which are generally harder.

Table 2.12 addresses the issue of course difficulty directly by predicting the number of courses students would take that are classified as "easy" and "hard" according to the criteria used in table 2.4. As can be seen, the only group systematically to avoid "easy" courses is Latinos, and the only background factors that really influence the number of such courses taken are gender, self-rated preparation, and susceptibility to peer influence. Males generally avoid high-grading, easy courses, whereas those who rate themselves as better prepared for college and more sensitive to the opinions of others take more of them.

In terms of the number of hard courses taken, Asians continue to stand out from other groups. Even after background differences are held constant, members of this group take many more courses classified as hard. Attraction to hard courses is also predicted by gender and academic preparation. Males take significantly more hard courses than do females, as do

Table 2.12
OLS equations estimating determinants of number of easy and hard courses taken during freshman and sophomore years

	Number of Easy Courses		*Number of Hard Courses*	
Independent Variables	B	SE	B	SE
Group				
White	—	—	—	—
Asian	−0.175	0.184	1.005***	0.183
Latino	−0.525***	0.112	−0.008	0.171
Black	0.121	0.167	0.277	0.213
Demographic Background				
Male	−0.604***	0.093	0.725***	0.133
Foreign-Born Parent	−0.107	0.165	0.457*	0.184
Two-Parent Family	−0.334*	0.143	0.244†	0.145
Siblings under 18	−0.041	0.033	0.034	0.089
Education of Parents				
No College Degrees	—	—	—	—
One College Degree	0.038	0.145	−0.223	0.201
Two College Degrees	−0.086	0.145	0.321	0.229
One Advanced Degree	−0.031	0.140	0.295	0.199
Two Advanced Degrees	0.111	0.187	0.106	0.243
Economic Status				
Home Value (000)	0.000	0.000	0.000	0.000
Ever on Welfare	0.062	0.204	−0.141	0.172
Income > $100,000	−0.281	0.154	0.236†	0.127
Academic Preparation				
AP Courses Taken	−0.014	0.047	0.091*	0.038
High School GPA	−0.289	0.243	1.475***	0.223
Self-rated Preparation	0.041*	0.019	−0.043†	0.021
Social Preparation				
Self-efficacy	−0.008	0.028	0.019	0.022
Self-esteem	−0.004	0.011	−0.002	0.013
Susceptibility to Peer Influence	0.036**	0.015	−0.019	0.015
Social Distance from Whites	−0.002	0.009	−0.021*	0.010
Intercept	3.817**	1.370	−1.808	1.183
R^2	0.039***		0.094***	
Number of Cases	2,955		2,955	

†$p<.10$ *$p<.05$ **$p<.01$ ***$p<.001$

students of immigrant origins and those who have taken more advanced placement courses and earned higher GPAs from high school. In contrast, taking hard courses is negatively predicted by perceived social distance from whites. Given that social distance from whites is measured using a three-item scale with a range of 0 to 30 (see Massey et al. 2003, appendix B) and that each point increase in perceived distance from whites lowers the likelihood of taking a hard course by .03 points, a person who felt maximally distant from whites would take about one fewer "hard" course ($30 \times .03 = 0.9$), suggesting that feelings of social alienation on campus can influence academic decision making. Indeed, referring back to table 2.11, we see that social distance from whites negatively predicts the taking of professional courses while positively predicting the taking of courses in area-ethnic-gender studies.

Origins of Efforts and Aspirations

Whatever the effect that perceptions of social distance have on *which* courses are taken, they have no apparent affect on either the *perceived* difficulty of courses or on the *effort* students report putting into them. Degree of perceived difficulty is measured using a twelve-item scale ranging from 0 to 120 with a reliability of .75, whereas degree of effort is measured using an eight-item scale varying from 0 to 80 with a reliability of .82 (see appendix C of this volume for details). Table 2.13 presents the results of OLS regressions estimated to predict these outcomes from group indicators and background characteristics.

The left-hand columns confirm our earlier observation of relatively minor differences between groups with respect to perceived difficulty. The only group-specific coefficient that is even marginally significant is that for Asians, and its effect is substantively quite small. However, once again males stand out: they systematically perceive courses to be less difficult than females, as do those who perceive themselves to be well-prepared academically for college. The equation predicting effort has more explanatory power than that predicting difficulty, as indicated by the higher R^2 and the greater preponderance of significant effects. Degree of effort is strongly and positively related to parental education and academic preparation as measured both by self-rating and grades earned in high school. Effort is negatively predicted by being male, coming from a welfare background, and by having taken a greater number of advanced placement courses. Once these various effects are controlled, we see that African Americans put in greater effort than whites whereas Asians put in significantly less.

Table 2.14 continues the analysis of academic integration by predicting the relative frequency with which students avail themselves of various

Table 2.13
OLS equations estimating determinants of perceived degree of difficulty and perceived degree of effort put into courses taken during freshman and sophomore years

	Degree of Difficulty		*Degree of Effort*	
Independent Variables	B	SE	B	SE
Group				
White	—	—	—	—
Asian	−0.127†	0.063	−0.187**	0.069
Latino	−0.016	0.065	0.104	0.085
Black	−0.128	0.083	0.170†	0.091
Demographic Background				
Male	−0.304***	0.049	−0.530***	0.057
Foreign-Born Parent	−0.119	0.083	−0.037	0.081
Two-Parent Family	0.111	0.066	0.092	0.074
Siblings under 18	−0.029	0.025	−0.022	0.025
Education of Parents				
No College Degrees	—	—	—	—
One College Degree	0.084	0.079	−0.012	0.089
Two College Degrees	0.137	0.094	0.113	0.114
One Advanced Degree	0.118	0.083	0.152	0.119
Two Advanced Degrees	0.126	0.097	0.267***	0.089
Economic Status				
Home Value (000)	0.000	0.000	0.000	0.000
Ever on Welfare	−0.022	0.074	−0.179*	0.080
Income > $100,000	−0.002	0.071	−0.076	0.073
Academic Preparation				
AP Courses Taken	−0.017	0.017	−0.058**	0.017
High School GPA	0.142	0.100	0.524***	0.141
Self-rated Preparation	−0.032**	0.010	0.041***	0.010
Social Preparation				
Self-efficacy	−0.008	0.012	0.016	0.014
Self-esteem	−0.001	0.005	0.009	0.007
Susceptibility to Peer Influence	0.006	0.006	0.006	0.009
Social Distance from Whites	−0.006	0.006	−0.003	0.007
Intercept	5.695***	0.439	4.074***	0.512
R^2	0.025***		0.059***	
Number of Cases	2,956		2,956	

†$p<.10$ *$p<.05$ **$p<.01$ ***$p<.001$

educational supports and services. Specifically, we regress the indexes described earlier and shown in figure 2.3 on group indicators and background characteristics. Across all estimated equations, group membership proves to be highly significant in predicting the seeking of academic support. As

Table 2.14
OLS equations estimating determinants of frequency with which students sought different kinds of assistance as freshmen and sophomores

	Kind of Assistance			
Independent Variables	Institutional	Professorial	Peer	Libraries and Laboratories
Group				
White	—	—	—	—
Asian	1.571†	−2.130*	2.050***	2.352**
Latino	3.407***	−0.654	1.431**	2.407***
Black	8.393***	4.019**	2.488***	4.025***
Demographic Background				
Male	−1.487***	−1.787*	−1.332**	−3.185***
Foreign-Born Parent	1.714†	2.072**	−0.625	2.869***
Two-Parent Family	0.178	−1.335	0.276	0.513
Siblings under 18	0.039	−0.541	−0.205	0.240
Education of Parents				
No College Degrees	—	—	—	—
One College Degree	−1.171	0.180	1.557**	−0.094
Two College Degrees	−2.385***	−0.102	−0.625	−0.974
One Advanced Degree	−2.706**	−0.152	0.234	−0.848
Two Advanced Degrees	−2.782**	2.539*	0.648	0.812
Economic Status				
Home Value (000)	0.001	−0.001	0.000	−0.001
Ever on Welfare	1.805	0.608	1.076†	1.122
Income > $100,000	0.379	−0.725	0.288	−0.283
Academic Preparation				
AP Courses Taken	−0.967***	−0.592*	0.017	−0.318†
High School GPA	−2.502	−0.923	1.001	1.326
Self-rated Preparation	−0.470***	0.255*	−0.232***	−0.108
Social Preparation				
Self-efficacy	−0.044	0.511**	0.023	0.189
Self-esteem	0.033	0.187**	0.058	−0.047
Susceptibility to Peer Influence	−0.072	0.261**	−0.166**	0.140*
Social Distance from Whites	0.095	0.136*	0.002	0.074
Intercept	27.819***	18.908***	15.453***	25.869***
R^2	0.135***	0.076***	0.040***	0.058
Number of Cases	2,797	2,795	2,798	2,795

†$p<.10$ *$p<.05$ **$p<.01$ ***$p<.001$

one might expect, accessing institutional resources such as tutoring, advising, and special instruction is negatively predicted by academic preparation and by parental education. Those students most likely to use institutional support services are those whose parents did not finish college, who took no advanced placement courses in high school, and who view their academic preparation as weak.

Even holding constant these effects, however, males are significantly less likely than females to seek out institutional assistance in support of their studies. Moreover, even after accounting for lower parental education and less academic preparation, minorities display a far greater tendency to make use of institutional supports than do whites. On the scale of institutional assistance, Asians use 2.5 points more of institutional services than whites, compared with 4.1 points among Latinos and 8.9 points among African Americans. Indeed, across all forms of assistance African Americans display the greatest usage levels. As the table clearly shows, blacks stand out from all other groups in making contact with professors and making use of libraries and laboratories. Although all minority groups, including Asians, display a greater proclivity than whites to turn to peers for academic assistance, the tendency is slightly greater for African Americans.

In sum, African Americans stand out for putting more effort into their studies than other groups as well as for making greater use of institutional and faculty resources for academic support. Based on these data, no one can say that black students are not taking their education seriously, a point that is buttressed by the analysis shown in table 2.15. This table presents a multinomial logit model estimated to predict educational aspirations. It shows the effect of group membership and background characteristics on the odds of aspiring to a master's degree or equivalent, or a Ph.D. degree or equivalent, compared with those who are satisfied with just a bachelor's degree.

As one might logically expect, aspirations to acquire an advanced degree are positively predicted by parental education and income, academic preparation, and self-esteem, but unlike results in the other models we have estimated to this point, we find no gender difference on this dimension. For both males and females, as family income and the number of parental degrees rise, the odds of seeking a master's and especially a doctorate increase sharply. Likewise, those earning higher grades in high school are more likely to seek an M.A. or Ph.D., and those completing advanced placement courses and rating themselves as well prepared academically are more likely to seek a doctorate or equivalent.

Table 2.15
Multinomial logistic regression estimating the determinants of educational aspirations

	Seeks to Earn M.A. or Equivalent		*Seeks to Earn Ph.D. or Equivalent*	
Independent Variables	B	SE	B	SE
Group				
White	—	—	—	—
Asian	−0.328**	0.133	−0.119	0.129
Latino	0.175	0.162	0.379**	0.150
Black	0.279*	0.136	0.366**	0.141
Demographic Background				
Male	0.091	0.071	−0.173	0.117
Foreign-Born Parent	0.083	0.179	0.005	0.155
Two-Parent Family	0.021	0.095	−0.109	0.118
Siblings under 18	−0.045	0.048	0.005	0.059
Education of Parents				
No College Degrees	—	—	—	—
One College Degree	0.270**	0.101	0.155	0.163
Two College Degrees	0.281*	0.132	0.347*	0.169
One Advanced Degree	0.399**	0.131	0.427**	0.135
Two Advanced Degrees	0.690***	0.166	0.831***	0.213
Economic Status				
Home Value (000)	0.000	0.000	0.000	0.000
Ever on Welfare	0.061	0.144	0.235	0.204
Income > $100,000	0.285**	0.103	0.521***	0.123
Academic Preparation				
AP Courses Taken	0.027	0.038	0.135***	0.032
High School GPA	0.472***	0.132	1.198***	0.177
Self-rated Preparation	0.026	0.016	0.033†	0.018
Social Preparation				
Self-efficacy	−0.015	0.019	0.014	0.021
Self-esteem	0.026***	0.008	0.036***	0.010
Susceptibility to Peer Influence	0.007	0.009	0.031**	0.011
Social Distance from Whites	−0.003	0.009	0.016†	0.010
Intercept	−2.699***	0.521	−7.511***	0.783
Log Likelihood	2931.112***			
Number of Cases	2,798			

†$p<.10$ *$p<.05$ **$p<.01$ ***$p<.001$

Holding constant these important effects, however, the very ambitious educational plans of Latinos and blacks still clearly stand out. Blacks are significantly more likely to aspire to an M.A. or equivalent, and both blacks and Latinos are much more likely than other groups to intend to pursue a doctorate or equivalent. This result suggests a potentially troubling paradox for underrepresented minorities. Although they are more likely than whites or Asians to aspire to attend graduate or professional school, they nonetheless earn significantly lower grades, which, of course, probably reduces their odds of admission to top programs.

Determinants of Majors Chosen and Grades Earned

The last facet of academic decision making we consider before turning to the subject of grades is the choice of a major. Table 2.16 presents the results of a multinomial logit model estimated to predict the major field selected by the spring of the sophomore year, with no major (undeclared) serving as the reference category. As with the selection of courses, in the choice of majors it is Asians who stand out most clearly from other groups, displaying a systematic and significant reluctance to declare a humanities major and a modest proclivity to select instead a math, computer science, or engineering major. Although Asians display a positive attraction to the biological and physical sciences, the effect is not significant after controlling for background differences; but compared with other groups Asians do tend to avoid the residual category of "other" majors.

Aside from the Asian avoidance of humanities and attraction to quantitative fields, the only other strong effect is the apparent avoidance by Latinos of the biological and physical sciences. In choosing a major, blacks and whites are indistinguishable once background characteristics are taken into account. As in most of the prior analyses done in this chapter, we find rather strong and significant effects of gender. Other things equal, male students avoid majors in the humanities and professions and seek out those in math, computer science, and engineering, again confirming the pattern reported by Jacobs (1986, 1999) of gender segregation by major.

Table 2.17 completes our analysis of academic currents by predicting the grade point average earned over the first two years of college. The analysis proceeds in stages moving from left to right across columns in the table. The leftmost pair of columns regresses group indicators on GPA

Table 2.16

Multinomial logit regression estimating determinants of major declared by end of sophomore year

Independent Variable	Humanities	Biological & Physical Sciences	Social & Behavioral Sciences	Math, Computer Science, & Engineering	Profession	Other
Group						
White	—	—	—	—	—	—
Asian	−0.713***	0.077	−0.239	0.292†	0.270	−1.754†
Latino	−0.085	−0.481*	0.012	−0.107	−0.127	−0.027
Black	−0.341	−0.134	−0.028	−0.054	−0.285	0.538
Demographic Background						
Male	−0.370**	−0.028	−0.137	0.802***	−0.359†	0.130
Foreign-Born Parent	−0.141	−0.043	0.054	0.070	−0.091	−1.217†
Two-Parent Family	0.006	−0.057	−0.114	0.240	−0.175	0.170
Siblings under 18	−0.053	−0.034	−0.063	0.046	−0.025	0.130
Education of Parents						
No College Degrees	—	—	—	—	—	—
One College Degree	0.220	−0.300	0.128	0.079	0.180	−0.049
Two College Degrees	0.200	−0.016	0.350*	0.074	0.037	−0.272
One Advanced Degree	0.085	−0.326	−0.012	0.003	−0.074	−1.199*
Two Advanced Degrees	0.461	−0.228	0.288	0.219	−0.559†	−0.772
Economic Status						
Home Value (000)	0.000	−0.001**	0.000	−0.001*	0.000	0.000
Ever on Welfare	−0.142	−0.389†	−0.267	−0.126	−0.415	−0.377
Income > $100,000	−0.036	0.281	0.126	0.047	0.110	0.347

(continued)

Table 2.16 *(continued)*

Independent Variable	Humanities	Biological & Physical Sciences	Social & Behavioral Sciences	Math, Computer Science, & Engineering	Profession	Other
Academic Preparation						
AP Courses Taken	0.008	0.053	0.040	0.016	−0.214**	−0.282***
High School GPA	−0.723***	0.629†	−0.448†	0.109	−0.679*	−0.485
Self-rated Preparation	0.065**	0.037	0.032	0.013	0.069**	0.060
Social Preparation						
Self-efficacy	0.027	0.016	0.018	0.034	0.027	0.042
Self-esteem	−0.008	−0.001	0.032*	0.003	0.014	−0.019
Susceptibility to Peer Influence	0.040**	−0.003	0.005	0.011	−0.048***	0.019
Social Distance from Whites	−0.022*	−0.034**	0.004	−0.004	−0.040***	0.027
Intercept	1.414	−3.016*	0.009	−2.707	3.731*	−1.250
Log Likelihood	4777.93***					
Number of Cases	2,782					

†$p < .10$ *$p < .05$ **$p < .01$ ***$p < .001$

Table 2.17

OLS model estimating determinants of GPA earned during freshman and sophomore years

	Group + Controls		*Major + Group + Controls*		*Difficulty + Major + Group + Controls*		*Full Model*	
Independent Variables	B	SE	B	SE	B	SE	B	SE
Key Indicators								
Group								
White	—	—	—	—	—	—	—	—
Asian	0.031	0.015	0.042*	0.016	0.045**	0.014	0.059**	0.013
Latino	−0.090***	0.019	−0.089**	0.021	−0.076***	0.021	−0.071*	0.019
Black	−0.186***	0.034	−0.185***	0.034	−0.189***	0.032	−0.182***	0.027
Major								
None Declared	—	—	—	—	—	—	—	—
Biological-Physical Sciences	—	—	0.091**	0.033	0.104**	0.031	0.053†	0.031
Math–Comp Sci–Engineering	—	—	0.039†	0.021	0.062**	0.020	0.050*	0.019
Social-Behavioral Sciences	—	—	0.101***	0.033	0.093**	0.032	0.056*	0.025
Humanities	—	—	0.181***	0.027	0.131***	0.026	0.089***	0.019
Professions	—	—	0.128***	0.033	0.130***	0.034	0.109***	0.029
Other	—	—	0.111*	0.053	0.074	0.053	0.027	0.051
Measured Difficulty of Courses								
Number of Easy Courses	—	—	—	—	0.023***	0.004	0.022***	0.003
Number of Hard Courses	—	—	—	—	−0.006†	0.003	−0.004	0.002
Subjective Perceptions								
Difficulty of Courses	—	—	—	—	—	—	−0.027**	0.009
Degree of Effort	—	—	—	—	—	—	0.048***	0.007

(continued)

Table 2.17 *(continued)*

	Group + Controls		*Major + Group + Controls*		*Difficulty + Major + Group + Controls*		*Full Model*	
Independent Variables	B	SE	B	SE	B	SE	B	SE
Academic Assistance								
Institutional Help	—	—	—	—	—	—	−0.003***	0.0005
Professorial Help	—	—	—	—	—	—	0.003***	0.0005
Peer Help	—	—	—	—	—	—	−0.003**	0.0009
Use of Libraries and Labs	—	—	—	—	—	—	0.000	0.0006
Academic Aspirations								
M.A. or Equivalent	—	—	—	—	—	—	0.012	0.020
Ph.D. or Equivalent	—	—	—	—	—	—	0.061**	0.023
Control Variables								
Demographic Background								
Male	−0.073***	0.014	−0.058***	0.012	−0.044**	0.013	−0.027*	0.012
Foreign-Born Parent	0.004	0.019	−0.001	0.020	0.002	0.019	0.003	0.017
Two-Parent Family	0.019	0.020	0.026	0.020	0.035†	0.020	0.041†	0.021
Siblings under 18	−0.009	0.008	−0.008	0.007	−0.007	0.007	−0.005	0.007
Education of Parents								
No College Degrees	—	—	—	—	—	—	—	—
One College Degree	0.037	0.025	0.038	0.024	0.037	0.024	0.032	0.025
Two College Degrees	0.102***	0.022	0.086***	0.021	0.092***	0.020	0.068**	0.021
One Advanced Degree	0.099**	0.026	0.095***	0.024	0.099***	0.023	0.078**	0.024
Two Advanced Degrees	0.166***	0.032	0.159***	0.027	0.161***	0.025	0.134***	0.029

Economic Status								
Home Value (000)	0.000	0.000	0.000	0.000	0.000	0.000	0.000	0.000
Ever on Welfare	−0.014	0.023	−0.009	0.021	−0.011	0.022	0.004	0.022
Income > $100,000	0.036	0.021	0.028	0.021	0.036†	0.020	0.033	0.021
Academic Preparation								
AP Courses Taken	0.014*	0.005	0.015**	0.005	0.016**	0.006	0.014***	0.004
High School GPA	0.427***	0.030	0.447***	0.032	0.457***	0.029	0.421***	0.026
Self-rated Preparation	0.032***	0.003	0.028***	0.003	0.027***	0.003	0.021***	0.003
Social Preparation								
Self-efficacy	−0.004†	0.003	−0.006*	0.003	−0.006*	0.003	−0.008**	0.002
Self-esteem	0.004*	0.002	0.005**	0.002	0.005**	0.002	0.003	0.002
Susceptibility to Peer Influence	0.010***	0.001	0.010***	0.001	0.010***	0.001	0.008***	0.001
Social Distance from Whites	0.001	0.002	0.002	0.002	0.002	0.002	0.002	0.002
Intercept	1.060***	0.148	1.050***	0.152	0.971***	0.154	1.109***	0.140
R^2	0.294		0.323***		0.343		0.389	
Number of Cases	2,943		2,832		2,832		2,787	

†$p<.10$ *$p<.05$ **$p<.01$ ***$p<.001$

while controlling for the background factors considered in the foregoing tables. This equation thus offers a baseline of group-specific differences in grade performance holding constant family demography, parental education, economic status, academic preparation, and social preparation. As can be seen, with these background conditions equalized, Asians and whites earn roughly the same GPA, whereas that earned by Latinos is 0.09 points lower and that of blacks 0.19 points lower on a conventional 0 to 4 grade scale, where 4 is an A and 0 is an F.

The next pair of columns adds the student's declared major to the set of predictor variables. This does little to change the relative grade performance of Latinos and African Americans, but it does push the Asian coefficient upward to achieve statistical significance. Once the choice of major is controlled, in other words, Asians earn significantly higher grades than whites, suggesting that the concentration of Asians in science and math depresses their performance relative to whites. In general, students who declare a disciplinary major by the end of their sophomore year earn higher grades than those who do not, suggesting that high academic achievers tend to pick their major field earlier than others. Among the disciplines, grade points are highest in the humanities, followed by the professions, the social sciences, the biological and physical sciences, and finally math, computer science, and engineering.

The third pair of columns adds controls for the number of easy and hard courses taken, based on the criteria used earlier in table 2.4. Controlling for the difficulty of courses reduces the range of variation by major. Compared with undeclared majors, all disciplinary majors earn GPAs that range from 0.06 to 0.13 points higher than nonmajors (compared with a range of 0.04 to 0.16 in the prior equation). Thus some of the disparity in grade performance across majors is explained by the relative difficulty of courses across disciplines.

As one would expect, taking more relatively hard courses depresses the GPA earned by students; but the effect is not strong and is only marginally significant. Average grades are much more strongly determined by the relative number of easy courses taken. Indeed, each additional easy course taken raises a student's GPA by 0.022 points, whereas each hard course lowers GPA by just 0.005 points. The effect of easy courses on grades is thus more than four times greater than that of hard courses.

Controlling for course difficulty also increases, very slightly, the apparent grade performance of Asians, consistent with our earlier suggestion that the superior grade performance of Asians is masked by their greater proclivity to take hard courses. Our ultimate conclusion is that because Asians are more likely to take "hard" courses in math, science, and engineering and less likely to take "easy" courses in the humanities, they earn lower grades relative to whites than they otherwise would. Once one adjusts for this difference in course distribution, Asians seem to perform *better* academically than whites.

The last pair of columns adds in the self-reports of students about perceived difficulty, use of academic services, and educational aspirations. The addition of these controls increases even further the grade performance of Asians relative to whites while leaving the relative performance of Latinos and blacks unchanged. Other things equal, Asians earn GPAs that are nearly 0.06 points greater than those of whites, which is quite similar to the deficit exhibited by Latinos. Although we already introduced controls in prior equations for the "objective" difficulty of courses, adding in the students' subjective perceptions of difficulty further increases the explanatory power of the model without significantly reducing the effect of the earlier measure. Thus our objective and subjective measures of difficulty complement rather than duplicate one another. As expected, the more difficult that students perceive courses to be, the lower the GPA of students who take them.

As one would logically expect, the degree of academic effort reported by students has a significant and positive effect on grades, as do contacts with professors in- and outside class and aspirations to study at the doctoral level. The use of libraries and laboratories is unrelated to grade performance, however, and greater usage of institutional services and peers is associated with lower grades. This negative effect probably does not mean that getting institutional help lowers grades but, rather, that students with poor academic preparation and, hence, lower grades seek institutional assistance. The same could equally be said about peer support: those who turn to peers for support are those who are already in trouble academically. Though a negative peer influence on grades is also possible, research to date is quite consistent in finding that learning is improved, not hampered, when students work together and teach each other (Chickering and Gamson 1991; Brufee 1993; Cottell 1996; Hagedorn et al. 1999; Pascarella and Terenzini 2005). Being tutored by peers has also been shown repeatedly to produce academic outcomes that are as good as or better than those produced by studying alone (Fantuzzo, Dimeff, and Fox 1989; Riggio et al. 1991; Topping 1996; Pascarella and Terenzini 2005).

Battling the Academic Currents

Plunging into the first two years of higher education at a selective institution is a daunting task for most students. Not only do they shift from an environment where they were likely an academic star to one where almost everyone was a high school star of some sort, but they also acquire a new freedom of choice. Beyond meeting general requirements, they can take whatever courses they wish and specialize in whichever field interests them. With no parent watching over them, at least directly, and little adult supervision, it is they who decide when and if to go to the library, how long to work in the laboratory, how much effort to put into studying, and how many easy versus hard courses to take. They make these decisions on a daily basis, given their tastes, aspirations, abilities, perceptions of course difficulty, and judgments of the probability of success.

During the freshman year, students in all groups pursued similar course-taking strategies as they focused on meeting general requirements and exploring the curriculum. Although relatively minor intergroup differences were apparent in the first year, by the sophomore year group-specific strategies of course selection had become better defined. Asians displayed a clear tendency to avoid humanities courses and gravitated instead toward courses in technical, quantitative disciplines such as math, the sciences, and engineering, as well as the professions. They also displayed a modest attraction to area studies courses, focused on Asian and Asian-American studies. African Americans likewise displayed a strong attraction toward African and African American studies as well as gender studies courses, and like Asians they tended to avoid humanities courses. Although blacks signed up for health and physical education courses in relatively large numbers, this proclivity reflects lower levels of preparation and parental education rather than group membership per se. Latinos and whites displayed no differences in course-taking patterns once background differences were held constant.

Patterns of course selection were generally consistent with the majors that students in different groups ultimately declared. Thus, controlling for background characteristics, Asians were significantly less likely than other groups to declare a humanities major and significantly more likely to declare a major in mathematics, computer science, or engineering. Latinos were less likely than other groups to declare a major in the social or behavioral sciences. Aside from these tendencies, however, the attraction to various majors was generally quite similar across groups.

By the end of the sophomore year, students in different groups had accumulated significantly different numbers of course credits. Given the rate of course taking observed among NLSF students, a cohort of 1,000 Asian students would have accumulated a total of 19,327 courses by the end of their sophomore year, followed in descending order by whites at 19,159, Latinos at 18,647, and African Americans at 18,586. In terms of courses taken per student per year, these numbers work out to 9.7 for Asians, 9.6 for whites, and 9.3 each for Latinos and African Americans. Although not exceptionally large, the differences are significant statistically and suggest that as sophomores blacks and Latinos were beginning to lag behind whites and Asians in accumulating the number of courses necessary for graduation.

We also found significant intergroup differences in the distribution of courses by degree of difficulty. In general, Asians were strongly attracted to hard courses, and Latinos displayed a tendency to eschew easy courses but were no different from whites or blacks in their propensity to take hard courses. Students in different groups responded to the challenge of college course work with different degrees of effort. Other things equal, African Americans reported a higher degree of academic effort than whites, whereas Asians reported a lower effort level. Latinos and especially African Americans were also more likely to make use of institutional services such as tutoring and special support classes, as well as library and laboratory facilities. Black students were also most likely to engage professors in- and outside class. All minority groups—Asians as well as blacks and Latinos—were more likely than white students to turn to peers for academic support. Black and Latino students also had somewhat higher educational aspirations than either whites or Asians, being more likely to aspire to postgraduate studies at both the master's and doctoral levels.

Prior research using data from the NLSF revealed clear differences in first-term grade performance between groups, a tendency that did not change with the passage of time. By the end of the sophomore year, whites and Asians were still earning roughly the same grades, whereas Latinos averaged 0.09 points lower and blacks around 0.19 points lower, controlling for differences in demographic background, parental education, economic status, academic preparation, and social preparation. The addition of further controls for course difficulty, subjective effort, academic assistance, and educational aspirations did not affect the relative standing of Latino or black students compared with whites, but it reduced their respective gaps slightly to 0.07 and 0.18 grade points.

The addition of controls did, however, significantly affect the relative grade performance of Asians. As noted above, Asians took more courses in mathematics, the sciences, and engineering than other students and fewer courses in the humanities, and as a result of this course distribution they ended up taking relatively larger numbers of classes that were "hard" in the sense that students tend to earn lower grades in them, whereas they took fewer courses that were "easy." Adjusting for course difficult improves the grade performance of Asians relative to whites. Although Asians and whites appear to earn the same grades in raw comparisons, this equivalence seems to result from the fact that Asians take more difficult courses, on average, than whites. Once one adjusts statistically for this fact, Asians are found to outperform whites slightly with respect to GPA. In sum, based on early patterns of course selection, choice of major, and grades earned, Asians appear to be best prepared for occupations and careers that demand technical training and expertise, and they are in the best position to pursue advanced degrees in these fields.

3 Staying Afloat Socially

For most 18-year-olds who head off to college, arriving on campus is the first step on a long road to adulthood and independence. Until that moment, the vast majority of students lived with one or both of their parents in a household composed primarily of kin—mainly parents and siblings (full, half, and step) but sometimes grandparents, aunts, uncles, and cousins as well. Although prior work with the NLSF has shown that parents in different racial-ethnic groups participate in the lives of their children to different degrees, all were in a position to monitor their children's behavior on a day-to-day basis. Although coresident parents cannot control their children's behavior absolutely, they are uniquely positioned to notice subtle changes in comportment, to observe whether children are working hard on their studies or spending more time with friends, and to take note of the date, time, frequency, and duration of their comings and goings.

None of the selective colleges and universities included in the NLSF are commuter institutions. By accepting admission into these schools, most students are implicitly agreeing to move out of their parents' home and into a radically different social environment, one inhabited by a new and quite selective group of peers (fellow students, all presumably exceptional in some way). In doing so, they will acquire a new set of authority figures who are far more distant than parents (professors, counselors, and school administrators), and they will experience little direct supervision. For the first time in their lives they will share living space with people who are not close relatives, and their behavior will not be monitored on a daily basis by older adults. Although professors may issue periodic evaluations that trigger closer supervision by a dean, coach, or counselor, in general the day-to-day habits of college students will be witnessed only by roommates or close friends of the same age and experience.

Freshmen arriving on campus thus enter a new social world in which the influence of parents wanes, that of peers rises, exposure to formal authority becomes more indirect, and far more responsibility falls on individual shoulders. The choices made by students in responding to these new social circumstances carry serious implications for their subsequent academic careers. Although studies have generally found that living off versus on campus has no effect on collegiate learning once other factors are controlled (Kuh 1993; Pascarella et al. 1993; Pascarella and Terenzini 2005), participation in fraternities and sororities does lower scholastic achievement along a variety of academic dimensions (Pike and Askew 1990; Anaya 1992; Pascarella et al. 1996; Pascarella, Flowers, and Whitt 2001). While a Greek affiliation may be hazardous to students' academic health, however, it does increase their sense of community and raise their level of social integration on campus (Pike and Askew 1990; Lounsbury and DeNeui 1995).

Apart from cavorting with fraternities and sororities, interacting with peers outside the classroom seems generally to have a positive effect on collegiate learning (Kuh et al. 1991; Arnold et al. 1993; Astin 1993; Davis and Murrell 1993; Pascarella and Terenzini 2005; Whitt et al. 1999). Likewise, participation in campus service organizations is associated with higher academic achievement (Markus, Howard, and King 1993; Gray et al. 1996; Astin and Sax 1998), especially, of course, if the service involved occurs in the context of a course (Eyler 1993, 1994; Eyler and Giles 1999). As with fraternities and sororities, however, participation in student clubs and social organizations appears to have a small but significant negative influence on academic achievement as assessed (Anaya 1992, 1996; Astin 1993). Although working for pay does reduce time spent studying, it does not appear to detract significantly from learning as measured by standardized tests (Pascarella et al. 1994, 1998; Pascarella and Terenzini 2005).

Taking the Plunge Socially

Ultimately, of course, each student must rely on his or her own judgment in managing the transition to social independence; but navigating the social currents of campus life is no easy task. Not only must students negotiate a highly competitive academic environment; they must also manage a perplexing social environment that is at once more diverse (containing people of different racial, ethnic, regional, and class backgrounds) but also more homogeneous (composed of fellow students of the same age, all selected for their academic ability). For these reasons, the living situations that students encounter as freshmen and sophomores are likely to play a key role in conditioning their social and academic progress.

Most students' introduction to social life on campus begins in a college dormitory, which is certainly true of students in the NLSF regardless of their race or ethnicity. As table 3.1 shows, 97% to 98% of all freshmen across all groups lived on campus in a dormitory during their first year of college. Thus, the initial experience of student residential life was rather uniform, occurring within institutional quarters in the company of one or two roommates (the average was 1.2 to 1.3 persons). By sophomore year, however, intergroup differences in living arrangements had begun to emerge. Whereas one-third of whites and Latinos shifted out of dorms and into other kinds of housing during the second year, 80% of blacks and 75%

Table 3.1
Information by race and ethnicity about living situation of freshmen attending 28 selective colleges and universities (percent)

Variable	Whites	Asians	Latinos	Blacks
Freshman Year				
On Campus				
Dormitory	98.2	97.3	97.1	96.9
Apartment	0.1	0.3	0.1	0.2
Off Campus				
Apartment	0.6	0.5	0.5	0.6
Fraternity/Sorority	0.3	0.0	0.0	0.1
Parents/Relatives	0.8	1.9	2.1	2.1
Sophomore Year				
On Campus				
Dormitory	66.8	75.1	66.8	79.6
Apartment	6.2	5.3	7.1	5.4
Off Campus				
Apartment	16.3	13.8	16.1	8.4
Fraternity/Sorority	8.9	2.8	6.8	1.2
Parents/Relatives	1.7	2.7	3.2	5.3

of Asians remained in school-sponsored dormitories, a significant set of differences ($F = 16.0$, $p < .001$). Instead of dorm life, 16% of whites and Latinos chose an off-campus apartment, 7% to 9% picked a fraternity or sorority, and 6% to 7% selected an on-campus apartment; a very small number (2% to 3%) lived with relatives (virtually all parents).

With two exceptions, the living choices made by Asians are similar to those made by whites and Latinos. The main difference between Asians and the other groups is their avoidance of fraternities and sororities. Whereas 9% of whites selected this living option, only 3% of Asians did so ($t = -5.4$, $p < .001$). This difference in proclivity toward Greek life accounts for most of Asians' greater representation in dorms relative to whites. The distribution of Asians across other housing conditions is quite similar, with 5% residing in on-campus apartments (compared with 6% for whites) and 14% in off-campus apartments (16% for whites). As with whites and Latinos, few very Asians (3%) lived with relatives (again almost all parents).

African Americans evince the most distinctive pattern of housing in the sophomore year. As already noted, a significantly higher fraction (80%) remained in campus dormitories as sophomores, and whereas the share occupying on-campus apartments is roughly comparable to that evinced by other groups (5% compared with 5% to 7%), the percentage who lived in off-campus apartments or sororities and fraternities is much lower. Only 8% of black sophomores lived in an off-campus apartment, compared with 16% of whites ($t = -4.4$, $p < .001$), and whereas 9% of whites inhabited a sorority or fraternity only 1% of African Americans did so ($t = -7.6$, $p < .001$).

The great exception to the rule of African Americans eschewing off-campus housing is their greater propensity to live with relatives, though the relative share living with family is still small. Whereas 5% of black sophomores lived with a family member (nearly all parents), only 2% of whites did so ($t = 4.8$, $p < .001$). Thus, compared with other groups, African Americans appear to be more reluctant, or perhaps less able, to venture off campus to live on their own as sophomores. Although there is a modest shift between the freshman and sophomore years away from on-campus dorms to off-campus arrangements, 90% of black sophomores still lived on campus or with a parent.

Despite the foregoing differentials in the propensity to live on and off campus, most freshmen and sophomores continued to inhabit institutional settings, and the overwhelming majority continued to have roommates. Living in multiunit settings with roommates means that students lack full

Table 3.2
Distractions experienced very Frequently by race and ethnicity

Variable	Whites	Asians	Latinos	Blacks
Freshman Year				
Percentage Very Frequently Distracted By:				
Talking or Conversation	40.0	39.4	39.1	36.0
Someone Playing a Stereo	19.7	22.3	18.5	18.1
Someone Watching TV	8.2	7.9	9.1	8.3
Friends Partying	5.4	6.9	6.8	5.6
Being Talked into Going Out	17.1	18.2	17.7	14.5
Percentage Saying They Very Frequently:				
Had to Leave to Do Schoolwork	19.7	22.3	22.6	24.0
Had to Stay Late at Library to Work	8.0	12.0	12.5	12.9
Sophomore Year				
Percentage Very Frequently Distracted By:				
Talking or Conversation	33.3	32.8	32.8	29.8
Someone Playing a Stereo	17.3	15.6	16.2	15.8
Someone Watching TV	9.6	10.6	10.3	10.0
Friends Partying	7.1	5.6	6.5	5.2
Being Talked into Going Out	18.6	20.8	20.4	14.7
Percentage Saying They Very Frequently:				
Had to Leave to Do Schoolwork	27.1	26.9	25.2	28.0
Had to Stay Late at Library to Work	9.0	14.4	13.3	13.5

Note: "Very frequently" is defined by a rating of 7 or greater on a 0–10 frequency scale.

control over their home environment, raising the possibility of ongoing distractions that potentially compete with schoolwork. In recognition of this fact, the NLSF asked students how frequently they experienced various kinds of distracting events, and these data are summarized in table 3.2.

Respondents were asked to rate on a 0 to 10 scale how frequently they found themselves distracted at home by talking or conversation, the playing of a stereo, someone watching TV, and friends partying. In the table we show the percentages who experienced these distractions "very frequently," meaning that they assigned the distraction a frequency rating of 7 or greater. Among freshmen living in dormitories for the first time, distractions from talking or conversation were most common and were reported with considerable frequency. Some 40% of whites reported experiencing this distraction with high frequency, whereas for Asians and Latinos the figure is 39% and for African Americans it is 36% (the latter difference significant at $p < 0.01$).

Other distractions were generally reported less frequently. Among whites, 20% reported being distracted frequently by someone playing a stereo, 8% by someone watching TV, and 5% by friends partying. The percentages are similar among other groups, and the same patterns prevail in the sophomore year. During the second year of college, distraction by talking or conversation continued to be most common, followed by stereo playing, TV watching, and partying. Once again the intergroup differences are minor, though African Americans do display slightly lower levels of distraction by talking and conversation.

Across all groups, there is a decline between the freshman and sophomore years in the level of distraction from conversation or stereo playing. For example, whereas 40% of white freshmen reported being frequently distracted by talking or conversation, only 33% of white sophomores did so. Among Asians and Latinos, the decline from freshman to sophomore year is 39% to 33%, and among African Americans it goes from 36% to 30%, all shifts that are statistically significant at conventional levels. Likewise, the share of whites who were frequently distracted by someone playing a stereo drops slightly from 20% among white freshmen to 17% among white sophomores, with corresponding shifts of 22% to 16% among Asians, 19% to 16% among Latinos, and 18% to 16% among African Americans, shifts that are generally below or on the margins of statistical significance.

In contrast, the frequency of distraction from TV watching and friends partying seems to increase slightly or stay the same. Whereas 8% of white freshmen said they were distracted by someone watching TV and 5% by friends partying, among white sophomores the respective figures are 10% and 7%. Among Asians the shift in distraction is from 8% TV watching and 7% partying in the freshman year to 11% and 6% in the sophomore year. These small shifts are again on the margins of statistical significance. However, the frequency of distraction from partying and television is generally stable between freshman and sophomore Latinos and blacks. As freshmen, 9% of Latinos and 8% of African Americans said they were frequently distracted by someone watching TV, whereas among sophomores the figure for both groups stands at around 10%. Likewise, 7% of Latino freshmen and 6% of black freshmen reported very frequent distraction by friends partying, compared with respective figures of 7% and 5% in the sophomore year.

These patterns are consistent with what one might expect given the fact that within each group a significant (though variable) fraction of students shifted from dormitory to apartment living between the freshmen and sophomore years. Thus distractions associated with high-density institutional living—loud hallway conversations and stereos blasting away next door—declined in frequency, whereas those associated with roommates—TV watching and partying—did not necessarily decline, and in some cases increased slightly.

Associated with friends partying is the possibility of being talked into going out to have fun rather than staying at home to study. Among freshmen, 17% of whites admitted to succumbing to this temptation frequently (that is, they reported a frequency rating of 7 or more on the 0 to 10 scale), with similar figures for the other groups (18% for Asians and Latinos and 15% for African Americans). Thus, all groups appear to display similar levels of resolve in the face of temptations to go out and have fun; and, if anything, blacks are slightly less prone to this kind of temptation than others. Essentially the same pattern of group-specific differentials prevails among sophomores.

The second panel in table 3.2 presents information on behaviors that students might adopt to avoid the distractions we have considered: leaving home to do schoolwork somewhere else and staying late at the library to work rather than coming home. As freshmen, 20% of whites reported frequently leaving home to get schoolwork done, compared with 22% of Asians, 23% of Latinos, and 24% of blacks, differences that are not significant ($p > .10$). Although black freshmen appear to be slightly more likely to leave home to study as freshmen, by the sophomore year even this small difference has disappeared, though the frequency of leaving home to pursue schoolwork does increase significantly for all groups. Among whites, 27% said they frequently left home to do schoolwork, compared with 27% of Asians, 25% of Latinos, and 28% of blacks. Apparently students in all groups found roommates more distracting as sophomores than as freshmen.

Another way of avoiding distractions at home is to stay late at the library, and here whites seem to be the outliers. Whereas 8% of white freshmen reported that they frequently stayed late at the library, 12% of Asians and 13% of both Latinos and African Americans did so ($F = 5.5, p < .001$). By sophomore year, the figures had risen to 9% for whites, 13% for Latinos, and 14% for Asians and blacks. In general, therefore, blacks seem to be slightly more sensitive to potential distractions at home and most inclined to take evasive action, whereas whites are least affected and least inclined to eschew home for study purposes, but the differences are fairly modest in substantive terms.

Navigating Peer Cultures

Perhaps more important than what college friends and roommates do is what they think and, specifically, the traits and behaviors they appear to value, for it is the values held by friends and associates that determine the normative context within which students make choices about how to allocate their time among the myriad possibilities available to them—studying, reading, socializing, volunteering, extracurricular participation, and so forth (Hallinan 1982, 1983). Although we later measure what students actually *do* with the time at their disposal, here we focus on their perceptions of what others around them *think*. As the sociologist W. I. Thomas long ago pointed out, things that are perceived as real are often real in their consequences (Thomas and Thomas 1929).

Table 3.3 reports how students in the various racial and ethnic groups perceived their fellow students valued selected aspects of academic and

Table 3.3
Percentage of respondents who said that various activities were very important to their peers during the spring of the sophomore year

Variable	Whites	Asians	Latinos	Blacks
Academic Culture				
Attend Class Regularly	53.1	54.9	58.1	55.5
Study Hard	69.6	68.3	71.8	74.3
Get Good Grades	74.5	75.9	79.0	85.8
Graduate from College	94.6	93.0	93.9	95.1
Go to Graduate/Professional School	38.7	49.6	50.8	54.8
Social Life				
Have Steady Boy- or Girlfriend	10.5	12.7	11.6	13.8
Be Willing to Party	43.5	35.7	40.9	36.4
Play Sports	11.2	10.3	9.3	11.7
Be Popular	35.0	30.7	31.2	30.6
Hang Out with Friends	76.9	71.8	67.2	61.8
Beyond Academics				
Participate in Religious Activities	9.9	18.0	14.3	26.9
Do Volunteer Work in Community	13.2	17.9	15.1	21.2
Have Job to Help Pay for Education	9.6	13.5	15.3	23.2

Note: "Very important" is defined by a rating of 7 or greater on a 0–10 importance scale.

social life. The specific wording of the question, posed at the end of the sophomore year, was "considering the views of your friends and close acquaintances here at (name of college), how important is it to them to . . . ," followed by a list of attitudes and behaviors. The top panel focuses on academic outcomes. Given the fact that students attending very selective schools must already have put in considerable effort to gain admission, it is not surprising that most respondents perceive their peers to put a high premium on graduation. Thus, the share stating that it is very important to graduate from college (i.e., those rating it 7 or more on the 0 to 10 scale) is universally high at 93% to 95% for all groups.

The relative number saying it is very important to attend classes regularly is somewhat lower and more variable across groups: 53% for whites, 55% for Asians, 56% for blacks, and 58% for Latinos ($F = 2.3, p < .10$). Although these group differentials may seem small, they hint at a greater attention to academic achievement in the peer cultures of Latino and black students compared with whites and Asians. Indeed, whereas 70% of whites and 68% of Asians reported that their friends and close acquaintances felt it was very important to study hard, the respective figures for Latinos and African Americans are 72% and 74% ($F = 6.8, p < .001$).

Likewise, whereas only 75% of whites and 76% of Asians said their peers viewed getting good grades as being very important, the figures were 79% among Latinos and 86% among African Americans ($F = 27.8, p < .001$). The reason why the peers of minorities appear to put greater emphasis on academics is suggested by the data shown in the bottom line of the top panel of table 3.3. Among African Americans and Latinos, there is much greater peer pressure to go on to a graduate or professional school. Whereas only 39% of whites said their peers felt it was very important to go to graduate or professional school, 50% of Asians, 51% of Latinos, and 55% of African Americans did so ($F = 18.6, p < .001$).

In other words, although the peers of all racial and ethnic groups strongly endorse the importance of college graduation, the friends and close acquaintances of African Americans, Latinos, and Asians place a greater emphasis (compared with whites) on academic achievement, emphasizing the importance of studying hard and getting good grades in order to get into a good graduate or professional school. Indeed, the latter represents a goal that a majority of black, Latino, and Asian students, but a minority of white students, perceive to be very important among their peers.

The lower importance assigned by white peers to academics is paralleled by a greater emphasis on social life. While few consistent intergroup differences emerge with respect to the importance of having a steady romantic partner or playing sports, there are clear differences with respect to the importance of partying, being popular, and hanging out with friends. Whereas just 11% to 14% of respondents in any group reported that their peers viewed a steady boy- or girlfriend as very important, and just 9% to 12% said that playing sports was important, among whites 44% said their friends and close acquaintances viewed being willing to party as being very important, 35% said being popular was important, and 77% said hanging out with friends was important. In contrast, the respective figures for African Americans were 36% for partying ($t = -5.6$, $p < .001$), 31% for being popular ($t = -6.2$, $p < .001$), and 62% for hanging out with friends ($t = -7.5$, $p < .001$). Among Latinos the respective percentages were 41%, 31%, and 67%, and among Asians they were 36%, 31%, and 72% (all significantly different from those of whites at $p < .05$). Thus white peers seem to place the most emphasis on deriving social satisfaction from college life and black peers the least, with the peers of Latinos and Asians lying in between.

The final panel of the table shows how respondents viewed friends' and acquaintances' perceptions with respect to other activities involving religion, work, and volunteering in the community. Once again whites and blacks line up at opposite ends of the spectrum with the other two groups in between. Whereas just 10% of whites reported that their peers saw religious participation as very important, the figure is 27% for African Americans, compared with 14% for Latinos and 18% for Asians ($F = 39.4$, $p < .001$). Likewise, whereas only 13% of whites perceived peers to weigh volunteer work as important, 21% of African Americans did so, compared with 15% of Latinos and 18% of Asians ($F = 10.5$, $p < .001$). Finally, just 10% of whites said their peers valued a job to pay for education as very important, compared with 23% of black peers, 14% of Asian peers, 15% of Latino peers ($F = 5.1$, $p < .001$).

Patterns of Participation

The foregoing tabulations suggest that white and black students lie at different ends of a continuum of peer culture. The friends and close associates of white students value social life highly, and academic achievement is seen

Table 3.4
Percentage of students in different groups who said they were involved in selected activities during their sophomore year

Variable	Whites	Asians	Latinos	Blacks
Academic				
Career Development Group	7.6	12.8	11.3	17.8
Foreign-Language Group	5.1	9.0	10.4	5.0
Music, Arts, Theater Group	19.2	17.8	18.1	23.1
Social				
Varsity or JV Sports Team	10.8	5.0	5.7	13.1
Intramural Sports Team	30.9	21.6	24.2	14.5
Fraternity or Sorority	26.6	15.2	20.8	10.7
Organizational				
Environmental or Political Group	17.2	16.1	16.3	19.6
Religious Group	18.4	25.6	18.3	27.2
Community Group	37.1	45.8	35.7	44.1

as relatively less important; they also place a relatively low emphasis on participation in religious and community activities. In contrast, the friends and close acquaintances of black students place high emphasis on academic achievement while giving less weight to social life and placing greater emphasis on participation in religious and community activities. Latinos and Asians generally fall between these extremes, with Latinos generally being closer to blacks and Asians closer to whites.

Here we consider whether the foregoing differences in social context are paralleled by concrete differences in behavior with respect to participation. The simplest way of assessing patterns of student participation is simply to ask respondents which groups they currently belong to. Table 3.4 presents the results of this exercise, which was carried out in the spring of the sophomore year. For ease of interpretation, activities are divided into three categories: academic, social, and community.

The first activity we consider under the academic heading is participation in a group or organization devoted to career development, such as a "sociology club" for sociology majors or "future CPAs" for accounting majors. Peer interactions in contexts that reinforce what happens in the academic program have been shown to facilitate knowledge acquisition among college students (Astin 1993; Arnold et al. 1993; Davis and Murrell 1993; Watson and Kuh 1996; Whitt et al. 1999). As one might expect given the emphasis of black peers on graduate or professional education, African Americans are the most likely to be active in career development groups.

Whereas 18% of black students reported belonging to such a group, only 8% of whites did so, compared with 13% of Asians and 11% of Latinos ($F = 14.8$, $p < .001$). Likewise, 23% of black students said they were involved with a music, arts, or theater group compared with 19% of whites and 18% of the other groups ($F = 9.5$, $p < .001$). The only activity that constitutes an exception to the pattern of greater black participation is membership in a foreign-language organization, where Asians and Latinos stand out, reflecting their immigrant roots ($F = 3.2$, $p < .05$).

As the second panel of the table shows, with the exception of varsity sports whites clearly dominate other groups when it comes to participation in social activities. Whereas 27% of whites belonged to a fraternity or sorority, the frequency was only 11% for African Americans, 15% for Asians, and 21% for Latinos ($F = 28.9$, $p < .001$). Likewise 31% of whites participated in intramural sports, compared with just 15% of blacks, 22% of Asians, and 24% of Latinos ($F = 23.8$, $p < .001$). The only exception to the greater involvement of whites than blacks in social activities is in varsity or junior varsity sports. In this case, 13% of black students reported participation, compared with 11% of whites, 6% of Latinos, and just 5% of Asians ($F = 16.8$, $p < .001$), and the black-white differential is not statistically significant ($t = 1.5$, $p > .10$).

The third panel considers the rate of participation in other community-oriented groups. Although we observe few differences in the rate of participation in environmental or political organizations (with rates of 16% to 19% across groups), clear differentials emerge with respect to religious participation and the residual "other" category. In keeping with the peer cultures described earlier, we see that just 18% of white students reported involvement in a religious organization compared with 27% of blacks ($t = 4.5$, $p < .001$); and whereas 37% of whites reported an affiliation with some kind of "other" organization, 44% of blacks did so ($t = 3.0$, $p < .001$). Asians also evinced relatively high levels of participation, 26% for religious groups and 46% for other organizations, compared with figures of 18% and 36% among Latinos.

Allocation of Time

Although the foregoing intergroup differentials paint a general picture of the degree to which members of various groups are involved in different kinds of campus activities and organizations, they reveal little about the intensity of that involvement or how—when push comes to shove—students make tradeoffs between competing demands. To derive a more concrete, detailed, and accurate picture of student behavior on campus, we turn to time-use analysis (see Michelson 2005).

Time is the ultimate scarce resource. The amount of time at anyone's disposal is ultimately fixed by the bookend events of life and death, and the daily time available to each person in between is just twenty-four hours. If one spends a dollar today, one can always earn another dollar tomorrow; but spending an hour on some activity means that it is gone forever and can never be recovered. The scarcity of time and the need for its strategic allocation are brought home to human beings every day. Upon waking, each human being is faced with the task of how to allocate an inelastic amount of time available in the diurnal cycle. The number of potential activities greatly exceeds the number of available hours. Some of these activities are mutually exclusive and some not, but all place absolute demands on the fixed amount of time at one's disposal.

Choices made about the allocation of time thus reveal in very concrete terms what actions are deemed important and which activities are valued more than others. In both the freshmen and sophomore follow-up surveys, therefore, we asked respondents "to consider the last week, from Monday through Friday, on which classes were held" and to "estimate the total number of hours that you spent" in different activities, which were then listed for them. Table 3.5 presents average amounts of time spent by freshmen in different activities classified according to major categories relevant in the life of a college student: academic, extracurricular, recreational, life maintenance, and income generation.

Academic activities are obviously central to scholarly achievement, and in the top panel of the table we display average amounts of time that whites, Asians, Latinos, and blacks reported they spent attending class or lab, studying, computing, and reading or writing. The total amount of time allocated to these four activities reveals small differences by race and ethnicity. Across all groups, students devoted an average of 38 to 41 hours to academic activities during the typical five-day school week. Asians allocated the greatest amount of time to academic pursuits, 40.5 hours, followed by Latinos at 40 hours and blacks at 38.8 hours, and whites were lowest at 37.5 hours ($F = 3.3$, $p < .05$). This rough parity in total hours spent on academic pursuits is paralleled by general similarities in the amounts of time allocated to specific activities under this heading: all groups spent an

Table 3.5
Average amount of hours during most recent full week of classes (Monday–Friday) that freshmen spent engaged in different activities

Variable	Whites	Asians	Latinos	Blacks
Academic Activities				
Attending Class or Lab	17.7	18.8	18.1	18.5
Studying	18.2	19.7	20.1	18.9
Computing	1.3	1.8	1.2	0.9
Reading or Writing	0.3	0.2	0.6	0.5
Total	*37.5*	*40.5*	*40.0*	*38.8*
Extracurricular Activities				
General Extracurricular	8.4	8.5	8.4	9.0
Playing or Practicing Sports	4.2	3.2	3.2	3.9
Doing Volunteer Work in Community	0.9	1.3	1.3	1.5
Total	*13.5*	*13.0*	*12.9*	*14.4*
Recreational Activities				
Watching Television	3.9	3.7	4.0	5.4
Listening to Music	9.5	10.8	11.9	12.5
Attending Parties	4.2	3.3	4.2	3.1
Socializing with Friends	12.9	12.8	13.1	12.8
Other Recreation	1.1	0.8	1.2	1.1
Total	*31.6*	*31.4*	*34.4*	*34.9*
Income-Generating Activities				
Working for Pay	2.9	3.2	5.3	5.7
Life Maintenance Activities				
Sleeping	35.1	34.6	34.8	32.4
Other Maintenance	1.5	1.5	1.3	1.4
Total	*36.6*	*36.1*	*36.1*	*34.2*
Other	3.3	3.5	2.9	2.7
Assessment of Time Stress				
Actual Hours in Week	120.0	120.0	120.0	120.0
Total Hours Reported	125.4	127.7	131.6	130.7
Ratio Total/Actual Hours	1.05	1.06	1.10	1.09
Estimated Waking Hours	84.9	85.4	85.2	87.6
Total Hours of Waking Activity	90.3	93.1	96.8	98.3
Ratio Waking Activity/Waking Hours	1.06	1.09	1.14	1.12

average of 18 to 19 hours per week attending class or lab ($F = 3.8, p < .01$), 18 to 20 hours studying ($F = 2.74$, $p < .05$), 1 to 2 hours computing ($F = 4.2, p < .01$), and 0 to 1 hours reading or writing ($F = 2.5, p < .10$).

We also found relatively modest intergroup differences with respect to extracurricular activities ($F = 5.0$, $p < .01$), which took up an average of 13 to 14 hours per week across groups, including 1 to 2 hours of volunteer work ($F = 6.2$, $p < .001$), 3 to 4 hours playing sports ($F = 6.8$, $p < .001$), and 8 to 9 hours in different extracurricular endeavors ($F = 2.0$, $p = .11$). Sharper differences emerge with respect to recreation, however. Whereas white students reported spending an average of just under 32 hours per week on recreational activities, black students reported spending around 35 hours per week, compared with around 31 hours for Asians and 34 hours for Latinos ($F = 11.3$, $p < .001$).

Although African Americans spend about the same amount of time as whites and other group members socializing with friends and engaging in "other" recreational activities, and they spend slightly less time attending parties, blacks allocate relatively more time to watching television and listening to music, and these activities account for most of the greater amount of total time they devote to recreation. Whereas whites, Asians, and Latinos spent only around 4 hours per week watching television, black students spent more than 5 hours in TV viewing ($F = 18.6$, $p < .001$); and whereas whites spent 9.5 hours listening to music, blacks spent some 12.5 hours, on average, compared with 11.9 hours for Latinos and 10.8 for Asians ($F = 7.0$, $p < .001$).

Consistent with the greater support evinced by black peers for employment, black students allocated more time than other groups to paid work. On average, they reported spending 5.7 hours per week on the job, compared with just 2.9 hours for whites, 3.2 hours for Asians, and 5.3 hours for Latinos ($F = 43.2$, $p < .001$). However, the number of hours devoted to activities in the residual "other" category and in life maintenance activities (e.g., grooming, showering, washing clothes, etc.) differed little between groups. In general, miscellaneous "other" activities took up 2.7 to 3.3 hours per week, and general life maintenance activities accounted for another 1.3 to 1.5 hours.

In sum, black students appear to devote more time during the school week than whites and other groups to recreational activities and working for pay, and about the same amount of time to academic pursuits, general life maintenance activities, and "other" obligations. Possibly in order to compensate for the greater pressure on their time, black students appear to sleep less than other groups. During a normal school week, for example, the average black respondent reported sleeping 32.4 hours, compared with 35.1 hours for whites, 34.6 hours for Asians, and 34.8 hours for Latinos ($F = 14.5$, $p < .001$). Blacks thus sleep 2.0 to 2.5 hours less per week than other groups attending selective schools.

We hypothesize that attempting to fit more activities into a fixed amount of time causes a certain amount of stress. Within any five-day week there are no more than 120 hours available to allocate to any combination of activities. The degree to which the foregoing time allocations contribute to time stress can be seen from the calculations shown at the bottom of table 3.5. Whereas all groups attempt to fit more activities into a fixed week of 120 hours than is ideal, Latinos and African Americans stand out as trying to do more than others. Whereas whites reported a total of 125.4 hours of activities per week, African Americans reported 130.7 hours, compared with 127.7 for Asians and 131.6 for Latinos. These excesses over 120 hours are possible only because some activities are not mutually exclusive (e.g., one can study and listen to music at the same time), and the gap between total hours reported and total available is finessed by multitasking.

Attempting to cram more and more activities into a fixed amount of time creates stress, which we indicate by the ratio of the total hours of reported activity to the actual number of hours per week. Among Latinos and African Americans the ratio of reported to actual hours is 1.10 and 1.09 respectively, compared with values of 1.05 and 1.06 among whites and Asians. As we have noted, however, African Americans apparently seek to overcome this time crunch by sleeping less, so in the bottom three lines we recompute our measure of time stress for waking hours only. As can be seen, sleeping less does not eliminate the time stress that black students experience relative to others. The ratio of waking activities to waking hours is 1.12 for blacks compared with just 1.06 for whites; the same ratio is 1.14 for Latinos and 1.09 for Asians.

Whereas the foregoing table provides clear results for a typical Monday-through-Friday school week, students also have the weekend at their disposal to make appropriate adjustments for purposes of time management. In addition to asking students to estimate the amount of time spent on different activities during the school week, therefore, the NLSF also asked freshmen to "think about the most recent weekend between two weeks when classes were being held and you were on campus" and then, "beginning on Saturday morning and continuing through Sunday night," to estimate how many hours they spent on different activities.

The results of this time allocation exercise appear in table 3.6. In general, they reinforce the impression that blacks and Latinos experience greater time stress than whites or Asians. Black students report spending 9.2 hours per weekend on academic activities compared with just 8.3 hours

Table 3.6
Average amount of hours during most recent weekend (Saturday and Sunday) that freshmen spent engaged in different activities

Variable	Whites	Asians	Latinos	Blacks
Academic Activities				
Attending Class or Lab	0.1	0.2	0.2	0.5
Studying	7.6	8.3	8.7	8.3
Computing	0.4	0.5	0.3	0.3
Reading or Writing	0.2	0.1	0.1	0.1
Total	*8.3*	*9.1*	*9.3*	*9.2*
Extracurricular Activities				
General Extracurricular	3.7	4.1	3.9	4.9
Playing or Practicing Sports	1.8	1.4	1.4	1.4
Doing Volunteer Work in Community	0.4	0.5	0.5	0.6
Total	*5.9*	*6.0*	*5.8*	*6.9*
Recreational Activities				
Watching Television	2.7	2.6	2.9	4.0
Listening to Music	5.0	5.3	5.9	6.9
Attending Parties	4.1	3.2	4.0	3.3
Socializing with Friends	7.9	7.4	8.0	8.2
Other Recreation	1.3	1.1	1.1	1.2
Total	*21.0*	*19.6*	*21.9*	*23.6*
Life Maintenance Activities				
Sleeping	14.3	14.7	14.3	14.2
Other Maintenance	0.6	0.7	0.5	0.6
Total	*14.9*	*15.4*	*14.8*	*14.8*
Income-Generating Activities				
Working for Pay	0.7	1.0	1.2	1.4
Other	0.7	0.7	0.7	0.7
Assessment of Time Stress				
Actual Hours in Weekend	48.0	48.0	48.0	48.0
Total Hours Reported	51.5	51.8	53.7	56.6
Ratio Total/Actual Hours	1.07	1.08	1.12	1.18
Estimated Waking Hours	33.7	33.3	33.7	33.8
Total Hours of Waking Activity	37.4	37.1	38.9	42.4
Ratio Waking Activities/Waking Hours	1.11	1.11	1.15	1.25

for whites. In this case, however, both Asians and Latinos more closely approximate blacks than whites, with respective totals of 9.1 and 9.3 hours spent on academic pursuits ($F = 4.0, p < .01$).

A similar pattern of time allocation emerges with respect to extracurricular activities, with blacks reporting a total of 6.9 hours over the weekend compared with 5.9 hours for whites. Asians and Latinos are in between with 6.0 and 5.8 hours, respectively ($F = 4.0$, $p < .01$). As during the school week, blacks spent more time on the weekend in recreational activities, owing primarily to the larger number of hours logged listening to music or watching television rather than attending parties, socializing with friends, or engaging in other forms of recreation. Black students reported a total of 23.6 hours of weekend time spent on recreation compared with 21 hours for whites, 19.6 hours for Asians, and 21.9 hours for Latinos ($F = 16.7$, $p < .001$).

There is little evidence that black students sought to adapt to time pressures by sleeping less on the weekend. All groups slept 14 to 15 hours over the course of the weekend, or roughly seven hours per night; and there are no differences between groups in time allocated to general life maintenance activities or to activities in the residual "other" category. As before, there is a clear progression from whites to blacks in terms of time spent working, with whites reporting just 0.7 hours, Asians 1.0 hours, Latinos 1.2 hours, and blacks 1.4 hours ($F = 0.2$, $p < .001$).

The exposure of different groups to time stress is summarized at the bottom of the table. Every weekend, of course, has 48 hours available, but whites report activities accounting for 51.5 hours, Asians 51.8 hours, Latinos 53.7 hours, and African Americans 56.6 hours, yielding respective time stress ratios of 1.07, 1.08, 1.12, and 1.18. Limiting calculations to waking hours by no means eliminates group differences in exposure to time stress. When the computations are confined to time spent not sleeping, whites and Asians evince time stress ratios of 1.11, whereas Latinos and African Americans display ratios of 1.15 and 1.25 respectively.

In sum, students in all groups seem to be trying to fit more activities into a fixed amount of time than is really feasible, both during the week and on weekends; but the resulting time pressures are more severe for blacks and Latinos than for whites and Asians. Taking a full seven-day week and computing time stress ratios for waking hours yields indexes of 1.08 for whites, 1.10 for Asians, 1.14 for Latinos, and 1.16 for African Americans. Put another way: by multitasking, black students at selective schools appear to be trying to shoehorn 16% more activities into the seven-day week than are readily doable, Latinos are trying cram in 14% more, Asians 10% more, and whites just 8% more. All groups are burning both ends of the candle, but among minorities the flames seem to be burning the wick down faster.

The foregoing time budgets were constructed by students for a typical weekend and school week. Naturally they constitute subjective evaluations rather than objective measures of time allocated to different activities. In an effort to measure the use of time more concretely and more exactly, the NLSF also had students reconstruct a recent weekday on an hour-by-hour basis, using the following question:

> I want you to think back to the most recent Tuesday on which school was in session. Beginning at the time you awakened, could you please tell me what you did during each hour of the day until you retired for the night. On that Tuesday, what time did you awake? At what time did you retire for the evening to go to sleep? For simplicity, let's classify your activities into a few general categories: Grooming, Eating, Sleeping, Attending Class, Playing Sports, Studying, Working for Pay, Socializing, Relaxing, Doing Volunteer Work, Other.
>
> Beginning at (*next whole hour from wake up time*), take me through that most recent Tuesday when school was in session and account for your time. During the first hour, from *X to X + 1*, were you mostly grooming yourself, eating, sleeping, attending class, studying, socializing, or relaxing? How about from *X + 1 to X + 2*? What was your principal activity then? Continue hour by hour from *X + 2* to bedtime.

The results of this detailed analysis are summarized in figure 3.1, which shows, on average, how each group of students allocated the 24 hours beginning from the time they awoke on the most recent Tuesday morning. These detailed reconstructions generally accord well with the data in table 3.5, which presents students' subjective estimates of time spent on different activities during a typical Monday-through-Friday period; and all the significant intergroup differences are replicated. As can be seen from the figure, the detailed reconstructions for the most recent Tuesday yield a range of time spent on academic activities of 7.8 to 8.4 hours, compared with a range of 37.5 to 40.5 hours estimated for a five-day school week. Dividing the latter figures by five yields a range of 7.5 to 8.1 hours per day during the school week, which is remarkably close to the range reported for Tuesday.

Reports of sleep time are likewise very similar to the subjective estimates. The 32.4 to 35.1 hours per week reported in table 3.5 translate into a daily average of 6.5 to 7.0 hours, compared with a range of 7.2 to 7.4 hours on the most recent Tuesday. The main difference between the two sets of

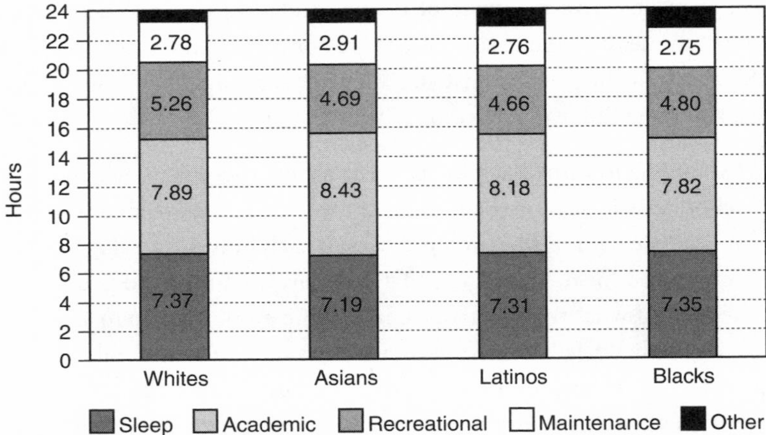

Figure 3.1.
Allocation among daily activities of the 24 hours on the most recent Tuesday that school was in session, by racial-ethic group

estimates is the greater amount of time spent on recreational activities in the subjective weekly estimates (6.3 to 7.0 hours per day) compared with the objective reconstruction of the last Tuesday (4.7 to 5.3 hours). This difference stems from a greater tendency to report time spent in life maintenance activities in the Tuesday time budget than in weekly estimates, and more time spent in extracurricular activities in the former compared with the latter.

Data from the NLSF thus suggest that the weekly subjective estimates may understate the time spent on life maintenance activities, but the difference in reports of time spent on extracurricular activities may simply reflect the Tuesday focus of the hourly reconstruction, which would miss such activities done on Monday, Wednesday, Thursday, or Friday. The critical variables of study time and hours spent on academic activities are reported reliably and consistently in both the single-day time budget and the weekly subjective estimates.

Social Currents and Grade Achievement

The descriptive data reviewed in the foregoing sections do not reveal huge differences between groups in living situations, peer cultures, participation in campus activities, or in the allocation of time among social, academic, and other pursuits; but they do suggest different emphases within different student populations. Compared with other students, whites generally place more weight on social than academic concerns and are generally unconcerned with working to pay for college. In contrast, blacks place considerable emphasis on academic achievement and hold community participation in high esteem while paying less attention to social life. Black students also spend more time in recreational activities than whites, though they generally study as much as or more than other groups. In general, Asians and Latinos fall between these contrasting types, with Asians being more similar to whites and Latinos to blacks.

Although we may have documented modest differences between groups with respect living situations, values, and behavior on campus, the more important question is whether these differences make any difference academically. We therefore conclude this chapter by measuring how housing, distractions, peers, participation, and time allocation affect the grades earned by students in their sophomore and junior years. Table 3.7 (discussed later in this section) presents the estimate for a multivariate regression equation that predicts cumulative grade point average from the variables described in the foregoing section.

We measured each student's housing situation using a series of dichotomous 0 or 1 variables. Compared to living in a dormitory during the freshman and sophomore years, we assessed whether respondents had ever lived in an apartment, in a fraternity or sorority, or with relatives. We also created dichotomous measures to indicate whether a student was involved in different kinds of organizations: career development, varsity or junior varsity sports, intramural sports, a fraternity or sorority, a religious group, an environmental or political group, or some other organization. Finally, we measured the hours of time that respondents said they spent in academic pursuits, extracurricular activities, recreational activities, paid employment, and life maintenance activities (with the latter category including sleep).

Using methods outlined in appendix C, we created a series of summated ratings scales to indicate the degree to which students experienced various situations during their freshman and sophomore years at college. The distraction index added together frequency ratings for distractions such as talking, stereo playing, TV watching, partying, and being talked into going out, yielding a 0 to 100 scale over the two years. The evasive action index added up the frequency with which students reported taking

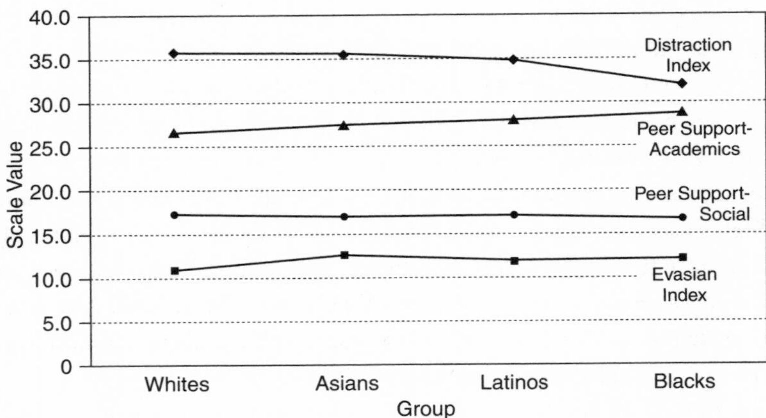

Figure 3.2.
Indexes of distraction from studies, evasive actions taken, peer support for academics, and peer support for socializing, by racial-ethnic group

evasive measures to avoid distraction each year, such as leaving home to do schoolwork and staying late at the library, yielding a 0 to 40 scale over freshman and sophomore years. The index of peer support for academics combined ratings of the perceived importance among friends of attending class, studying hard, getting good grades, and getting postgraduate training, which produced a 0 to 40 scale; and the index of peer support for social activities combined ratings of how important it was among friends to party, be popular, and hang out with friends, yielding a 0 to 30 scale.

Figure 3.2 shows the average values obtained on each of these scales as constructed for whites, Asians, Latinos, and African Americans. The scale measuring the frequency of distraction is highly reliable (Cronbach's alpha = .77), and using this measure whites are seen to be distracted most frequently, with a scale value of 35.8, followed by Asians at 35.4, Latinos at 34.8, and African Americans 32.0 ($F = 12.3, p < .001$). There are relatively few differences between groups in terms of evasive actions taken in response to distractions at home (alpha = .71) or peer support for social life (which unfortunately has a low alpha of .41); but consistent with the data adduced so far, peer support for academics generally increases as one moves from whites, with a scale value 26.7, through Asians at 27.5 and Latinos at 28.0 to blacks at 28.8 ($F = 19.3, p < .001$), and the latter scale is highly reliable (alpha = .76).

Table 3.7 shows the estimated effects of these scales and other social factors on freshman and sophomore GPA, controlling for background variables that prior work has shown to be important in determining academic achievement. Although the frequency of distractions and evasive actions have no significant effect on grade performance, housing circumstances do appear to make a difference. Just as Pascarella and Terenzini (2005) found in their review of the literature, we find that students living in fraternities and sororities earn modestly lower grades, compared with students who live in campus dorms or apartments. From these estimates, we cannot determine whether the negative effect of living in a fraternity or sorority is achieved through selection (wherein those less motivated to study self-select into Greek life) or whether it reflects something about the living environments such organizations offer. We have independently controlled for the frequency of distractions and allocation of time, so whatever the mechanism is, it does not occur as a result of mechanisms involving these factors. Living with relatives is likewise associated with lower grades, but again it is not clear whether this reflects a direct effect or the influence of selection.

The effects of peer culture might at first appear to be paradoxical, in that support for academics significantly and strongly *reduces* grade performance whereas support for social life increases it. The positive relationship between support for social life and grades is consistent with the work of Tinto (1993), however, who views institutional attachment is a primary determinant of college success. He shows that students who are more engaged socially at an institution tend to display higher a likelihood of progressing from year to year and of continuing on to graduation. The significant effect found here suggests that social engagement also predicts grade performance—that is, social integration promotes academic integration. This interpretation is supported by the effects of participation in various campus organizations, which are also generally positive. Joining a political or environmental group on campus is associated with significantly higher grades, as is membership in other community organizations or in career development groups.

Although seemingly anomalous, the negative effect of peer support for academics on GPA is also consistent with Massey and Fischer's (2005) finding that feeling a strong psychological burden to perform can, under certain circumstances, undermine academic performance. If good grades are held in high regard by high-achieving peers, students may inflict on themselves considerable pressure to perform just as well, and this pressure

Table 3.7
Effect of selected variables on grade point average through end of sophomore year

Independent Variables	B	SE	*P* Value
Key Indicators			
Group			
Whites	—	—	
Asians	0.020	0.019	.316
Latinos	−0.075**	0.026	.008
Blacks	−0.210***	0.028	.000
Kind of Housing			
Always in Dormitory	—	—	—
Ever in Apartment	−0.026	0.024	.297
Ever in Fraternity/Sorority	−0.065†	0.036	.083
Ever with Relatives	−0.062†	0.032	.062
Distractions			
Frequency of Distraction	−0.001	0.001	.339
Frequency of Evasive Action	−0.001	0.001	.357
Peer Culture			
Support for Academics	−0.006***	0.001	.000
Support for Social Life	0.005***	0.001	.001
Involvement in Activities			
Career Development	0.045†	0.024	.071
Varsity or Junior Varsity Sports	0.001	0.023	.969
Intramural Sports	0.032*	0.014	.034
Fraternity or Sorority	−0.027	0.020	.195
Religious Group	0.015	0.015	.327
Environmental or Political Group	0.039*	0.016	.025
Other Community Group	0.042**	0.012	.002
Time Allocation			
Academic	0.0017***	0.0004	.000
Extracurricular	0.0003	0.0007	.665
Recreational	−0.0010***	0.0002	.000
Work	−0.0002	0.0016	.876
Maintenance	−0.0017	0.0018	.342
Sleep	0.0010	0.0006	.118
Time Stress Index	−0.0732	0.0773	.353
Control Variables			
Difficulty of Courses			
Number of Easy Courses	0.023***	0.003	.000
Number of Hard Courses	−0.010**	0.003	.006
Demographic Background			
Male	−0.041**	0.013	.005
Foreign-Born Parent	0.007	0.018	.695
Two-Parent Family	0.032	0.020	.120
Siblings under 18	−0.012†	0.007	.085

Table 3.7 *(continued)*

Independent Variables	B	SE	*P* Value
Education of Parents			
No College Degrees	—	—	—
One College Degree	0.029	0.021	.192
Two College Degrees	0.092***	0.019	.000
One Advanced Degree	0.070***	0.016	.000
Two Advanced Degrees	0.152***	0.022	.000
Economic Status			
Home Value (000)	0.000	0.000	.860
Ever on Welfare	−0.013	0.019	.504
Income > $100,000	0.029†	0.016	.087
Academic Preparation			
AP Courses Taken	0.012**	0.005	.014
High School GPA	0.427***	0.024	.000
Self-rated Preparation	0.026***	0.003	.000
Social Preparation			
Self-efficacy	−0.005†	0.002	.055
Self-esteem	0.005**	0.002	.010
Susceptibility to Peer Influence	0.008***	0.002	.000
Social Distance from Whites	0.001	0.001	.479
Intercept	1.306***	0.128	.000
R^2	0.365		
Number of Cases	2,891		

†$p<.10$ *$p<.05$ **$p<.01$ ***$p<.001$

could, in turn, lead to lower grades. Although a little pressure may serve as an important motivator for students, too much pressure may inhibit student performance to the point where grades actually suffer.

Although prior work has generally found athletic participation to have a negative influence on college achievement (Astin 1993; Pascarella et al. 1995; Pascarella et al. 1999), here we find that participation in varsity sports has no effect on grades and participation in intramural sports has a significant positive effect. The positive effect of intramural participation is consistent with Tinto's theory of student integration, of course, and the lack of effect for varsity sports may reflect the fact that we have strong controls in place for students' use of time. If the negative effect of varsity sports occurs by taking time away from studies, it will be picked up in the time allocation variables instead.

Indeed, the amounts of time spent both in academic and in recreational pursuits have strong and highly significant relationships on grades earned, and in the directions one would expect: time spent in academic activities raises GPA, whereas time spent in recreational activities reduces it. Interestingly, time stress does not appear to affect grade performance in and of itself. Our measure of time stress—the ratio of reported time expended on different activities to total time available—manifests no significant effect on students' grades through the freshman and sophomore years. It seems that what really matters for students is the absolute amount of time spent on academics versus recreation.

Entering the Social Stream

This chapter examined the living situations and social lives of college students during their freshman and sophomore years. We found that whites are the most likely of all groups to move off campus in the sophomore year, the most likely to admit to being talked into going out with friends rather than studying, the most likely to play intramural sports, the most likely to join a fraternity or sorority, and the most likely to report that partying, being popular, and hanging out are important among their friends and acquaintances on campus. At the same time, they are the least likely of all groups to stay late at the library to do schoolwork, the least likely to leave their dorm or apartment to get work done, the least likely to participate in a career development group, the least likely to work for pay, the least likely to say their peers value getting good grades and going to graduate or professional school, and the least likely to say their peers value holding a job to help pay for college.

At the other end of the spectrum we found African Americans, who are the least likely to move off campus as sophomores, the least likely to be talked into going out, the least likely to play intramural sports, the least likely to join a fraternity or sorority, and the least likely to report that being popular and hanging out are important among their peers. African Americans are, in contrast, the most likely to stay late at the library to do schoolwork, the most likely to leave home in order to get work done, the most likely to participate in a career development group, the most likely to work to pay for school, and the most likely to say their peers value getting good grades and going on to graduate or professional school.

In sum, although whites do not necessarily neglect their studies, they clearly place relatively more weight on having fun and socializing while in school. Likewise, while African Americans do not necessarily abjure relaxing and socializing, they clearly subordinate these pleasures to working hard academically, doing well in school, and supporting their education through gainful employment.

Although these profiles emerge from students' professed beliefs about themselves and their friends, they are remarkably consistent with the concrete ways that respondents reported spending their time. Compared with white students, African Americans allocate more time during the week and on weekends to academic pursuits, extracurricular activities, and working for pay but spend less time sleeping, attending parties, and playing sports. At the same time, however, black students did report spending more time watching television, listening to music, doing volunteer work, and attending religious activities than other students.

On the whole, we found that black students try to cram more activities into a fixed amount of time than white students. In a typical seven-day week, the ratio of time spent on various activities to total waking time available—a measure of time stress—is 1.08 for whites, 1.10 for Asians, 1.14 for Latinos, and 1.16 for African Americans. Fortunately, this time crunch in itself is not a detriment to academic achievement. In multivariate analyses of grade performance, the ratio of time expended to time available has no significant effect on the GPA earned through the freshman and sophomore years, other things equal. What matters is the *absolute* time spent undertaking academic activities and the *absolute* time devoted to recreation. Compared with whites, black students spend more time studying, which enhances their grade performance; but they also spend more time watching television, listening to music, and other recreations, and these activities reduce grade achievement.

The greater time devoted to recreational activities by black students may reflect the greater pressure they feel to perform academically and the lower degree of connection they feel with respect to campus social life. In order to blow off steam and relax in a context of social marginalization, they may watch more television and listen to more music on their own, perhaps while they study. In the end, the effect of greater study time is offset by the greater time they spend in such recreational activities, and the net result seems to be close to a wash. In balancing study time with recreational time, black students end up doing as well as other students.

What is more important is the direct effect of psychological pressure, whose importance has already been documented by Massey and Fischer

(2005). Here we found that black students perceive a great deal of pressure from their peers to perform well in school, are more oriented toward graduate and professional education than whites, and that the more they perceive their peers to value educational achievement, the worse they perform in terms of grades. This effect is diametrically opposed to Ogbu's (1977, 1981, 1991) argument that black academic performance is suppressed because peers perceive it as "acting white." Among black students attending selective schools, there is no evidence for such an effect (see also Massey et al. 2003). On the contrary, it is precisely because academic performance is so valued among black students that academic performance is compromised, an effect that is much more in line with the social psychological effect of stereotype threat described by Steele (1992), an issue we take up in a later chapter.

In keeping with the arguments and results of Tinto (1993), we also found evidence that social connection to an institution enhances performance. However, whereas Tinto focused mainly on staying in school, we showed here that social attachment also affects grade achievement to some extent. Specifically, students who report membership in environmental, political, or community groups in and around campus earn higher grades than those who do not. Moreover, those students who feel their peers value social engagement likewise do better in terms of grades. The only apparent downside of social engagement seems to occur when students enter more intensively into Greek life by moving into a fraternity or sorority, which has a marginally significant negative effect on grades. It is not clear, however, whether this negative effect represents the selective entry of less serious students into the fraternity and sorority scene, or whether living in the Greek system itself has some causal influence.

In the end, the social estrangement that black students appear to experience at selective institutions of higher education may have very real academic consequences. To the extent that they are less connected socially, perceive their peers not to value social engagement, and resist involvement in environmental or political groups on campus, they will tend to do less well academically. Instead of undermining them academically, participation in various community groups cements them socially to the institution to yield better scholastic outcomes.

4 Staying Afloat Financially

Getting into a selective college or university is one thing; paying for it is something else entirely. Most of the institutions included in the NLSF have a policy of need-blind admissions, which, in theory, means that the admissions and financial aid offices operate independently and without collusion (Springer and Franck 2005). Applications for college entry are evaluated by admissions officers, and the decision to admit is made on the basis of whatever combination of subjective and objective criteria the institution deems relevant, not including, of course, the applicant's socioeconomic status. If the applicant has applied for financial aid, then once the admission decision is made, the file is sent over to the financial aid office, where officers tailor a package of grants, loans, and work-study employment sufficient to meet the financial needs of each student (see Steinberg 2002).

For most colleges, the goal of the financial aid office is to attract the most desirable students at the least cost to the institution, which in practice means getting the family to absorb whatever cost that it realistically can. According to the College Board's annual survey, average tuition and fees for the 2005–2006 academic year were $21,235 for private institutions and $5,491 for public institutions. When room and board are taken into account, total charges averaged $29,026 in the private sector and $12,127 in the public (College Board 2005b). These figures constituted 43% and 27%, respectively, of the U.S. median household income of $44,385 in 2005. Thus, except for parents who are independently wealthy or who enjoy extraordinarily high incomes, the cost of supporting a child for four years at a selective institution can be expected to constitute a significant financial burden; and for students coming from poor or working-class families, the costs to parents will seem daunting indeed.

Although many studies have examined the influence of financial factors on decisions about whether and where to attend college (see McDonough 1997; Heller 1997, 2002; Hoxby 2004), fewer have considered how financial issues affect academic outcomes and behavior after matriculation (Pascarella and Terenzini 2005). Most of these studies simply attempt to measure how financial aid affects year-to-year persistence, and they generally confirm the commonsense wisdom that receiving financial aid increases persistence and raises the likelihood of graduation, especially for low-income students (Astin 1993; St. John and Masten 1990). This conclusion appears to hold whether one considers the amount of the support received or the simple receipt of aid itself (St. John 1990; Somers 1995).

However, one might also expect the *form* of financial assistance—grants versus loans or work-study packages—to have an effect on academic outcomes; and research indeed suggests that grants have a significant and positive influence on the likelihood of college progression and graduation (St. John 1990, 1991; Clotfelter 1991; Cofer and Somers 1999; Heller 2003). The size of the effect, however, seems to be greatest during the first two years (Heller 2003) and may even disappear thereafter (U.S. General Accounting Office 1995). Participation in work-study programs likewise appears to enhance rates of college persistence and completion (St. John 1990; Wilkie and Jones 1994; Adelman 1999; Beeson and Wessel 2002; Heller 2003). In contrast, off-campus employment generally has been found to have negative effects on enrollment (Astin 1993; Stage and Rushin 1993; Nora et al. 1996; Gleason 1993; Leppel 2002). The effect of holding an off-campus job, however, is nonlinear and depends on the number of hours worked (Horn and Berktold 1998; King 2002). The evidence on the effects of college loans is less consistent, with some studies finding negative effects of indebtedness on persistence, others finding positive effects, and still others no effect at all (Pascarella and Terenzini 2005).

The Financial Challenge

Given continuing inequalities by race and ethnicity with respect to income and wealth, it is inevitable that the financial burdens of an elite education will fall more heavily on African Americans and Latinos than on whites or

Table 4.1
Financial status of families of respondents to the National Longitudinal Survey of Freshmen by race and ethnicity

Economic Indicator	Whites	Asians	Latinos	Blacks
Income				
Mean Income (000)	$101.2	$92.3	$76.5	$68.8
Ever on Welfare (%)	5.3	7.3	14.0	18.9
Assets				
Own Home (%)	93.8	86.9	80.7	72.4
Mean Home Value (000)	$304.2	$275.7	$191.5	$136.9
Financial Capacity				
Number of Children 18 or Younger	1.9	1.7	1.9	1.9
Income per Child (000)	$65.1	$64.3	$50.1	$47.0
Home Value per Child (000)	$196.0	$190.3	$121.8	$91.7

Asians. Table 4.1 considers intergroup differences in financial capacity by examining the incomes and assets of white, Asian, Latino, and black households, as reported by respondents in the fall of 1999. As expected, these data reveal very clear differences by race and ethnicity. At the top of the socioeconomic ladder are white students, whose households earned an average of $101,00 per year and 94% of whom owned a home with an estimated average value of $304,000. A few rungs down the ladder are Asians, with a mean household income of $92,000, an 87% home ownership rate, and a median home value of $276,000. At the bottom of the ladder are black and Latino households, which earned average incomes of just $69,000 and $77,000 respectively, and whose corresponding home ownership rates were 72% and 81%, with median home values of $137,000 and $192,000.

Clearly, then, compared with whites and Asians, black and Latino students at selective institutions have less income and fewer assets at their disposal to finance their schooling. Intergroup differences in income, home ownership, and home value are all highly significant, with robust F-scores and p values well under .001. Of course, the ability to deploy financial resources in support of a college education is not simply a matter of income and assets. It also depends on the number of children the family must potentially send to college. Intergroup differences in family size are small, however, with white, black, and Latino students each reporting around 1.9 children per family, compared with 1.7 for Asians.

The bottom two lines of the table offer crude indexes of financial capacity by dividing average household income and home value (coded as 0 if the family did not own a home) by the number of children potentially to be educated. As can be seen, the financial capacity of black households was about 28% less than that of white families in terms of income, with an income around $47,000 versus $65,000 per child ($t = -9.5$, $p < .001$) and about half as much in relative home value ($92,000 versus $196,000 per child, $t = -12.8$, $p < .001$). Thus, in absolute terms, compared with African Americans white students could count on some $18,000 more in income and $104,000 more in home value to help finance their education.

The financial situation of Latino families was not much better, as they lagged behind white families by $15,000 in income per child ($t = -7.4$, $p < .001$) and $74,000 in home value ($t = -8.6$, $p < .001$). In contrast, the slightly smaller number of children in Asian families offset their slightly lower income and assets to render their financial capacity virtually equal to that of whites (significance tests not significant), thus illustrating the quality-quantity tradeoff noted by economists when it comes to childbearing decisions (see Becker and Lewis 1973; Willis 1973; Rosenzweig and Wolpin 1980; Hanushek 1992).

Table 4.2 continues our assessment of financial issues by examining the cost of attending the selective, and predominantly private, colleges and universities represented in the NLSF. The baseline survey asked each respondent: "About how much money do you think you will need to attend college this academic year, including tuition, academic fees, room and board, and your daily expenses for living and entertainment?" And then: "Of this total amount, how much will be funded from each of the following sources? Parental contributions, contributions from other family members, grant or fellowship from university, grant or fellowship from other funding agency, student loan, personal savings, earnings from work/study job, earnings from other work, or some other source?" The top panel of the table summarizes the data arising from this query.

The total cost of college estimated by students was remarkably and reassuringly consistent by race and ethnicity, with each group estimating the cost to average between $28,000 and $29,000, meaning that the cost of an elite education was basically the same for students in all groups. How this fixed cost was financed differed substantially by group, however. The top panel allocates the total cost of college in absolute dollars to different funding sources, but it is easier to describe intergroup differences in the support package using data in the second panel, which shows the percentage contribution from each source.

Table 4.2
Average cost of attending college or university and the source of funds to meet college costs by group

Source of Funds	Whites	Asians	Latinos	Blacks
Absolute Cost				
Family Payments	$20,703	$19,625	$13,658	$10,301
Grants	5,926	6,818	11,717	13,804
Loans	1,578	1,620	2,386	2,909
Work	493	640	852	1,048
Other	100	110	138	100
Total Cost	*$28,800*	*$28,813*	*$28,751*	*$28,162*
Percentage Distribution				
Family Payments	71.8%	68.1%	47.5%	36.6%
Grants	20.7	23.7	40.8	49.0
Loans	5.5	5.6	8.3	10.3
Work	1.7	2.2	3.0	3.7
Other	0.3	0.4	0.4	0.4
Total Cost	*100.0*	*100.0*	*100.0*	*100.0*
Median Cost Burden per Child				
Cost/Income	0.50	0.49	0.67	0.70
Cost/Home Value	0.18	0.19	0.34	0.55
Family Payments/Income	0.31	0.31	0.24	0.17
Family Payments/Home Value	0.12	0.12	0.13	0.15

These percentages clearly show that share of total funds contributed from family sources declines steadily as one moves from left to right, going from whites to Asians to Latinos and, finally, to blacks. Whereas nearly three-quarters of the cost of college was borne by the families of white students (72%), the share was two-thirds for Asians (68%), about half for Latinos (48%), and closer to one-third for African Americans (37%). Differences in family financial contributions across groups were made up for through various forms of financial aid. Whereas grants covered only around 21% of the college costs of white students, the figure was 49% for African Americans, 41% for Latinos, and 24% for Asians. Likewise, loans contributed only about 6% toward the cost of college for whites and Asians but 8% for Latinos and 10% for black students. Paid employment was relatively unimportant in enabling students to afford higher education, accounting for just 4% of the cost of college for African Americans and 3% for Latinos, compared with just 2% for whites and Asians. This differences are all highly significant statistically (F-tests all over 9.0, $p < .001$).

Thus a principal difference between whites and Asians, on the one hand, and African Americans and Latinos, on the other, is that the former rely primarily on family resources to cover two-thirds or more of the cost of college whereas the latter rely on a combination of grants (40% to 50% of the cost) and loans (8% to 12%) to meet the financial challenge. The computations at the bottom of table 4.2 suggest that these adjustments, presumably arranged through each school's financial aid office, are quite successful in mitigating the relatively greater cost burden faced by black and Latino students.

Naturally, if one takes the total cost of college and divides it by the amount of income and assets available per child, one finds much higher cost-to-resources ratios among blacks and Latinos than among whites and Asians. Thus the ratio of cost per unit of income was 0.70 for blacks and 0.67 for Latinos, but only 0.50 for whites and 0.49 for Asians. If, however, we take the ratio of costs actually paid by family members to income, we obtain a ratio of 0.31 for whites and Asians but only 0.24 for Latinos and just 0.17 for blacks. In other words, because of financial aid the real cost to families was reduced to around one-third of family income for whites and Asians, and less than a quarter for Latino families and just 17% for black families. Likewise, once financial aid is taken into account, the ratio of family payments to home value was equalized across groups to the narrow range of 0.12 to 0.15. In sum, the financial aid packages being constructed in support of the principle of need-blind admissions seem to be functioning effectively to equalize the cost burden across families based on their varying financial capacities.

Making Ends Meet

Just because out-of-pocket costs to families are relatively equal does not necessarily mean that the financial burdens of college are equally distributed across groups. Our crude estimates of financial capacity do not fully take into consideration savings accounts, home equity, stocks, bonds, and other investments, much less liabilities. It is well established that net financial assets rise markedly with income among whites but not among African Americans (Oliver and Shapiro 1997; Conley 1999). As a result, the net wealth owned by African Americans remains a small fraction of that owned by whites, with smaller but still significant differentials between Asians and Latinos (Keister 2000).

Thus, by underassessing the wealth of whites, who have much, and blacks, who have little, we most likely do not paint a true picture of the more precarious financial circumstances of black families sending a child to a selective college or university. Indeed, nearly a fifth (19%) of black families in our sample had spent some time on welfare, compared with just 5% of white families (see table 4.1 here and, for more background, Massey et al. 2003). Families with fewer assets, less wealth, and prior brushes with poverty are likely to be far more risk averse than families within which significant wealth has accumulated over generations, and the simple cost/resource ratios we report in table 4.2 cannot capture fully how hard-pressed low-income families might really be in sending a child to an expensive school, even given generous financial assistance. In an effort to delve more deeply in to the financial circumstances, we consider in more detail three ways that students and their families might take action to make ends meet.

Financial Aid

The most obvious means of financing an expensive college education is to apply for financial aid, which is offered to varying degrees by all the institutions included in the NLSF. As shown in table 4.3, a majority of students in all groups applied for financial aid, thus underscoring the significance of the financial commitment involved. Among whites, 62% said they had applied for financial aid, compared with 67% of Asians. What is perhaps most surprising is not that a majority of students from these groups applied for assistance but that such a large fraction did not. Nearly 40% of whites and about one-third of Asians said that they or their families were paying the full cost of nearly $30,000 per year. Again, these differences are highly significant statistically (the F-tests for amount paid by family and amount paid by grants both exceed 125.0).

Naturally, among Latinos and Asians the relative share paying the full cost was much smaller: 83% of Asians and 90% of African Americans reported applying for financial aid in the course of the admissions process. The critical nature of this assistance is indicated by the second line in table 4.3, which shows the average importance rating assigned to financial aid by the members of each group. On the baseline survey, respondents were asked: "On a scale of 0 to 10, how important were the following considerations in choosing where to attend college, where 0 indicates it was extremely unimportant and 10 indicates it was extremely important?" One of the options was availability of financial aid.

Table 4.3
Indicators of role played by financial aid in financing college costs of different groups

Indicator	Whites	Asians	Latinos	Blacks
Prior to Acceptance				
Applied for Aid (%)	62.3	66.7	82.6	90.0
Importance in Decision (0–10)	4.1	4.9	6.7	7.4
Degree of Family Sacrifice (0–10)	6.1	6.6	7.0	7.0
Freshman Year				
Grants Received ($)	5,926	6,818	11,716	13,804
Amount in Loans ($)	1,578	1,620	2,386	2,909
Total Financial Aid ($)	7,505	8,438	14,102	16,713
Share of Aid Borrowed (%)	21.0	19.2	16.9	18.6
Frequency of Visits re Aid (0–10)	0.7	0.9	1.7	2.4
Frequency of Aid Problems (0–10)	1.5	2.0	2.4	2.7
Sophomore Year				
Grants Received ($)	5,356	6,893	11,069	13,896
Amount in Loans ($)	1,735	2,097	2,773	3,297
Total Financial Aid	7,091	8,990	13,842	17,193
Share of Aid Borrowed (%)	24.5	23.3	20.0	19.2
Frequency of Visits re Aid (0–10)	0.8	0.9	1.7	2.8
Frequency of Aid Problems (0–10)	1.8	2.1	2.4	3.2
Mean Debt Burden				
Cumulative Debt ($)	3,313	3,717	5,159	6,206
Debt/Income per Child	0.11	0.14	0.20	0.28
Debt/Home Value per Child	0.05	0.04	0.41	0.64

With average ratings 7.4 and 6.7 for African Americans and Latinos, respectively, access to financial aid was obviously high on the list of considerations for minority groups. In contrast, the importance rating assigned to financial aid by whites was just 4.1, and the Asian rating was only 4.9 ($F = 178.4$, $p < .001$). By way of contrast, the importance assigned to the schools' academic reputation in deciding where to attend college ranged from 6.5 to 7.5 across groups, that given to curricular issues ranged from 3.5 to 4.5, and that given to social considerations ranged from 4.0 to 5.1 (see Massey and Mooney 2006). For black and Latino students, therefore, financial considerations loom large, and the availability of aid is among the most important factors in deciding which school to attend.

Despite the cushion of financial aid, students in all groups believed their families were making a financial sacrifice to pay for their college education and that this sacrifice created a moral obligation to study hard. To estimate the perceived degree of the sacrifice, respondents were asked, "in thinking about how hard to try in your college studies, how important for you is each of the following considerations?" Students were then told to use a 0 to 10 scale, and one of the items rated was "my family is making sacrifices for my education." Although African Americans and Latinos offered the highest ratings for family sacrifice, averaging 7.0 in both cases, even the relatively well-off Asians and whites perceived considerable financial sacrifice on the part of their families, with respective ratings of 6.6 and 6.1, which is perhaps not surprising given the large share of the cost actually being assumed by their families. At the very least, students perceive the cost to create a moral debt. Nonetheless, the intergroup differences are significant ($F = 21.7, p < .001$).

The second panel in table 4.3 shows the amount of aid received and the relative amount received in loans rather than outright grants. As already noted, far more of the cost of college for minorities, compared with whites, comes from financial aid. Whereas the average value of grants and loans given to white freshmen was $7,505—not a trivial sum in itself—the average value of the aid package for blacks was $16,713, and for Latinos $14,102. Asians were much closer to whites at $8,438 ($F = 21.8, p < .001$). Although there were not large differences between groups with respect to the relative amount of aid given in the form of loans rather than grants, minority students were generally called on to assume proportionately less debt than whites. Thus, the share of aid given in the form of loans was 17% for Latinos and 19% for African Americans and Asians, compared with 21% for whites ($F = 21.7, p < .001$).

Although the share of the financial aid that came in the form of loans may have been slightly lower for black and Latino students compared with whites, the lower factions were not enough to offset the greater absolute amounts, putting minority students in greater total debt. In round numbers, the total debt accumulated by black students during their freshman year was $2,900, compared with $2,400 for Latinos but only around $1,600 for whites and Asians ($F = 21.8, p < .001$). From the very beginning, therefore, those students with the least financial capacity are put on a track to accumulate the greatest debt. Even though in proportional terms the loan amounts may seem quite small to financial aid officers making funding decisions, the amounts themselves may appear more daunting to minority students and their families.

The next panel down repeats the financial analysis using data for the sophomore year. These data suggest that to some degree the institutions under study are playing a game of "bait and switch," enticing students into school as freshmen with relatively generous aid packages skewed toward grants rather than loans but then, in the sophomore year, holding the grants fixed or reducing them while increasing the amount covered by loans. Black students, for example, received an average of $13,804 in grants and $2,909 in loans as freshmen, but as sophomores the amount of aid in the form of grants increased by only $92 whereas the amount covered by loans grew by $388.

Although the total aid offered to African Americans increased from the freshman to the sophomore years, that offered to Latinos actually decreased slightly, thereby raising the financial burden on their families. Whereas grants and loans to Latino students totaled $14,102 as freshmen, they summed to just $13,842 as sophomores. Moreover, whereas the amount of aid offered through grants fell by $647, the amount coming in the form of loans grew by $387. Because the increase in loans did not equal the decline in grants, the total value of the aid package fell, and at the same time the share given in loans increased from 17% to 20%. Although, like African Americans, Asians enjoyed a total increase in financial aid, they too experienced a shift from grants toward loans, with the share of aid borrowed going from 19% to 23%; and like Latinos, white students experienced a falling level of financial aid and a rising debt burden, with the value of the aid package shrinking by $414 and the share financed through loans going from 21% to 25%.

The bottom panel of the table illustrates the cumulative effect of these aid practices through the first two years of college. By the end of their sophomore year, black students had racked up debts totaling roughly $6,200 compared with $5,200 for Latinos, $3,700 for Asians, and $3,300 for whites ($F = 19.1$, $p < .001$) Thus, in absolute terms the greatest debt was accumulated by those students whose families were least able to repay it. The bottom two lines of the table illustrate this fact by computing the ratio of debt to available income and assets. As can be seen, in terms of income the relative debt for blacks was 2.5 times that of whites, with a ratio of debt to income of 0.28 compared with just 0.11 for whites, with corresponding values of 0.14 and 0.20 for Asians and Latinos, respectively ($F = 33.7$, $p < .001$). The ratio of debt to housing assets was even more extreme for blacks compared with whites, exceeding it by a factor of nearly 13 (0.64 compared with 0.05 for whites, $t = 2.4$, $p < .05$). The debt ratio for Asians was similar to that of whites at 0.04, but that of Latinos was much greater at 0.41 ($t = 3.0$, $p < .01$). Even though relatively lower *percentages* of the aid given to blacks and Latinos came in the form of student loans, therefore, they accumulated greater *total* debt both in absolute terms and as a fraction of their ability to pay.

The difficulty and consternation potentially caused by the reliance of minorities on financial aid and their relatively greater assumption of debt is indicated by the relative frequency of visits to aid counselors and reported issues with their aid package. On both the freshman and sophomore follow-up surveys, respondents were asked: "On a scale of 0 to 10, where 0 indicates you never engage in a behavior and 10 indicates you always do it, please indicate the frequency with which you . . . ," and one of the response categories was "speak to a financial aid counselor about money matters." Likewise, respondents were also asked to use the same scale to rate "how much you agree or disagree with each of the following statements about college," one of which was "I am having problems with my financial aid."

Average ratings for these two scales are presented for the freshman and sophomore years in table 4.3. As can be seen, the frequency of visits to financial aid offices and of problems with financial aid either stayed constant or increased between the first and second years of college, and were always worse for minorities than whites, though happily were apparently not very severe for any group. Thus, in the sophomore year the frequency of visits on a 0 to 10 scale was 0.8 for whites, 0.9 for Asians, 1.7 for Latinos, and 2.8 for African Americans ($F = 103.9$, $p < .001$), and the corresponding frequency ratings for aid problems were 1.8, 2.1, 2.4, and 3.2 ($F = 30.3$, $p < .001$). Despite the modest size of the ratings, these intergroup differences are highly significant statistically and indicate that the greater reliance on financial aid and larger amounts of assistance given to minority students do come at a cost. In addition to increasing their relative debt burden, they also bring more frequent problems and headaches with financial aid offices.

Working to Study

Besides taking out more loans, another way that students can respond to the falling generosity of aid packages is to increase their amount of paid employment to generate additional funds in the form of earnings. Table 4.4 takes an in-depth look at paid employment by students in each of the groups to discern the role of work in student financial strategies. The top panel summarizes the situation of freshmen with respect to work during

Table 4.4
Indicators of role played by employment in financing college costs of different groups

Indicator	Whites	Asians	Latinos	Blacks
Freshman Year				
Work Required for Aid (%)	16.9	26.1	36.8	39.2
Felt That Needed to Work (%)	56.6	52.6	68.8	66.1
Held Paying Job (%)	46.3	46.3	61.3	62.5
Work Contributions ($)	492	640	852	1,047
Sophomore Year				
Work Required for Aid (%)	13.1	22.3	31.3	33.5
Felt That Needed to Work (%)	55.2	52.4	67.0	66.8
Held Paying Job (%)	64.5	59.6	72.0	73.0
Work Contributions ($)	784	696	1,078	1,098
Total				
Worked Both Years (%)	40.0	36.3	52.4	55.0
Mean Hours per Week	18.4	15.2	19.0	20.4
Mean Weeks Worked	35.1	35.1	38.4	39.6
Total Work Hours	348	309	379	410
Work Hours/Academic Hours	0.09	0.10	0.16	0.17
Work Contributions ($)	1,276	1,336	1,930	2,145

the school year and reveals that black and Latino students are more often *required* to work as part of their financial aid package compared with white and Asian students. Whereas 39% of African Americans and 37% of Latinos reported having a work requirement, only 26% of Asians and just 17% of whites did so ($F = 25.2$, $p < .001$).

Although a minority of students in each group may have been required to work, most nonetheless felt under some pressure to get a job given their financial circumstances. When respondents were asked whether "apart from financial aid requirements, do *you* feel it is necessary to work to finance your college education," 57% of whites, 53% of Asians, 69% of Latinos, and 66% of African Americans responded affirmatively ($F = 12.2$, $p < .001$). However, the relative number of students who actually acted on these feelings to get a job differed sharply by group. Whereas 63% of blacks and 61% of Latinos actually worked at a job during their freshman year, only 46% of whites and Asians did so ($F = 31.5$, $p < .001$). The gap between the percentage feeling pressured to get a job and the share actually working was just 3.6%, 6.3%, and 7.5% for blacks, Asians, and Latinos, respectively, but 10.3% for whites. Thus, feeling the need to work is obviously more immediate and concrete for blacks than for whites.

In the general scheme of things, however, the amount contributed by work to the cost of education was small. Compared with a bottom line of around \$29,000, the average freshman contributed no more than around \$1,000 through paid employment; but again minority students contributed more than others. The average contribution was \$1,047 for blacks and \$852 for Latinos, compared with \$492 for whites and \$640 for Asians ($F = 9.1$, $p < .001$).

The second panel in the table summarizes the work situation of sophomores. In general, though relatively fewer students were compelled to work as part of their aid package, the share who felt they should work held steady and the percentage who were, in fact, working generally rose, quite sharply in the case of whites and Asians. Thus 60% of Asians reported working in their sophomore year, compared with 65% of whites, 72% of Latinos, and 73% of African Americans ($F = 16.0$, $p < .001$). As a result, the average amounts contributed to the cost of college also increased, reaching \$1,098 for blacks, \$1,078 for Latinos, \$696 for Asians, and \$784 for whites ($F = 8.2$, $p < .001$).

The bottom panel summarizes students' work contributions over the first two years of college. As can be seen, 55% of black students and 52% of Latinos worked in both years, compared with figures of 40% and 36% for whites and Asians. The average hours worked per week was similar across all groups at 15 to 20 hours. Nonetheless hours worked by blacks were greatest at 20.4, followed by Latinos at 19.0, whites at 18.4, and Asians at 15.2. A similar pattern prevailed with respect to weeks worked during the school year. Whereas whites and Asians reported an average of around 35 weeks worked per year, the figure was around 38 for Latinos and 40 for African Americans. Black and Latino students thus put in 3 to 5 extra weeks of work at a slightly higher number of hours per week compared with whites.

When all is said and done, these modest intergroup differences accumulate to substantial discrepancies in work effort over the two school years. Whereas black students accumulate an estimated 410 hours of paid work during their freshman and sophomore years, and Latinos garner 379 hours, the totals are 348 hours for whites and 309 hours for Asians, figures 15% and 25% lower than the total for African Americans ($F = 3.7$, $p < .01$). A sense of the degree to which work might conflict with study efforts may be had by forming the ratio of hours worked to hours spent in academic pursuits. For Asians, this ratio is only 0.10 and for whites just 0.09, compared with figures of 0.16 and 0.17 for Latinos and African Americans ($F = 27.4$, $p < .001$). Although work efforts may carry a high opportunity cost in terms of attention to scholarship, the financial payoff is rather small, ranging from a two-year total of just $1,276 in the case of whites to $2,145 in the case of African Americans. The latter figure constitutes a mere 4% of the total cost of two years of college. Work during college thus disproportionately burdens minority students while providing relatively little actual financial benefit.

Consumer Credit and Family Transfers

One final way to meet the escalating financial demands of a college education is through family transfers—the receipt of private gifts from parents or other family members. The NLSF questionnaire asked freshmen and sophomores whether they had received any funds from family members other than birthday gifts or holiday presents, and whether or not they possessed a credit card paid by a family member (typically parents). The top panel of table 4.5 summarizes this information for the freshman year. As first-year college students, Asians were least likely to report a family transfer whereas blacks were most likely. Some 54% of black students said they

Table 4.5
Indicators of role played by family transfers and personal credit cards in financing college costs of different groups

Indicator	Whites	Asians	Latinos	Blacks
Family Transfers				
Freshman Year				
Received Money from Family	43.6%	32.4%	37.7%	54.3%
Amount of Money Received	$436	$274	$234	$302
Has Credit Card Paid by Relative	55.9%	63.5%	48.9%	43.4%
Amount Charged per Month	$48	$73	$47	$32
Sophomore Year				
Received Money from Family	27.8%	25.7%	29.2%	44.2%
Amount of Money Received	$1,251	$2,117	$3,162	$3,760
Personal Debt				
Freshman Year				
Has Credit Card Paid by Self	30.6%	28.7%	34.5%	33.2%
Amount Charged per Month	$118	$144	$143	$160

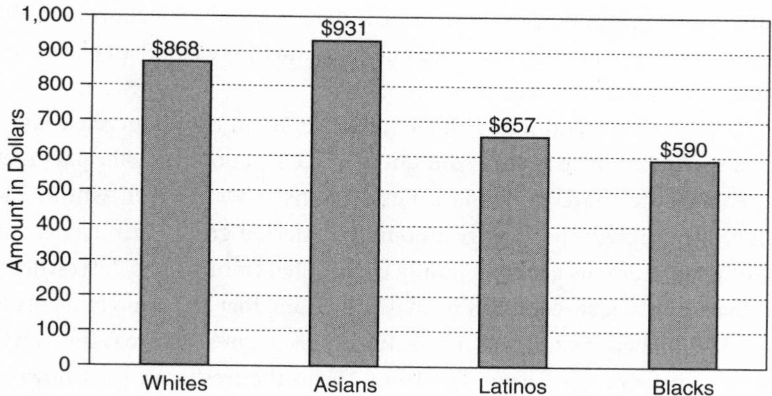

Figure 4.1
Total cash transfers expected by students from family members during freshman year, by racial-ethnic group

had received money from family members during their freshman year, compared with just 32% of Asian students; and the respective figures for whites and Latinos were 44% and 38% ($F = 35.9, p < .001$).

On average, however, family transfers did not amount to much. The average sum received by black students was just $302, and Latinos got only $234, compared with $436 for whites and $274 for Asians, differences that are marginally significant in statistical terms ($F = 2.5$, $p = .06$). A less visible transfer occurs, however, when parents or other family members regularly pay off credit card charges made by students, and there were substantial differences in access to such cards. Whereas 56% of whites and 64% of Asians reported access to a family-paid credit card, the figures were only 49% for Latinos and 43% for African Americans ($F = 20.1, p < .001$). The amount charged per month averaged $48 for whites, $73 for Asians, $47 for Latinos, and $32 for African Americans ($F = 10.2$, $p < .001$). Having a credit card paid by parents is obviously another form of transfer, and the total expected amount of this transfer equals the proportion of students having such a card times the average charged per month times nine months. For whites, this calculation works out to $432 per school year, compared with values of $657 for Asians, $423 for Latinos, and $288 for blacks.

Figure 4.1 shows the total amount that students in each group could expect to receive from family members during their freshman year, either as a cash transfer or as an amount charged to a credit card paid by parents. Obviously, African Americans could expect the least support from family sources, only around \$590. In contrast, Asians could expect around \$931 dollars per year and whites around \$868. Latinos were closer to blacks with an expected value of \$657.

The NLSF questionnaire did not ask sophomores about their use of credit cards, but once again it did query students about transfer payments. In general, the share receiving a family transfer went down within each group, even though the average amount transferred grew. Thus the percentage of white students getting a family transfer fell from 44% to 28%, whereas the share of black students fell from 44% to 33%, that of Latino students fell from 38% to 29%, and that of Asians from 32% to 26%. Whereas the average size of transfers ranged from \$234 to \$436 in the freshman year, however, among sophomores the range increased substantially to \$1,251 to \$3,760.

The NLSF questionnaire also asked freshmen whether they possessed a credit card that they themselves paid, and roughly a third of students in each group admitted to having such a card. The group figures were about 33% of blacks, 35% of Latinos, 29% of Asians, and 31% of whites ($F = 2.9$, $p < .05$), and the respective amounts charged per month were \$160, \$143, \$144, and \$118 ($F = 1.5$, not significant). Unfortunately we do not know how much of the amount charged per month was paid off, but given the financial constraints under which black and Latino students were operating, it is likely that some portion of the amount charged accumulated over time as added debt.

Financial Stress and Grade Achievement

The foregoing analyses clearly indicate that the burdens of financing an elite college education fall more heavily on black and Latino students and their families. Although some of their financial pressures are mitigated by more generous financial aid packages, these students nonetheless accumulated greater debt in both relative and absolute terms, were more likely to be compelled to work to support their studies, were more likely actually to be working, and were less likely to receive transfers of various sorts from their families. The question we now address is whether financial issues faced by students in paying for college affected their academic performance.

We indicate each student's financial circumstances using a battery of measures derived from earlier results. To express the overall burden of the cost of college faced by families, we use a ratio of the amount of the cost contributed by families to their earnings and assets, as measured by household income per child and home value per child. We also express the amount of debt accumulated over the first two years of college as a ratio of the same denominators. To capture the effect of students' work efforts, we measure the number of hours worked compared to the number of hours spent in academic pursuits. To measure the effect of family transfers, we use the absolute amount transferred from family members during the freshman and sophomore years and the average amount charged each month to a family-paid credit card during the freshman year.

We then regressed the freshman-sophomore GPA on these indicators with and without controls for demographic background, parental education, socioeconomic status, academic preparation, and social preparation, along with the numbers of easy and hard courses taken. The results of these two OLS regressions are presented in table 4.6. The left two columns show regression coefficients (B) and standard errors (SE) for each group and financial indicator without background controls, and the right two columns show these figures with controls. They reveal that the relative size of family payments had no effect on grades earned, suggesting that financial aid programs were successful in mitigating the financial pressures on students, at least as far as grades were concerned. Although debt expressed as a fraction of income is negatively associated with grades earned in the left-hand equation, the effect disappears once controls are applied, suggesting a spurious association attributable to some background factor such as parental education or academic preparation.

Once controls are applied, only one factor seems to have a strong and significant effect on grades: the frequency that students experience problems with financial aid. The more frequently they report problems and difficulties arising from their financial aid package, the lower the grades earned during their freshman and sophomore years. Although it may help to alleviate financial pressures on students and their families, financial aid does come at a cost in the form of aggravation and worry that undermine grade performance. Family transfers have marginally significant effects on grades, but they are in the opposite direction depending on whether the transfer took the form of a cash gift (negative) or credit card payment (positive). In general, therefore, the biggest academic effect of students' financial circumstances appears to occur because poorer students are forced to interact more frequently with financial aid officers to deal with problems arising with respect to their aid packages.

Table 4.6
Effect of budgetary constraints on grade point average through end of sophomore year

Independent Variables	B	SE	B	SE
Key Indicators				
Group				
Whites	—	—	—	—
Asians	−0.001	0.021	0.000	0.018
Latinos	−0.180***	0.022	−0.106***	0.024
Blacks	−0.317***	0.022	−0.230***	0.034
Budget Indicators				
Family Cost/Income per Child	0.008	0.006	0.005	0.012
Family Cost/Home Value per Child	0.000	0.001	0.000	0.001
Cumulative Debt/Income per Child	−0.079**	0.026	−0.031	0.025
Cumulative Debt/Home Value per Child	0.000	0.001	0.002	0.002
Hours Worked/Hours Spent on Academics	−0.076*	0.034	−0.040	0.036
Money Received from Family (000)	−0.001*	0.0004	−0.001†	0.0005
Credit Card Payment by Family (000)	−0.007	0.005	0.059†	0.032
Frequency of Financial Aid Problems	−0.004***	0.001	−0.003*	0.001
Control Variables				
Difficulty of Courses				
Number of Easy Courses	—	—	0.023***	0.003
Number of Hard Courses	—	—	−0.008**	0.003
Demographic Background				
Male	—	—	−0.035*	0.013
Foreign-Born Parent	—	—	0.019	0.021
Two-Parent Family	—	—	0.020	0.021
Siblings under 18			−0.004	0.007
Education of Parents				
No College Degrees	—	—	—	—
One College Degree	—	—	0.043†	0.024
Two College Degrees	—	—	0.088**	0.026
One Advanced Degree	—	—	0.098***	0.025
Two Advanced Degrees	—	—	0.169***	0.030
Economic Status				
Home Value (000)	—	—	0.000	0.000
Ever on Welfare	—	—	−0.014	0.026
Income > $100,000	—	—	0.010	0.018
Academic Preparation				
AP Courses Taken	—	—	0.017***	0.004
High School GPA	—	—	0.442***	0.025
Self-rated Preparation	—	—	0.027***	0.003)

Table 4.6 *(continued)*

Independent Variables	B	SE	B	SE
Social Preparation				
Self-efficacy	—	—	−0.003	0.003
Self-esteem	—	—	0.003†	0.002
Susceptibility to Peer Influence	—	—	0.010***	0.001
Social Distance from Whites	—	—	0.002	0.002
Intercept	3.408***	0.016	1.191***	0.119
R^2	0.138		0.354	
Number of Cases	2,790		2,588	

†$p<.10$ *$p<.05$ **$p<.01$ ***$p<.001$

Calming the Financial Waters

Our in-depth probing into the financial circumstances of students attending selective colleges and universities in the United States reveals large gaps by race and ethnicity in the ability to finance an elite education. Compared with whites and Asians, black and Latino students had fewer resources at their disposal to pay college costs that averaged between $28,000 and $29,000 per year. They came from families with substantially lower household incomes who lived in lower-value houses that yielded fewer assets in the form of home equity. As a result, much higher fractions of African Americans and Latinos applied for financial aid during the admissions process, and the availability of such aid played a more central role in deciding which school to attend.

Nonetheless, data from the NLSF suggest that the financial aid packages put together by universities for low-income students were relatively successful in mitigating the financial pressures experienced by black and Latino students. Through grants and loans, the out-of-pocket costs absorbed by black and Latino families were reduced to levels below those experienced by white and Asian families, when expressed relative to household income. Possibly as a result, in the end the relative financial burden faced by students and their families had no direct effect on academic achievement, with no significant effect on grades earned through the sophomore year. Financial aid was thus successful in calming potentially troubled financial waters and enabling students to stay afloat financially through two years of college.

However, one downside to the financial aid packages used by these selective schools was their reliance on loans for a portion of the aid and the increase in the degree of that reliance from the freshman to the sophomore year. By the sophomore year, loans had come to comprise between 20% and 25% of the aid given to students. Although loans accounted for less than 4% of the total cost of attending college, and in absolute terms averaged just $1,600 to $3,300 per year, borrowing did cumulate to significant amounts for minority students from lower-income families. After two years of college, black students had accumulated an average of around $6,200 in debt that constituted 28% of available household income and 64% of home value. In contrast, white students had accumulated just $3,300 in debt that represented only 11% of household income and just 5% of home value. A possible area for reform in financial aid policy is to reduce the use of loans in financing the education of low-income students.

Although relative debt accumulated had a negative effect on grades in uncontrolled models, once background characteristics were added in, the negative effect remained but was reduced to statistical insignificance. The main academic effect of financial aid seems to come as a result of the contact it requires with the financial aid bureaucracy on campus. Given their higher rates of aid receipt and greater levels of financial dependency, Latinos and African Americans reported more frequent problems with financial aid officials than whites or Asians, and these aggravations had a significant negative effect on grades earned through the sophomore year.

5 Battling Social Undercurrents

The formation of friendships represents an important step in adapting to college life, especially at academically competitive institutions. Having friends helps smooth the transition to the college setting. Friends help one another figure out how the institution works; friends encourage one another academically; and friends share new academic and social experiences. When problems arise, friends are there to offer support and assistance to make them easier to bear. For these and other reasons, the development of a supportive network of friends has been found to increase persistence in college (Grosset 1991; Terenzini et al. 1994) and foster greater social integration on campus (Christie and Dinham 1991). Rather than being a sideshow to academic achievement, social relationships—with classmates, professors, friends, and romantic partners—in a very real way constitute the foundation upon which scholarly achievement is built. Students who feel marginalized socially and alienated interpersonally are at heightened risk of dropping out (Tinto 1993).

Because minority students at selective schools are entering a rarefied environment from which they were once excluded, they are naturally prone to perceive social undercurrents to social interactions they experience on campus. As social psychologists have long emphasized, negotiating the social world is problematic for all human beings (see Fiske and Taylor 1991; E. Fiske 2005); but for nonwhite students who are aware of past racism and sensitive to its continuing expression in American society, the possibilities for social misunderstanding and interpersonal confusion are multiplied (Devine and Vasquez 1998). Especially within elite, wealthy, and predominantly white settings, the social waters may be muddy and the rules of interpersonal behavior far from clear (Pettigrew 1998).

Studies have indeed documented many problems and issues faced by minority students on predominantly white campuses, which range from subtle slights and exclusions to overt expressions of racial hostility and apparent discrimination (see Allen, Epps, and Haniff 1991; Feagin, Vera, and Imani 1996). Compared with white-majority schools, historically black colleges and universities (HBCUs) have been shown to provide a social and intellectual climate that is more conducive to the academic and psychological well-being of African American students (Bohr, Nora, and Terenzini 1995; Pascarella and Terenzini 2005). That a school's racial climate can affect academic outcomes is suggested by quantitative studies showing that black students at HBCUs exhibit greater improvement on standardized measures of achievement than those attending majority-white schools (Bohr, Nora, and Terenzini 1995; DeSousa and Kuh 1996; Flowers and Pascarella 1999). Despite some progress, U.S. colleges and universities have by no means fully resolved the American dilemma, and race remains an issue on most campuses.

Crews and Captains

There is an element of truth in the timeworn admonition that it is important "to make a good first impression." First encounters carry disproportionate weight in conditioning future social judgments and significantly affect the course of later social interactions. The first formal encounter that students experience under the auspices of the institution occurs when they walk into their very first class as brand-new freshmen. The second wave of the NLSF therefore asked respondents to think back to the first class they attended at their college or university and to estimate the rough percentage of students in different racial and ethnic groups they saw sitting in the seats around them—their first glimpse at the crew that would accompany them in their journey across the academic river. Responses to this question are summarized by group in table 5.1, with the diagonal cells highlighted to underscore within-group contacts.

With the exception of Howard University, all the institutions in the NLSF are majority-white. It is not surprising, therefore, that all groups report very similar levels of exposure to white students in their first college-level

Table 5.1
Race-ethnicity of classes and professors during freshman and sophomore years

	Whites	Asians	Latinos	Blacks
Composition of First Class				
% White	**64.7**	65.5	63.3	64.2
% Asian	15.6	**17.2**	16.1	12.8
% Latino	5.6	5.1	**6.7**	4.1
% Black	10.1	8.4	9.5	**15.1**
Number of Professors in Freshman Classes Who Were:				
White	**7.4**	6.9	6.6	6.2
Asian	0.5	**0.7**	0.5	0.4
Latino	0.4	0.2	**0.5**	0.4
Black	0.3	0.3	0.3	**1.1**

class, with the precise percentage varying narrowly from 63% to 66% ($F = 0.3$, $p > .25$). In other words, for all freshmen walking into their first classroom at the beginning of the fall term, the sea of faces on which they gazed was almost two-thirds white. Most of the variation between groups occurred with respect to the relative share of nonwhite students reportedly seen on that first day of class.

Reflecting the demographic composition of elite educational institutions, all groups reported that the second most frequently encountered group was Asians, who were followed by African Americans and, finally, Latinos. Thus the typical white student walked into a classroom that was about 16% Asian, 10% black, and 6% Latino. Among minority groups, the greatest tendency toward own-group exposure in class was for Asians at 17%, followed by African Americans at 15% and Latinos at 7%. The elevated rates of within-group exposure for black and Asian students probably reflects the selective attraction of Asians to science, math, and Asian studies courses where, as we have seen, Asian students are fairly common, and the selective attraction of black students to African and African American studies courses.

These courses are also probably likely to have Asian and black faculty, as suggested by the lower panel of table 5.1, which shows the *number* of professors that students encountered from various racial and ethnic backgrounds across *all* freshman classes. Both Asians and African Americans reported elevated rates of exposure to own-group faculty as freshmen. Black students reported being taught by an average of 1.1 black faculty, compared with a figure of only 0.3 for all other groups ($F = 95.8$, $p < .001$).

Thus the typical black freshman took at least one class taught by a black professor, whereas white, Asian, and Latino freshmen did not. Asians reported having an average of 0.7 Asian professors as freshmen, compared with an average of 0.4 to 0.5 for other groups ($F = 38.4, p < .001$).

The rate of within-group exposure for Asians is obviously not as great as that evinced by African Americans, either in relative or absolute terms. As already noted, Asians are probably exposed to Asian faculty members in science and math courses and not just Asian studies courses. Since other students also take science and math in large numbers, however, they are also exposed to Asian faculty. In contrast, African Americans are exposed to black faculty primarily when they take courses on race, African studies, or African American studies. These tend to be elective courses that students in other groups do not take with the same frequency, especially as freshmen, thus missing a major venue for exposure to black faculty.

In keeping with the overwhelmingly European origins of the American professorate, each group reported by far the greatest number of encounters with white professors. As might be expected, white students reported the most white professors at 7.4, followed by Asians at 6.9, Latinos at 6.6, and African Americans at 6.2 ($F = 44.1, p < .001$). Indeed, whites were unlikely to encounter *any* nonwhite faculty members during their first year of college, with the average number of Asian professors being 0.5, compared with 0.4 Latino professors and just 0.3 black professors, figures roughly equal to those reported by Latinos. Of all groups, Latinos reported the lowest exposure to own-group members within classes, whether students or faculty.

Lifesavers

Once decisions about which courses to take have been made, the composition of classmates and professors—the crews and captains for their academic journey downriver—lies largely outside the student's control, stemming from decisions made by institutions about which faculty candidates to hire and which aspiring students to admit from pools that are already skewed with respect to race and ethnicity. To consider that portion of college social life over which students have more direct control, at several junctures the NLSF asked students to describe their personal relationships. In the spring of their freshman year, for example, students were asked to identify

Table 5.2
Characteristics of social networks reported by students as freshmen and sophomores

	White	Asian	Latino	Black
Ten Closest Friends in Freshman Year				
# White	**7.45**	4.95	5.34	2.40
# Asian	1.20	**3.54**	1.15	0.75
# Latino	0.46	0.45	**1.88**	0.62
# Black	0.69	0.75	1.22	**5.77**
Four Closest Contacts in Sophomore Year				
# White	**3.14**	1.40	1.70	0.63
# Asian	0.26	**1.70**	0.27	0.14
# Latino	0.08	0.10	**1.09**	0.08
# Black	0.05	0.10	0.16	**2.54**
Of Four Closest Contacts				
# On Campus	2.10	2.15	1.97	1.73
# Off Campus	1.90	1.85	2.03	2.27
# Relatives	0.81	0.66	0.81	1.12
# Adults Aged 26+	0.60	0.41	0.56	0.81
Scale of Social Support (0–64)	14.3	15.0	13.4	14.0

their ten closest friends by race and ethnicity, and these data are summarized in the top panel of table 5.2. The diagonal cells are once again highlighted to underscore within-group relationships.

Given the predominance of white students on most of the campuses, it is not surprising that a large majority of white students' reported friendships are with other whites and that they display by far the highest frequency of within-group relationships. Among the ten closest friends reported by white freshmen, 7.5 were white. The only other group with which they reported a significant number of friendships was Asians, who accounted for 1.2 friends, on average. Thus, in round numbers, the typical white student had eight white friends and one Asian friend but was relatively unlikely to be friends with anyone who was black or Latino (as indicated by the fractional averages below 1.0).

In the self-contained world of college, opportunities for intergroup friendship are constrained by the demographics of the student body. For all groups except whites, therefore, most of the people that students encounter in classrooms, in dorms, and walking around campus will be outside their own group. It is thus not surprising that both Asians and Latinos reported a larger number of friendships with whites than within their own groups. On average, both groups reported having roughly five white friends. Where they differ is in the relative number of own-group friendships. Because Asians outnumber Latinos on most campuses, they have greater opportunities to form within-group friendships, and Asian respondents reported having an average of 3.5 Asian friends compared with an average 1.9 within-group friendships among Latinos ($t = 19.8$, $p < .001$). Compared with Asians and whites, Latinos show a stronger tendency to befriend African Americans, reporting an average of 1.2 black friends, compared with figures of 0.7 and 0.8 for the other two groups ($t = 9.4$, $p < .001$). Indeed, aside from African Americans themselves, Latinos were the only group at all likely to report an African American among their ten closest friends. Intergroup differences in the distribution of friends are all highly significant (with F-tests all in excess of 250.0, $p < .001$).

Although campus demographics impose the same constraints and opportunities on all minorities, blacks display by far the lowest frequency of friendships with white students. Among the ten closest friends, the average black student reported just 2.4 white friendships compared with 5.8 black friendships. This preponderance of black friendships and the scarcity of white friendships is far too skewed to be a result of random, race-neutral processes ($F = 587.7$, $p < .001$). On the contrary, it indicates a structured social process operating to overcome the constraints of campus demographics. Although we cannot identify the processes at this point, whatever they are they cause black freshmen to report the highest preponderance of own-group friendships, the fewest contacts with whites, and the fewest contacts with Asians.

In order to delve more deeply into the structure and composition of students' social networks, the NLSF posed additional questions in the sophomore wave of the survey. Students were asked to name the four people to whom they felt closest and then to identify each person's gender, race-ethnicity, duration of relationship, and place of acquaintance. In addition, students were asked to estimate the level of support and solidarity provided by each contact through four questions: How often do you go to this person for advice? How often does this person accept you no matter what you do? How often does this person understand what you are really like? How often do you share your inner feelings with this person? Students estimated each frequency on a 5-point scale from never to always, coded 0 to 4, yielding a scale of social support ranging from 0 to 64 (16 points for four students) with a reliability of 0.85 (Cronbach's alpha—see appendix C).

The second panel draws on these data by reporting the race and ethnicity of students' four closest contacts. With an average number of 3.1, whites overwhelmingly reported that their closest contacts were white ($F = 819.0$, $p < .001$). Blacks likewise reported a majority of their closest associates to be black, 2.5 out of 4 contacts ($F = 2{,}473.0$, $p < .001$). Asians and Latinos reported a more diverse mix of groups among their close contacts, with whites as the most frequent out-group in both cases ($F > 560.1$, $p < .001$). Among Asians, whites accounted for an average of 1.4 of the four closest contacts, whereas among Latinos the figure was 1.7. Once again the tendency toward within-group association was stronger among Asians than among Latinos, with the former reporting an average of 1.7 Asian contacts and the later just 1.1 Latinos. Latinos thus continue to stand out for having the most diverse social networks, whereas black and white networks are notable for their insularity. In the case of whites, of course, this insularity *reflects* campus demographics; but among blacks it occurs *despite* campus demographics.

Other group differences emerge when we consider the setting from which the four closest contacts are drawn. At one end the continuum are whites, who show a strong proclivity for on-campus versus off-campus relationships (2.1 on versus 1.9 off). At the other end are African Americans, who display more off-campus than on-campus relationships (2.3 off versus 1.7 on). In general, the predominance of on-campus relationships falls and that of off-campus relationships rises as one moves from white to Asian to Latino to black students. In general, black and Latino students evince a greater reliance on off-campus contacts for social support than do white and Asian students.

Not only were the close social contacts of African Americans likely to be located off campus; they were also more likely than those of other groups to be relatives. Whereas black students reported that 1.1 of their four closest contacts were family members, the figure was 0.8 for whites and Latinos, and only 0.7 for Asians. African Americans' social contacts also tended to be older. Whereas an average of 0.8 of black students' four closest contacts were aged 26 or older, the figure was just 0.6 for whites and Latinos and just 0.4 for Asians. Whatever the age, relationship, or location of students' closest contacts, the total amount of social support received was roughly the same across groups. On the 64-point index of social support received described earlier, all groups reported values ranging narrowly from 13.4 to 15.0. Although the intergroup differences are significant

Table 5.3
Racial exclusivity of voluntary groups that students joined as sophomores

Measure of Exclusivity	White	Asian	Latino	Black
Percentage of students involved only in:				
Majority-White Groups	**80.5**	45.3	50.3	27.9
Majority-Asian Groups	0.8	**14.8**	2.1	0.9
Majority-Latino Groups	0.1	0.4	**7.9**	0.6
Majority-Black Groups	0.1	0.3	0.9	**26.4**

statistically ($F = 6.7, p < .001$), in substantive terms the amount and quality of social support provided to students by their social networks did not differ very much, even if other characteristics of the network did.

Opportunities to meet and befriend other students on campus are not random, of course, but depend on choices made by students, not only about which classes to take but also about which organizations to join. For each of the voluntary organizations described in chapter 3, the NLSF asked which racial or ethnic group, if any, constituted a majority of members, and responses to this query are summarized in table 5.3. These data show that whites display by far the greatest proclivity for organizations dominated by their own group. Among white students, 81% belonged to organizations where whites constituted the majority of members, and tiny shares of whites belonged to organizations dominated by any other group ($F = 102.8, p < .001$). This pattern substantially reflects campus demographics, of course, but the very skewed nature of the distribution suggests an element of choice as well.

In keeping with campus demographics, Asians and Latinos also display rather strong proclivities toward majority white organizations. Half of all Latinos and 45% of all Asians belonged to a student organization in which whites were the majority. As in earlier tabulations, Asians display a stronger attraction to within-group organizations than do Latinos. Whereas 15% of Asians belonged to an organization in which Asians were a majority, only 8% of Latinos did so ($F = 228.3, p < .001$).

Among nonwhite groups, African Americans stand out for displaying the strongest proclivity toward in-group organizations, once again going against campus demographics. Some 26% of black students reported belonging to a majority-black organization on campus, a figure that almost equals the share who reported membership in a majority-white organization (28%). Indeed, the proclivity of black students to join majority-white groups was roughly half that of Latinos ($t = -10.1$, $p < .001$), and their proclivity to join organizations dominated by own-group members was more than three times that of Latinos ($t = 31.0$, $p < .001$). The only group that was more socially insular was whites, but that is only to be expected since they constituted an average of two-thirds of the student body.

Dating Whirlpools

Student body demographics also set important constraints on dating behavior and the pursuit of romantic relationships. As mentioned in chapter 1, one of the most striking facts reported in *The Source of the River* was the relative absence of males in the population of black students attending selective colleges and universities. The top panel of table 5.4 summarizes the gender balance among students within each group. Whereas the gender balance of white students in the NLSF was close to even at 47% male and 53% female, the balance among black students was very skewed at 33% male and 67% female. Among NLSF respondents, in other words, black females outnumbered black males by more than two to one, whereas the figure for white students was just 1.12 to one. The gender balance among Asians and Latinos was also skewed in the direction of females, but not nearly to the same extent as that among African Americans. Asian women outnumbered Asian men by 56% to 44% for a ratio of 1.25 females per male, whereas Latinas outnumber Latinos by 54% to 46%, yielding a ratio of 1.18 females per male.

These figures pertain to the NLSF sample as a whole, not to the specific situation on any given campus, which varies widely. Indeed, the NLSF includes two women's colleges (Barnard and Bryn Mawr) that have no men on campus (though Barnard is literally across the street from coeducational Columbia University). The bottom line of the top panel thus reports the average ratio of females to males on campus. Though the numbers are different, these data basically reinforce earlier impressions based on the NLSF sample as a whole. White students experience the closest thing to an even sex ratio with 1.03 women per man on the typical campus, whereas blacks display the most imbalanced ratio at 1.62 women per man on average. Asians and Latinos are in between but generally closer to the situation of whites, with on-campus sex ratios of 1.15 and 1.14 women per man, respectively.

Table 5.4
Dating and romantic experiences reported by students as freshmen and sophomores

	White	Asian	Latino	Black
Dating Demographics				
% Male in NLSF	47.1	44.5	45.8	32.8
% Female in NLSF	52.9	55.5	54.2	67.2
Ratio of Females/Males in NLSF	1.12	1.25	1.18	2.05
Ratio of Females/Males on Campus	1.03	1.15	1.14	1.62
Prior Dating Experience				
% Ever Dated outside Group	37.7	60.3	69.3	46.1
% with Whites	—	84.7	74.4	70.9
% with Asians	44.3	—	27.8	27.4
% with Latinos	31.3	15.0	—	53.7
% with Blacks	33.5	17.1	29.3	—
Relationships in Freshman Year				
% with Steady Partner	63.4	50.2	62.4	56.0
% Known before College	46.8	47.1	42.2	44.1
% Met off Campus	8.1	8.2	11.5	17.4
Dating in Sophomore Year				
% with Dates	50.5	43.0	48.5	46.6
% with Steady Partner	33.5	27.7	33.4	31.3
% with No Dates and No Partner	14.9	28.8	17.7	24.2
Composition of Sophomore Dates				
% White	**96.0**	64.5	82.0	34.3
% Asian	18.5	**58.3**	17.8	13.5
% Latino	9.3	7.5	**43.9**	19.2
% Black	9.9	5.3	16.9	**86.5**
Composition of Sophomore Partners				
% White	**88.0**	46.6	62.1	15.2
% Asian	6.3	**41.7**	3.9	2.7
% Latino	2.1	3.8	**25.5**	3.4
% Black	0.9	2.6	3.6	**69.3**
% Biracial	1.2	3.8	2.0	5.2
% Other	1.5	1.5	2.9	3.3
Ever Experienced Negative Reaction				
% from Friends in Own Group	6.5	25.9	18.1	42.6
% from Family	3.2	25.3	16.5	23.7
% from Strangers in Own Group	6.5	23.7	12.8	45.1
% from Strangers in Partner's Group	6.5	20.4	14.6	41.5
% from Other Strangers	3.2	15.3	9.7	37.5

If we assume that the vast majority of students are heterosexual, that the incidence of homosexuality does not vary significantly across groups, and that women and men aged 18 and 19 are strongly motivated to form romantic attachments, these figures imply that women in all groups face a relative scarcity of potential male partners but that the degree of scarcity varies substantially by race or ethnicity. In general, black women face the most stringent demographic constraints to dating and romance, followed quite distantly by Asian and Latino women, then white women—unless, of course, one allows for intergroup dating.

The second panel reports responses to a question on intergroup dating posed to students in the spring of their freshman year: Have you ever dated anyone from a racial or ethnic group different from your own? Since no time frame is specified, responses must be taken to represent lifetime experiences. As can be seen, Asians and Latinos reported the most extensive rate of intergroup romance. Some 60% of Asians and 69% of Latinos reported having dated outside their racial or ethnic group, compared with figures of only 46% for blacks and just 38% for whites ($F = 79.2, p < .001$). Since Latinos and African Americans comprise a similar share of the U.S. population, and Latinos are a smaller percentage of college students, something besides demographics must account for their different rates of experience with intergroup dating, such as the patterns of segregation they experienced before coming to college and the differential patterns of association at college.

The remaining lines in the second panel report which out-groups were ever dated among those who reported an out-group date. These figures need not sum to 100%, as students could have dated members of more than one group. The most balanced distribution of out-group dates was reported by whites, 44% of whom reported dating Asians, 31% of whom dated Latinos, and 34% of whom dated blacks. Thus, the relatively few whites who dated outside the group displayed a modest preference for Asians; but they nonetheless dated Latinos and blacks with significant frequency.

Among Asians and Latinos, in contrast, out-group dates were highly skewed toward one particular out-group: whites. Among those who dated outside the group, 85% of Asians and 74% of Latinos reported dating someone who was white. The predominance of whites was most apparent in the case of Asians, only 15% of whom reported dating a Latino and 17% dating an African American. Latinos were more open to dating other minority groups than Asians, however, with 28% dating Asians and 29% dating blacks. For their part, African Americans who dated outside their group also displayed a skew toward whites, but also a rather high incidence of dates with Latinos. Thus 71% reported dating whites, but 54% reported dating Latinos compared with just 27% dating Asians.

The third panel assesses how campus demographics actually play out during students' first year of college in terms of romantic relationships. Substantial shares of freshmen reported being in a steady relationship, with the rough percentages going from 50% among Asians to 63% among whites, while blacks and Latinos occupied intermediate positions at 56% and 62%, respectively ($F = 4.4$, $p < .01$). These high percentages in part reflect the continuation of relationships from before college, most of which presumably began in high school—between 42% and 47% of respondents said they knew their current partner before arriving on campus. Relatively small shares reported meeting their partner off campus, but Latinos and blacks were significantly more likely to have formed an off-campus relationship than either whites or Asians. Whereas 17% of African Americans and 12% of Latinos said they met their romantic partner off campus, the figure was only 8% for whites and Asians ($F = 10.4$, $p < .001$).

The remaining panels in the table shift to the sophomore year, when more detailed questions were posed to respondents about dating and relationships. Students were asked whether they had dated at all during the sophomore year and to report on the race or ethnicity of all those with whom they had gone out. Students were also asked whether they were in a long-term relationship and the race or ethnicity of their partner. As can be seen from the middle panel in table 5.4, whites dated most frequently as sophomores, with 51% reporting at least one date. Asians dated least, with 43% reporting a date. The figures for Latinos and blacks were 49% and 47%, respectively ($F = 20.0$, $p < .001$).

The relative number of respondents who said they were in a steady relationship dropped from the freshman year, possibly reflecting the breakup of relationships continuing from high school. Nonetheless, the share of people in long-term relationships is significant, fluctuating around 33% for all groups. Asians were lowest, with 28% reporting a steady partner, and whites were highest at 36%. As with the dating frequencies, Latinos and blacks were in between with figures of 33% and 31%, respectively ($F = 9.2$, $p < .001$).

The last line in the middle panel shows the percentage in each group who reported neither a date nor a relationship in the sophomore year. This cross-referencing of variables reveals that Asians were least likely to be romantically engaged, with 29% saying that they neither went on a date nor had a steady boyfriend or girlfriend. Black students were next in terms of romantic disengagement, with 24% sitting out of the dating and romance scene, followed by Latinos at 18% and whites at 15%. As with the campus social scene generally, whites appear to be more engaged than other groups when it comes to romance ($F = 19.9, p < .001$).

The fifth panel down shows the racial composition of dates during the sophomore year, which again do not necessarily add to 100%. Whites display the strongest pattern of homogamy when it comes to dating, with 96% of those who dated saying they went out with another white person, compared with 19% dating Asians, and around 9% dating blacks and Latinos. Asians and Latinos reported a preponderance of out-group dates with whites, one that exceeds even dates with members of their own group. Thus, some 65% of Asians reported dating a white person, compared who 58% who dated another Asian. Among Latinos, 82% said they dated whites, compared with just 44% who dated Latinos.

Once again, therefore, Asians display a greater tendency toward within-group relationships than Latinos; but also as before, African Americans display the strongest pattern of homogamy among any minority group. Whereas 87% of African Americans reported dating another black person, only 34% reported dating a white person, which goes strongly against the demographic grain on campus and represents by far the lowest rate of dating whites for any minority group. Around 19% of black students reported dating Latinos, and 14% said they dated Asians.

The next-to-last panel shows the racial-ethnic composition of partners, and these *do* add up to 100%, since respondents can be in only one steady relationship at a time. The imposition of exclusivity and permanence on romantic relationships reinforces the pattern of homogamy seen earlier. Although the diagonal cells fall somewhat in absolute value compared with the dating matrix, the off-diagonal cells fall even more. When it comes to forming steady romantic relationships, therefore, intergroup partnerships become relatively less common, a tendency that is especially marked among whites. Although 19% of whites *dated* Asians, 10% dated blacks, and 9% dated Latinos, when it came to picking a steady boyfriend or girlfriend, only 6% went with an Asian, 2% with a Latino, and just 0.9% with an African American. All told, 88% of the steady relationships formed by white students were with fellow whites ($F = 75.1, p < .001$).

The degree of homogamy in steady relationships for Asians and Latinos is greater than one would expect given their shares of the student population; but given the constraints of campus demographics, within-group relationships are still overrepresented relative to relationships with whites. Asians continue to display a greater tendency toward homogamy. Although 47% of steady relationships were with whites, nearly as many, 42%, were with other Asians. In contrast, 62% of the steady relationships reported by Latinos were with whites, compared with just 26% with other Latinos. As in previous tabulations, the overrepresentation of in-group relationships is by far the greatest among African Americans. Whereas 69% of their steady relationships were with other blacks, just 15% were with whites, and trivial numbers were reported with Latinos and Asians. Once again these numbers fly in the face of campus demographics, indicating that the high degree of segregation in black and white social networks that generally prevails in American society carries over onto campus.

Troubled Social Waters

Despite attitudinal changes since the civil rights era, going out with someone of another race or ethnicity still involves crossing a significant social boundary. According to recent data, one-third of whites and 17% of blacks disapprove of black-white intermarriage on principle (Schuman et al. 1997). In general, for whites, when it comes to crossing racial or ethnic boundaries, the social distance is greatest for blacks, less for Latinos, and least for Asians (see White, Kim, and Glick 2005). Whatever the social distance, however, crossing a social boundary always carries the risk of sanction from others, both within and outside the group, who care about maintaining racial and ethnic distinctions.

For those students who reported dating outside their group as sophomores, the NLSF followed up by asking how often they had "suffered negative reactions because you dated another racial or ethnic group." Several possible sources for these negative reactions were given: friends or acquaintances in their own group, family members (presumably in their group), strangers in their own group, strangers in their partner's group, and other strangers. The last panel in table 5.4 shows the share of those dating outside their group who said they had experienced a negative reaction from one of the foregoing sources.

Although they dated other groups the least, whites experienced by far the lowest frequency of social sanctioning for intergroup dating when they did so, probably because the social consequences are less immediate for the whites given their numerical dominance on campus and in society. Even if some whites date and marry outside the group, "white culture" will continue and white Americans will continue as a social group. Thus only around 7% of whites who dated nonwhites reported a negative reaction from either same-race friends or same-race strangers, and only 3% said they encountered negative reactions from family members (who could, of course, have been unaware of out-group dating by the respondent).

In contrast, given their minority status, intermarriage and out-group dating pose a more serious threat to the integrity of Latinos, Asians, and African Americans as social groups and the cultural forms they bear. For groups that are 12% or less of the total population, significant intermarriage carries the potential of obliterating the group demographically, along with its sociocultural attributes, within a few generations. Corresponding to this higher level of social and demographic threat, the reported incidence of negative reactions to intergroup dating was far greater among each of the minority groups than for whites. The associated F-tests ranged from a low of 6.0 for negative reactions from family ($p < .001$) to a high of 25.1 for negative reactions from own-group strangers ($p < .001$).

The lowest frequency of social sanctioning for dating outside the group occurred among Latinos. Just 18% reported any negative reaction from Latino friends, 17% reported a negative reaction from family members, 13% from Latino strangers, and just 10% from other strangers. Going out with Latinos also did not seem to bother members of their partner's group very much. Only 15% reported a negative reaction from their date's racial or ethnic group.

Compared with Latinos, Asians experienced significantly more sanctioning for dating outside the group, with negative reactions coming most frequently from other Asians. Some 24% reported encountering negative reactions from Asian strangers, 25% reported a negative reaction from family members, and 26% reported a negative reaction from Asian friends or acquaintances. Intergroup dating involving Asians did not seem to bother non-Asians nearly as much. Only 20% of Asians reported a negative reaction from strangers in the partner's group, and just 15% reported a negative reaction from other strangers.

Given the historical social distance between blacks and whites in the United States, it is not surprising, though no less troubling, that African Americans reported by far the highest rate of social sanctioning for having relationships outside the group. Thus 43% of those who dated interracially reported negative reactions from their black friends, and 45% reported negative reactions from black strangers. Unlike the case for Asians and Latinos, out-groups were also quite bothered by relationships with African Americans. Some 42% of black students said they experienced a negative reaction from their partner's group, and 38% encountered a negative response from other strangers. Among African Americans, families were more accepting of intergroup relationships. Only 24% of blacks with a nonblack date or partner reported a negative reaction from family members. Nonetheless, the foregoing data suggest once again that the social world of the college campus is far from being a "race-blind society."

Most social experiences are "gendered" in the sense that they are experienced differently by men and women, and are accompanied by different sets of risks, opportunities, and constraints. Romantic relationships are perhaps the most obvious instance where the view of males and females is likely to be quite different given divergent sets of risks (to pregnancy and venereal disease), different opportunities and constraints (grounded in patriarchal traditions), and contrasting expectations (the well-known double standard). On campus, the inherent asymmetry between men and women in terms of sex and dating is exacerbated by a demographic imbalance that ranges from mild in the case of whites to severe in the case of African Americans.

Table 5.5 thus focuses on dates and steady relationships reported among sophomores and contrasts the situation of male and female students within each group. The top panel shows the percentage within each gender-racial-ethnic category going on dates and in a steady romantic relationship during the second year of college. There are not large differences between males and females in these two series, and those that exist are difficult to interpret; for if one is in a steady relationship one is generally not dating, and if one is dating one is not in a steady relationship. A more telling indicator is the share who are *neither* dating *nor* involved in a steady relationship, a population we might call the romantically marginalized. Intergroup differences on this statistic are substantial and highly significant. Among males, the F-test for the share neither dating nor going steady is 13.7, and for females it is 5.3 (both $p < .001$).

The highest degree of alienation from the college mating market was among Asians, with males leading the way. Nearly 30% of Asian males neither dated nor had a steady girlfriend during their sophomore year. Next in romantic marginalization were Asian and black women, 22% of whom

Table 5.5
Dating and romantic experiences reported by minority males and females as freshmen and sophomores

	Males				*Females*			
	White	Asian	Latino	Black	White	Asian	Latina	Black
Dating in Sophomore Year								
% with Dates	51.4	44.4	51.8	48.9	49.7	41.9	46.1	45.4
% with Steady Partner	33.1	22.1	28.6	26.1	33.8	32.1	36.8	34.1
% with No Date or Partner	11.6	29.3	13.8	19.8	14.2	22.3	16.2	21.7
Composition of Sophomore Dates								
% White	**96.3**	63.2	85.9	46.1	**95.8**	65.6	78.8	27.4
% Asian	23.8	**64.3**	26.1	23.3	13.5	**53.3**	11.0	7.7
% Latino	9.4	8.1	**49.7**	27.8	9.2	7.0	**39.2**	14.2
% Black	7.4	4.3	14.1	**81.7**	12.3	11.5	19.2	**89.4**
Composition of Sophomore Partners								
% White	**85.4**	43.5	64.5	19.8	**90.4**	48.3	60.7	13.3
% Asian	8.3	**50.0**	5.5	10.4	4.5	**37.4**	3.1	0.9
% Latino	2.5	3.3	**25.5**	2.1	1.7	4.0	**25.5**	3.9
% Black	0.0	0.0	0.9	**52.1**	1.7	4.0	5.1	**76.4**
% Biracial	1.3	1.1	2.7	10.4	1.1	5.2	1.5	3.0
% Other	2.5	2.2	0.9	5.2	0.6	1.1	4.1	2.6
Ever Experienced Negative Reaction								
% Friends in Own Group	5.9	15.8	15.8	47.6	7.1	32.4	19.9	38.1
% Family	5.9	19.9	9.9	26.7	0.0	28.4	21.6	19.7
% Strangers in Own Group	6.3	13.0	9.5	41.9	0.0	25.8	15.4	47.0
% Strangers in Partner's Group	5.9	15.8	9.9	39.4	7.1	23.1	17.9	42.4
% Other Strangers	5.9	11.0	7.7	33.7	0.0	17.8	11.3	39.8

reported neither dates nor a steady relationship. Black males were close behind at around 20%, followed by Latino females at 16% and Latino males at 14%. Whites were least estranged from the romantic scene, with just 14% of females and 12% of males reporting no romantic involvement. There was thus a wide range of involvement in campus mating and dating behavior, ranging from a 70% participation rate among Asian males to an 88% rate among white males.

The next panel down looks at the racial composition of dates by gender. Intergroup differentials in the composition of dates is systematic and highly nonrandom, with F-tests among males ranging from 62.3 for dating whites to 243.6 for dating blacks, and among females from 36.8 for dating

Latinos to 281.3 for dating African Americans (all p values well under $p < .001$). There are also important gender asymmetries in intergroup dating. Although white males and females display very high and roughly equal tendencies toward homogamy, with about 96% in each category reporting dates with other whites, nearly a quarter of white males reported dating Asian females compared with only 14% of white females who said they dated Asian men.

The pattern of gender asymmetry is reversed among Asians. In contrast to their white counterparts, Asian males display a significantly higher level of dating homogamy than females. Whereas 64% of Asian males dated Asian females, only 53% of Asian females dated Asian males. Both Asian men and women reported dating a relatively large share of whites—63% in the case of males and 66% in the case of females—but Asian men were very unlikely to date black women. Just 4% of Asian males said they had dated a black women during the sophomore year, compared with 12% of females who said they had dated a black man.

Latinos reported much lower rates of homogamy and much higher rates of association with whites compared with Asians, though rates of within-group romance were greater for males than females. Thus 50% of Latinos but only 39% of Latinas reported dating others of Latino origin, whereas 79% of Latinas and 86% of Latinos dated whites. Latinos were more likely to date Asians than were Latinas, with a frequency of 26% compared with 11%; but Latinas were more likely to date African Americans than their male counterparts, with a frequency of 19% versus 14%.

Compared with the other minority groups, African Americans once again display by far the highest rates of dating homogamy, led by black females, 89% of whom reported dating black males, compared with 82% of black males dating black females. Black females were the least likely of any group to have a date with whites. Only 27% reported dating a white male, whereas 46% of black men reported dating a white female. In contrast, the rate of out-group dating with whites never fell below 63% for Latinos or Asians of either gender. Black females were also less likely than black males to report dating Asians or Latinos and are thus the most romantically segregated of all racial-ethnic-gender categories. If there is a pecking order in the mating and dating market on campus, black women would seem to be at the bottom.

This pattern of gender differentiation is enhanced when permanence and exclusivity are imposed on relationships. More than three-quarters of the steady boyfriends reported by black women were African American; just 13% were white; and very small shares (under 4%) were in other groups. In contrast, only 52% of black males reported a steady black girlfriend, compared with 20% reporting a steady white girlfriend, 10% a steady Asian girlfriend, and 10% a steady biracial girlfriend. Asian males reported a similar level of homogamy in their steady relationships, with 50% being in a steady relationship with an Asian female. But compared with black males, Asian males were much more likely to have white girlfriends—44% compared with 20% among black males.

Compared with African Americans, Asian females and Latinos of both genders reported much lower levels of homogamy with respect to their steady relationships; and in all cases the dominant relationship was with whites. Whereas 37% of Asian females had an Asian boyfriend, 48% had a white boyfriend. Likewise, although 26% of Latinos of both genders reported an in-group partner, more than 60% reported having a white boyfriend or girlfriend. As always, the most homogamous group was whites, led by females, 90% of whom reported white boyfriends. Likewise, 85% of white males reported white girlfriends, followed distantly by 8% who reported an Asian girlfriend.

The foregoing rates of intergroup partner formation by gender provide a lens on the social distances prevailing among racial and ethnic groups on selective college campuses. Figure 5.1 shows the results of a multidimensional scaling (MDS) analysis of the intergroup partner matrix shown in the third panel of table 5.5. MDS simply applies a mathematical algorithm to develop a relational picture of the relationships represented by a set of numerical proximities between objects—in this case, rates of intergroup partner formation. It gives a spatial form to the underlying numbers. The top half of the figure shows the spatial representation of intergroup distances implied by intergroup partnering reported by males. As can be seen, blacks and whites lie at opposite ends of the social space, separated by Latinos. Both Asians and whites are quite distant from other groups, though not that far from each other. The closest two groups are Latinos and African Americans.

The bottom half of the figure repeats the analysis for the partners reported by females in each group. Once again blacks and whites lie at the opposite ends of the social space, with Latinos and Asians in between but off to the sides. Whites are closest to Asians, and Latinos are closest to blacks. Asians are most distant from Latinos and roughly equidistant from

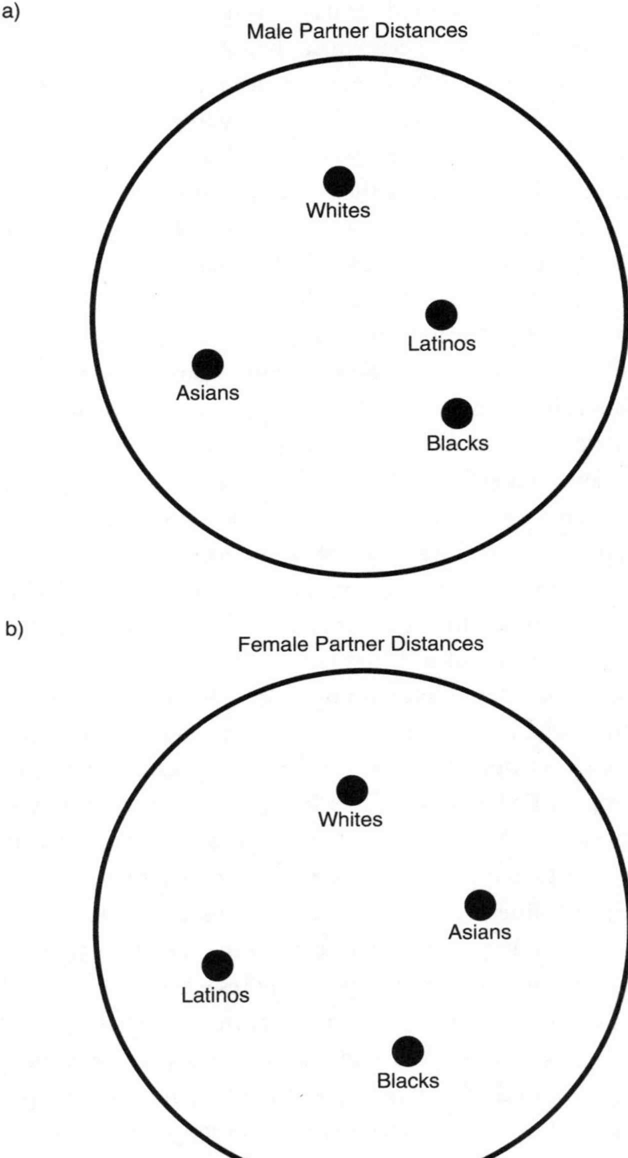

Figure 5.1.
Multidimensional scaling analysis of romantic distance between racial-ethnic groups

whites and blacks. Once again, in terms of mating and dating, the student bodies of selective colleges and universities are far from being race-blind societies.

The bottom panel of table 5.5 shows which racial-ethnic-gender groups experienced negative reactions as a result of intergroup dating. We already know the overall order of negative reactions from earlier analyses: whites experience the fewest social sanctions for dating across group lines, followed by Latinos and Asians, and finally African Americans. Although this general ordering is preserved when we consider males and females separately, the data reveal a significant contrast in the experience of Asian males and Asian females, one that suggests the existence of a double standard. Simply stated, Asian women are much more likely to experience negative reactions from other Asians for dating outside the group than are their male counterparts.

Whereas 16% of Asian men received a negative reaction from Asian friends or acquaintances, double that frequency of Asian women, 32%, encountered a negative reaction from their friends for out-group dating. Likewise, whereas only 13% of Asian men got a negative reaction from strangers in their own group and 16% from their partner's group, the respective figures for Asian women were 26% and 23%. Asian women also received more sanctions from family (28% compared with 20% among Asian males) as well other strangers (18% compared with 11%). Latinas also experienced more social sanctioning for intergroup dating than Latinos, but the discrepancy was not nearly as marked as among Asians. The biggest disparity in treatment came from families. Whereas 22% of Latinas reported a negative reaction from family members for dating outside the group, only 10% of Latinos did so.

Finally, although black males and females experienced about the same average level of social sanctioning for out-group dating, the pattern of negative reactions by source was quite different. Black males reported more negative reactions from black friends and family members, whereas black females reported more negative reactions from black strangers and other strangers. Thus, 48% of black males reported negative reactions from black friends and 27% from their families, compared with frequencies of 38% and 20% for black females. At the same time, 47% of black females reported a negative reaction from black strangers and 40% from other strangers, but the figures were 42% and 34% for black males.

Warmth of the Campus Waters

The foregoing analyses suggest the existence of palpable racial and ethnic undercurrents in the social interactions of students at selective colleges and universities. Mostly the undercurrents are implicit, observable only as differential propensities toward friendship, dating, and romance with various groups. Sometimes, however, the implicit becomes explicit, as when the crossing of a group boundary for purposes of romance triggers negative reactions from friends, family, and strangers. In addition to negative social sanctions triggered by specific behaviors, racial and ethnic undercurrents may also be expressed in less concrete, but no less real, ways. To assess these more subtle undercurrents the NLSF sophomore questionnaire asked students how often they had been made to feel self-conscious because of their race or ethnicity by classmates, professors, or "just walking around campus."

The top panel of table 5.6, for example, shows the percentage who said they had been made to feel self-conscious of their race or ethnicity at some point during their sophomore year. As might be expected, whites hardly felt uncomfortable on campus. Only 4% could recall ever being made to feel self-conscious because of race or ethnicity by classmates or just walking around campus, and virtually no one could recall being made to feel self-conscious because of something a professor said or did. Feelings of

Table 5.6
Perceptions of acceptance on campus during freshman year

Perception	Whites	Asians	Latinos	Blacks
% Made to Feel Self-Conscious of Race or Ethnicity from:				
Classmates	4.4	13.8	14.2	30.0
Professors	0.7	3.3	4.4	11.7
Just Walking around Campus	4.1	12.8	11.9	25.3
% Heard Derogatory Remarks about Race From:				
Students	9.6	16.0	22.6	23.3
Professors	1.0	1.4	2.9	2.9
Others	1.3	3.2	4.2	5.9
% Experience Harassment from:				
Campus Police Asking for ID	5.9	4.6	6.6	6.6
Professor Who Discouraged Participation	0.3	1.5	2.0	4.9
Professor Who Gave Unfair Grade	0.6	1.1	1.3	4.9
Own Group for Being with Others	3.0	9.9	7.4	16.9

social alienation were likewise relatively uncommon among Asians and Latinos. No more than 14% recalled being made to feel uncomfortable by classmates or just walking around campus, and no more than 4% ever felt uncomfortable because of a professor's behavior or demeanor.

Although a majority of African Americans also reported no discomfort, the incidence of discomfort was nonetheless higher for them. Some 30% said they had been made to feel uncomfortable because of race by their classmates ($t = 18.8$, $p < .001$) and 25% reported being made to feel self-conscious just walking around campus ($t = 14.8$, $p < .001$) . Whereas faculty-originated discomfort was extremely rare for other groups, some 12% of African Americans said that a professor had made them to feel uncomfortable because of their race at some point during the sophomore year ($F = 5.2$, $p < .001$).

Although these data clearly suggest the existence of racial and ethnic undercurrents on campus, feelings of self-consciousness are admittedly subjective and difficult to interpret—was the perceived racial slight real or imagined? The second panel of table 5.6 therefore focuses on something more concrete: whether students heard derogatory remarks about their group as sophomores. The most frequent source of derogatory comments was other students. Thus, 10% of whites, 16% of Asians, and 23% of Latinos and African Americans reported hearing derogatory remarks from fellow students. Fortunately, derogatory comments were very infrequently reported from professors, staff, or others on campus.

The last panel in table 5.6 begins by summarizing answers to the question: "Have the campus police ever asked you to present identification?" Notice that no mention is made of race or ethnicity in this query. It is just a sample question of fact, without going into underlying intentions or motivations. On this index, all groups look similar. Only 5% to 7% of respondents in any group could recall being asked by campus police to present identification. Likewise, although the figures are not identical, very few students in any group could recall being discouraged from asking a question in class by a professor, and very few felt they had ever been given an unfair grade because of race.

In the spring of the sophomore year the NLSF asked, "Have you ever experienced harassment from members of your own racial or ethnic group because you interacted or associated with members of some other group?" This turned out to be the most frequent form of social harassment. Responses to this question are shown in the last line of the table. Whereas only 3% of whites recalled such harassment, 17% of African Americans did so, compared with 10% of Asians and 7% of Latinos ($F = 59.1, p < .001$). These data, combined with earlier tabulations showing relatively high frequencies of negative reactions toward intergroup dating, suggest that whites are not the only ones involved in policing the categorical boundaries of race and ethnicity. Minority groups are substantially involved as well.

Undercurrents and Academics

While categorical distinctions based on race and ethnicity may be alive and well on college campuses, this fact does necessarily mean that the social undercurrents have any effect on academic performance. In order to measure the academic consequences of racial and ethnic undercurrents on campus, we developed a series of indicators based on the foregoing tabulations and regressed them on grades earned through the sophomore year while controlling for group membership and background characteristics.

We measured diversity in the classroom by indicating the percentage Asian, the percentage Latino, and the percentage African American in the respondent's first class. Faculty diversity was measured by whether or not the student had ever had an Asian professor, a Latino professor, or a black professor as a freshman. The diversity of friendship networks was measured by the number of Asian, Latino, and African Americans among the ten closest friends, and social support was measured using the summated rating scale described earlier. We also assessed whether or not the respondent belonged to a majority-white organization on campus, a majority-Asian organization, a majority-Latino organization, or majority-black organization. Romantic experience was measured by a dummy variable that equaled 1 if the student had neither a date nor a partner as a sophomore, and 0 otherwise. Among those who were involved romantically, we indicated whether or not the date or partner was outside the respondent's group.

In order to indicate the racial climate perceived by students, we created three scales that combined ratings across different sets of items. The scale of negative reactions from in-group members included four items measuring the frequency of negative reactions from own-group friends, family, and strangers, as well as the item indicating frequency of harassment by in-group members for associating with an out-group. The scale ranged from 0 to 16 and had a Cronbach's alpha of .68. The scale of negative reactions from out-group members included two items: one assessing the frequency of negative reactions from strangers in the partner's group and the other assessing the frequency of such reactions from other strangers, yielding an index that ranged from 0 to 8 with a Cronbach's alpha of .78.

Finally, we created a scale to measure the negativity of the campus climate for people of the respondent's race or ethnicity based on nine items assessing the frequency with which students were made to feel self-conscious by classmates, professors, and just walking around campus; the frequency with which they heard derogatory comments from students, professors, and others; and the frequency with which they were discouraged from speaking in class, discouraged from undertaking a course of study, or given a poor grade by a professor because of race or ethnicity. The resulting scale ranged from 0 to 64 with a Cronbach's alpha of .80. The construction of all scales is summarized in appendix C.

Table 5.7 regresses these variables on grades earned during the first two years of college along with dummy variables for group membership and standard controls. Looking at the coefficients, we can see right away that most social indicators have no significant effect on grade performance. Overall, the indicators of racial climate, romantic experience, group involvement, and class diversity play no significant role in determining grades earned by students. The only significant effect of faculty diversity is the positive effect of taking a course from a Latino faculty member, and the only significant effects of friendship diversity are negative. Having larger numbers of black and Latino friends tends to reduce grade performance, but social support has a marginally positive effect on achievement. Perhaps the most remarkable thing about these results is that once social factors are added to the mix of predictors, the heretofore resilient GPA gap between Latinos and whites disappears. Something about the social undercurrents we have identified appears to explain the lagging academic performance of Latino students compared with whites.

In order to shed light on how social undercurrents affect the grade performance of different groups, we regressed our GPA separately on social indicators for whites, Asians, Latinos, and African Americans; the results of this exercise are presented in table 5.8. Here we *do* find significant differences across groups in terms of which social factors influence grade performance and how. Classroom diversity appears to benefit white students in the sense that the presence of more Latino students increases

Table 5.7
Effect of social undercurrents on academic achievement

	Outcome: GPA through Sophomore Year		
Independent Variables	B	SE	*P* Value
Key Variables			
Group			
Whites	—	—	—
Asians	0.048**	0.015	.04
Latinos	−0.009	0.025	.717
Blacks	−0.142***	0.022	.000
Diversity of First Class			
% Asian	0.000	0.001	.795
% Latino	0.000	0.002	.775
% Black	0.002	0.002	.319
Faculty Diversity			
Had Asian Professor	−0.022	0.022	.327
Had Latino Professor	0.029*	0.011	.017
Had Black Professor	0.018	0.016	.278
Friends' Diversity			
# Asian Friends	0.005	0.005	.277
# Latino Friends	−0.026**	0.008	.003
# Black Friends	−0.009*	0.004	.050
Social Support			
Scale of Social Support	0.002†	0.001	0.063
Group Involvement			
In Majority-White Group	0.033	0.021	.125
In Majority-Asian Group	0.020	0.019	.296
In Majority-Latino Group	−0.001	0.036	.970
In Majority-black Group	−0.018	0.033	.588
Romantic Experience			
No Date or Partner	0.000	0.017	.999
Dated outside Group	−0.011	0.017	.506
Partner outside Group	−0.008	0.029	.778
Racial Climate on Campus			
Negative Reaction from In-group	−0.010	0.009	.280
Negative Reaction from Out-group	0.001	0.018	.964
Overall Racial Climate	0.000	0.001	.997
Control Variables			
Difficulty of Courses			
Number of Easy Courses	−0.005†	0.003	.093
Number of Hard Courses	0.023***	0.003	.000

Table 5.7 *(continued)*

Independent Variables	*Outcome: GPA through Sophomore Year*		
	B	SE	*P* Value
Demographic Background			
Male	−0.045**	0.014	.005
Foreign-Born Parent	0.019	0.017	.278
Two-Parent Family	0.012	0.020	.537
Siblings under 18	−0.009	0.007	.215
Education of Parents			
No College Degrees	—	—	—
One College Degree	0.025	0.024	.316
Two College Degrees	0.101***	0.024	.000
One Advanced Degree	0.108***	0.027	.000
Two Advanced Degrees	0.169***	0.030	.000
Economic Status			
Home Value (000)	0.000	0.000	.695
Ever on Welfare	−0.015	0.026	.565
Income > $100,000	0.029	0.023	.198
Academic Preparation			
AP Courses Taken	0.015***	0.004	.000
High School GPA	0.434***	0.030	.000
Self-rated Preparation	0.026***	0.003	.000
Social Preparation			
Self-efficacy	−0.005	0.003	.137
Self-esteem	0.005**	0.002	.006
Susceptibility to Peer Influence	0.009***	0.002	.000
Social Distance from Whites	0.001	0.002	.502
Intercept	1.101***	0.123	0.000
R^2	0.366***		
Number of Cases	2,213		

†$p<.10$ *$p<.05$ **$p<.01$ ***$p<.001$

the white students' grade performance. Conversely, a larger share of black students in the classroom has a negative effect on Asians' grade performance. Ironically, in no case does the presence of a minority's own in-group members in larger numbers improve the grade performance of that minority itself.

For the most part, the same is true of the presence of in-group faculty, with one important exception: having a Latino professor rather strongly improves the grade performance of Latino students. The presence or absence of Latino faculty as role models thus appears to play a significant role in explaining the Latino performance gap relative to whites. Although

Table 5.8
Effect of social undercurrents within groups on academic achievement

Independent Variables	Whites	Asians	Latinos	Blacks
Key Variables				
Diversity of First Class				
% Asian	0.000	0.000	0.000	0.001
% Latino	0.004**	0.005	0.001	−0.002
% Black	0.002	−0.005*	−0.002	0.003
Faculty Diversity				
Had Asian Professor	−0.027	0.021	−0.051	−0.019
Had Latino Professor	−0.011	−0.019	0.085**	0.049
Had Black Professor	−0.032	0.033	0.004	0.032
Friends' Diversity				
# Asian Friends	0.023**	0.008	0.019	0.004
# Latino Friends	−0.010	−0.048*	−0.019†	−0.023
# Black Friends	−0.030†	−0.004	−0.029*	0.006
Social Support				
Scale of Social Support	0.004*	0.004*	−0.002	0.001
Group Involvement				
In Majority-White Group	0.040	0.029	0.045	0.010
In Majority-Asian Group	−0.039	0.012	0.022	0.176***
In Majority-Latino Group	−0.005	−0.063	−0.008	0.274***
In Majority-Black Group	−0.141	0.082	0.132*	−0.042†
Romantic Experience				
No Date or Partner	−0.022	0.123***	−0.085*	0.001
Dated outside Group	−0.026	0.045	−0.045	0.063
Partner outside Group	−0.083	0.027	−0.020	0.014
Racial Climate on Campus				
Negative Reaction from In-group	−0.183	0.019	−0.031	−0.006
Negative Reaction from Out-group	0.162†	−0.034	0.024	−0.026
Overall Racial Climate	0.877	0.000	−0.002	0.001
Control Variables				
(Not Shown)				
Intercept	0.945**	0.813*	1.219***	1.391***
R^2	0.314	0.351	0.323	0.340
Number of Cases	592	563	493	565

†$p<.10$ *$p<.05$ **$p<.01$ ***$p<.001$

the effect of having a black professor is also positive for African Americans, it is smaller and not statistically significant. Having a Latino professor is also associated with better grades among African Americans, but again the effect is not significant. However, dividing the sample into race-specific groups for these regressions has severely curtailed the degrees of freedom, making it harder to attain statistical significance.

The effect of having friends of different race and ethnicity varies from group to group, as one might expect. Whites who report having more Asian friends earn higher grades, other things equal, whereas Asians with more Latino friends earn lower grades. The grade performance of Latinos also seems to be lower the more Latino and the more black friends they have, but black grade performance appears to be unaffected by the relative number of friends in different groups. Paradoxically, the degree of support received from one's social contacts seems to matter only for whites and Asians, the groups that need it least in terms of grade achievement. In both cases, more support from close contacts yields academic dividends in the form of higher grades, whereas such support has no significant effect on grade achievement among Latinos or African Americans.

In contrast, involvement in voluntary organizations dominated by one or another racial-ethnic group has no discernable effect on the grades earned by whites, but it does influence the grades earned by Latinos and blacks, though the direction of effects is not what one might expect: whereas Latinos benefit from membership in black-dominant organizations, African Americans experience a small penalty. Rather than being helped by joining black organizations, African Americans appear to benefit more from membership in organizations dominated by Asians and Latinos, and the effects are rather strong.

In terms of romantic experience, the only significant effects we observe are among Asians and Latinos. Asians who are not involved in dating or relationships earn higher grades. In contrast, Latinos with no dates or relationships earn lower grades. Thus romantic marginalization seems to work in different ways for Asians and Latinos. These associations could well represent the effect of a time trade-off, however. Those who apply themselves assiduously to their studies earn higher grades and have no time for dates or romance, whereas those who devote more time to pursuing a partner have romance but less time for studying, and hence, receive lower grades.

Navigating Racial Undercurrents

The baseline survey of the NLSF asked students a variety of questions about racial and ethnic attitudes; in feedback provided to interviewers and investigators, many students were upset and angry with the questions. The general viewpoint was that race and ethnicity no longer mattered, so why were we asking about it? Despite the ubiquity of this view among students, the data presented in this chapter indicate that race and ethnicity clearly *do* matter on the campuses of America's selective colleges and university.

Demography alone constrains the nature and frequency of intergroup relationships, and all groups reported that 60% to 70% of both classmates and professors where white. Under these circumstances, we would expect minority groups to report a preponderance of associations with whites, and this is generally what we observe among Asians and Latinos. In terms of close friendships, for example, the number of white friends exceeds the number of in-group friends, especially among Latinos. Blacks, however, go against the demographic grain. Among them black friendships outnumber white friendships by two to one.

When it comes to organizational memberships, we once again observe a greater preponderance of membership in white-dominant organizations among Asians and Latinos than blacks. Whereas 45% of Asians and 50% of Latinos said they belonged to a campus group or organization in which whites were the majority, the figure is just 28% for blacks. Moreover, whereas the ratio of white to in-group memberships is three to one among Asians and six to one among Latinos, it is roughly one to one for African Americans.

Similar intergroup contrasts prevail with respect to dating and mating. In terms of both dates and steady partners, Asians and Latinos are more likely to go out with whites than with members of their own group, but among African Americans the opposite is true. Among dates reported by African Americans in the sophomore year, dates with blacks outnumber dates with white by 2.5 to one; and among reported partners, blacks outnumber whites by 4.5 to one. One reason for the high rate of racial homogamy among African Americans is the reactions that they can expect for crossing group boundaries in choosing dates or partners. Of those dating interracially, African Americans reported by far the highest incidence of negative reactions, not just from members of their partner's group or others on campus but also from other black students on campus. Whereas

42% of African Americans who dated nonblacks reported a negative reaction from their partner's group, 45% reported one from their own group.

The dynamics of intergroup dating play out most cruelly in the case of black females, who outnumber black males by a substantial margin on most campuses. Because of this gender imbalance, many black women will have to remain dateless and mateless unless they cross a group boundary. Unfortunately, they are even more likely than black men to be sanctioned publicly for this transgression. As a result of the constraints of demography and the higher risk of social sanctioning, black females display the highest rate of in-group dating and partnership of any minority group, and the percentage of black females with neither dates nor steady partners in the sophomore year is exceeded only by that of Asian males, who seem to focus more on scholastic than romantic endeavors. When they do go on dates or form partnerships, Asian men are quite likely to do so with whites. Asians, however, appear to hold a double standard for out-group dating—females are more likely to be sanctioned by other Asians for dating outside the group—but despite this fact, the rate of dating and partnership formation with whites is very high among Asian women.

In addition to concrete and observable outcomes like intergroup dating, the undercurrents associated with race and ethnicity also play out in more subtle ways. Black students were far more likely than others to report being made to feel self-conscious by other students or by just walking around campus. Nearly a quarter reported hearing derogatory racial remarks from other students. But whites were not the only ones policing the color line—17% of black students reported being harassed by other African Americans for associating publicly with nonblacks. However lamentable such harassment might seem, and whatever the social and psychological consequences of negative reactions to out-group romance, they do not seem to have much effect on academic achievement. Experiencing negative reactions for intergroup romance has no discernible influence on grade point average, nor does the perceived negativity of the campus racial climate.

6 The Hidden Rocks of Segregation

Despite the *Brown* decision of 1954 and the passage of the Civil Rights Act of 1964, the Voting Rights Act of 1965, and the Fair Housing Act of 1968, U.S. society remains very segregated on the basis of race (Iceland, Weinberg, and Steinmetz 2002; Kozol 2005). Two-thirds of urban African Americans live under conditions of very high residential segregation (Massey 2004), and two-thirds of all African Americans attend minority-dominant schools (Orfield 2001). To a remarkable extent, black and white Americans, and increasingly Latinos, inhabit separate social worlds characterized by what Kozol (1991) has called "savage inequalities." Considerable research documents the disadvantaged conditions experienced by blacks and Latinos in segregated schools (Anderson and Byrne 2004) and neighborhoods (Sampson, Morenoff, and Gannon-Rowley 2002).

Black and Latino students at selective institutions are not immune from the forces promoting segregation elsewhere in U.S. society. Analyses done in *The Source of the River* confirmed this fact and elaborated some of its educational consequences. As seniors in high school, nearly half of all black students and roughly a quarter of Latinos in the NLSF inhabited predominantly minority neighborhoods; and given the strong correlation between neighborhoods and schools, it is only logical that a significant fraction—36% of African Americans and 23% of Latinos—likewise attended minority-dominant schools. These schools were characterized by fewer educational resources, lower-quality teachers, and more dilapidated infrastructures than majority-white schools. African Americans and Latinos who attended integrated high schools enjoyed the same resources, teachers, and infrastructure as white and Asian students.

As a result of these contrasting circumstances, minority students who grew up in segregated schools and neighborhoods were less prepared for the rigors of life at competitive academic institutions than whites, Asians, or minority students from integrated settings. Not surprisingly, Massey et al. (2003) found that this lack of preparation translated directly into lower collegiate grades. Here we consider other, more subtle, effects of segregation, assessing the degree to which its negative effects on grade achievement stem from consequences that are not as readily apparent as lower-quality schooling and thus, lurking beneath the surface, act as submerged rocks that might sink the academic hopes of minority students.

Submerged Dangers

It is well known that high levels of residential segregation interact with the distribution of income to concentrate poverty geographically (see Massey and Fischer 2000). When a relatively poor group is segregated on the basis of race or ethnicity, poverty is necessarily concentrated at high levels within minority schools and neighborhoods (Massey 1990). By concentrating poverty ecologically, segregation also concentrates anything associated with poverty, such as crime, delinquency, violence, family disruption, drug use, and welfare dependence (Massey and Denton 1993). The systematic segregation of African Americans and Latinos in the United States thus creates an unusually threatening and hostile social environment to which individual group members must adapt (Massey 2001).

People growing up in segregated schools and neighborhoods thus experience elevated levels of stress because of prolonged exposure to social disorder and violence (Massey 2004). To understand the manifold effects of stress on human beings, biomedical researchers have developed the concept of allostasis, which refers to the innate tendency of organisms to adapt bodily to threats in the environment (Sterling and Ayer 1988; McEwan and Lasley 2002). Whenever a human being perceives an external threat, a brain organ known as the hypothalamus triggers an allostatic response, which is a complex interaction involving the brain, the endocrine system, and the immune system. Upon perceiving a threat, the hypothalamus signals the adrenal glands to release adrenaline into the bloodstream, which activates the fight-or-flight response, accelerating heartbeat, constricting blood vessels, increasing the flow of blood to internal organs, dilating bronchial tubes, releasing fibrinogen into the bloodstream to enhance clotting, discharging glucose from stored fats to provide energy, and signaling the brain to produce endorphins to mitigate pain (McEwan and Lasley 2002).

While all these reactions are unfolding, the hypothalamus also signals the pituitary gland to release adrenocorticotropic hormone, which, in turn, causes the adrenal glands to secrete cortisol into the blood (McEwan and Lasley 2002). Cortisol is an important resource in threatening situations because it acts to replace energy stores depleted by adrenaline. It promotes the conversion of muscle protein to fat, blocks insulin from taking up glucose, subtracts minerals from bones, and changes the external texture of white blood cells to make them "stickier" and more adhesive, thus facilitating clotting. The allostatic response is nature's way of maximizing an organism's resources to meet an immediate, short-term threat. Long-term functions such as the building of muscle, bone, and brain cells are temporarily sacrificed to put more energy into the bloodstream for evasive or aggressive action (McEwan and Lasley 2002).

The hypothalamic-pituitary-adrenal axis is common to all mammals and is designed for infrequent and sporadic use. Unlike most mammals, however, humans are capable of keeping the HPA axis turned on indefinitely because they can experience stress from ideas in addition to actual events. Human beings can imagine threatening circumstances—mentally anticipating events that might occur or recalling past traumas. Repeated triggering of the allostatic response through chronic exposure to stressful events—as when someone is compelled by poverty and discrimination to live in a dangerous and violent neighborhood—yields a condition known as allostatic load (McEwan and Lasley 2002).

As a person's allostatic load increases and persists, it has powerful negative effects on a variety of bodily systems, raising the risk of cardiovascular and autoimmune diseases such as diabetes and asthma (McEwan and Lasley 2002). In addition, chronic exposure to stress hormones has profound effects on cognition, reducing long- and short-term memory, lowering frustration thresholds, limiting attention spans, and interfering with the neural chemistry of learning itself (Bremner 2002).

The part of the brain that is primarily responsible for the consolidation and storage of memory is the hippocampus (Carter 1999). Because stressful events are important to remember, the hippocampus is rich in cortisol receptors, making people more likely to remember things and events that are associated with strong emotions (McEwan and Lasley 2002). In evolutionary terms, human beings who recalled where and under what circumstances danger occurred were more likely to survive and pass on their genes. Chronically elevated cortisol, however, causes the receptors to become saturated, leading to atrophy of the hippocampus and impairment of memory, both short-term and long-term (Bremner 2002).

Excessive cortisol also interferes with the normal operation of neurotransmitters such as glutamate, which is a critical ingredient in the formation of synaptic connections. By disrupting the production and operation of glutamate at the synapse, allostatic load inhibits long-term potentiation—the formation of a relatively permanent neural connection—which is the fundamental chemical event in human learning. Thus chronic exposure to disorder and violence can compromise the very biochemical foundation of human learning (McEwan and Lasley 2002).

Finally, the hippocampus plays an important role in shutting down the hypothalamic-pituitary-adrenal axis by reducing cortisol production. As a result, damage to it is doubly detrimental. Through its effect on the hippocampus, chronic stress creates a vicious cycle whereby excessive cortisol causes shrinkage of the hippocampus, which causes less inhibition of cortisol production, which causes more hippocampal shrinkage (McEwan and Lasley 2002). Over the long run, this cycle leads to dendritic remodeling, wherein neurons become shorter and sprout fewer branches, as well as the suppression of neurogenesis, or the creation of new brain cells (Gould et al. 1998). Simply put, people who are exposed to high levels of stress over a prolonged period of time are at risk of having their brains rewired in a way that leaves them with fewer cognitive resources (McEwan and Lasley 2002; Bremner 2002). Students growing up in a segregated environment characterized by high levels of disorder and violence are at elevated risk of cognitive impairments capable of undermining academic performance in important but subtle ways years later.

In addition to these long-term effects, segregation has other, more immediate effects on academic performance through contemporaneous pathways. Even though all NLSF respondents personally inhabit a safe and secure campus environment, many of their friends and relatives do not. Because of the pervasiveness of segregation in American life, the interpersonal networks of many African Americans and Latinos inevitably include friends and relatives who attend minority-dominant schools, inhabit racially isolated neighborhoods, and thus continue to experience the risks of life in a poor, segregated setting. Even if black and Latino students themselves grew up under conditions of integration, many people within their extended network of friends and relatives will still live in segregated communities.

Because black and Latino students are disproportionately connected to people inhabiting disadvantaged ecological settings, they are at much greater risk of experiencing stress through their social networks. That is, the friends and relatives of minority students are much more likely to become victims of crime or violence, and to be affected by problems such as gangs or drugs; and this is true across all levels of socioeconomic status because segregation is only weakly related to income among African Americans. Indeed, the most affluent black families are virtually as segregated as the poorest African Americans (Massey and Fischer 1999; Wilkes and Iceland 2004).

Segregation thus represents an exogenous fact of American life that disproportionately exposes the friends and relatives of minority students to social problems, thereby increasing the odds that someone in their social network will experience a stressful life event. In this way, segregation, in combination with high rates of black and Latino poverty, produces elevated rates of social stress, which undermines academic performance in several ways: by distracting students psychologically from their studies; by compromising their physical and emotional well-being; and by necessitating competing investments of time, money, and energy to attend to family and personal issues. Through no fault of their own, minority students continue to be enmeshed in a web of social relationships that, owing to the pernicious effects of segregation, undermine their academic performance on campus.

The ways in which segregation affects academic performance in the short and long term are summarized in figure 6.1. The long-term effects occur through segregation's influence on cognitive skills, as indicated by the upper pathway in the diagram. Students who come of age in segregated schools and neighborhoods experience higher levels of disorder and violence than those in integrated settings and, hence, incur higher allostatic loads, thus increasing the risk of cognitive adaptations that inhibit academic performance. The short-term effects of segregation are shown by the bottom pathway. Segregation increases the frequency with which negative events occur to people in students' social networks, which undermines

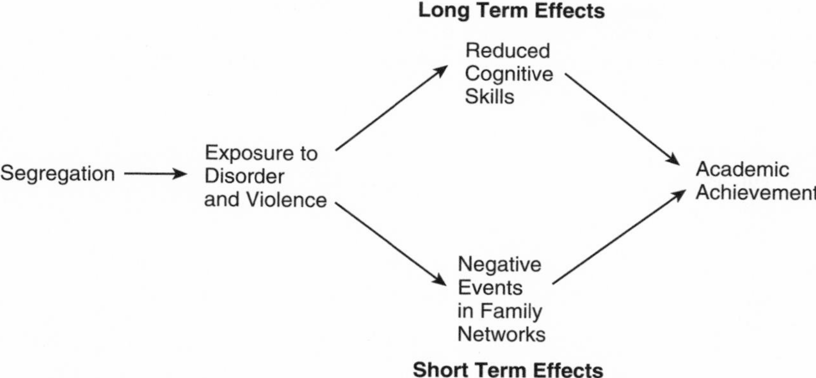

Figure 6.1.
The effects of racial segregation on academic achievement

their academic achievement by compromising health and promoting greater involvement with interpersonal issues off campus, taking time and energy away from their studies.

Sharp Rocks of Violence

The differential exposure of NLSF students to school and neighborhood segregation is well documented in *The Source of the River* and has been further elaborated in several articles (see Charles, Massey, and Dinwiddie 2004; Fischer and Massey 2005; Massey 2006). There is no need to repeat those analyses here. Table 6.1 simply recaps the contrasting situations of the four groups with respect to school and neighborhood segregation. Based on the average percentage of blacks and Hispanics present in each ecological setting at ages 6, 13, and 18, we classified schools and neighborhoods into one of three categories: integrated (those averaging under 30% minority presence, i.e., Hispanic plus black); segregated (those averaging more than 70% minority); and mixed (those averaging between 30% and 70% minority).

The top panel of the table shows the share of NLSF students coming from each kind of neighborhood by race and ethnicity. Obviously, the vast majority of whites and Asians—92% of the former and 89% of the latter—came of age within integrated neighborhoods that contained very few Latinos or African Americans. Exceedingly few even grew up in mixed

Table 6.1
Relative integration of neighborhoods and schools inhabited by respondents to the National Longitudinal Survey of Freshmen while growing up (percent)

Level of Segregation	Whites	Asians	Latinos	Blacks
Neighborhood				
Integrated	91.8	88.5	53.1	33.4
Mixed	5.5	9.5	22.3	27.9
Segregated	0.7	0.6	23.9	38.0
School				
Integrated	83.4	81.8	46.9	35.1
Mixed	16.6	18.1	32.8	41.9
Segregated	0.4	0.6	20.6	23.1

Note: Integrated: < 30% minority. Mixed: 30%–69% minority. Segregated: 70+ % minority.

neighborhoods (just 5.5% of whites and 9.5% of Asians), and virtually none came of age in segregated settings. In contrast, 24% of Latinos and 38% of African Americans grew up in segregated neighborhoods, and among African Americans, a segregated neighborhood was the modal category of residential experience. Only 28% of black students came from mixed neighborhoods and 33% from integrated residential areas. Among Latinos, 53% experienced an integrated neighborhood and 22% grew up in mixed circumstances. These differences are highly significant statistically ($F = 498.4, p < .001$).

The bottom panel of the table repeats the analysis for schools instead of neighborhoods. In general, we observe more integration and mixing in schools than in neighborhoods. Again these differences are highly significant ($F = 306.4, p < .001$). Whereas only 6% of whites and 10% of Asians came from mixed *neighborhoods*, 17% and 18%, respectively, attended mixed *schools*. Still, virtually no member of either group attended a segregated school, making integration by far the most common educational experience, accounting for more than 80% of cases in both groups.

Blacks and Latinos also move toward greater mixing when the focus shifts from neighborhoods to schools, but they come from the other direction: their movement is from segregated to mixed rather than integrated to mixed. Whereas 38% of African Americans and 24% of Latinos came from segregated neighborhoods, only 23% and 21%, respectively, attended segregated schools; and whereas only 28% of African Americans and 22% of Latinos came from mixed neighborhoods, 42% and 33% attended mixed schools.

Table 6.2
Index of disorder and violence experienced in neighborhoods and schools by respondents to the National Longitudinal Survey of Freshmen while growing up

			Latinos and Blacks by Segregation		
Indicator	Whites	Asians	Integrated	Mixed	Segregated
Disorder Index					
Neighborhood	5.4	5.4	6.9	14.2	25.5
School	33.0	32.6	34.1	36.7	39.2
Violence Index					
Neighborhood	12.0	13.7	18.4	42.4	85.1
School	47.0	48.6	51.3	61.8	69.6
Effects of Segregation					
Mean Disorder-Violence	24.3	25.1	27.6	38.8	54.8
SAT Score	1361	1375	1275	1233	1188

As already noted, intergroup differences with respect to segregation are associated with sharp differentials in the level of exposure to crime and violence. In *The Source of the River*, Massey et al. (2003) developed a set of severity-weighted indexes to capture the degree of exposure to violence and social disorder (see appendix B, pp. 258–61). These indexes weighted the frequency that transgressions were experienced at different ages by each event's severity using a ratio-level severity scale of crime and delinquency developed by Sellin and Wolfgang (1964) and standardized nationally by Wolfgang et al. (1985).

Using this severity-weighted scale, the top panel of table 6.2 shows the degree to which whites, Asians, Latinos, and African Americans were exposed to disorder in schools and neighborhoods while growing up. Latinos and blacks have been combined and their results broken down by average level of segregation. As can be seen, whites and Asians, as well as blacks and Latinos from integrated circumstances, generally experienced similar and relatively low levels of exposure to disorder, but blacks and Latinos growing up in mixed and especially segregated settings experienced very high levels. Within neighborhoods, the severity-weighted disorder index stands at 5.4 for whites and Asians, and at 6.9 for Latinos and blacks from an integrated background. For Latinos and blacks growing up in mixed residential areas, however, the disorder index is 14.2, and it rises to a value of 25.5 among those from segregated neighborhoods ($F = 252.5$, $p < .001$). In other words, Latinos and African Americans from a segregated residential background were exposed to 3.5 times more disorder while growing up than their counterparts from integrated neighborhoods. Within schools, the overall exposure to disorder was greater across all groups, but the ordering remains the same: whites and Asians, as well as Latinos and African Americans from integrated schools, experienced relatively lower exposure to disorder than Latinos and blacks from mixed or segregated schools ($F = 17.3, p < .001$).

The middle panel shows variation in the degree of exposure to violence rather than disorder. The severity-weighted index of violence within neighborhoods stands at 12.0 for whites and 13.7 for Asians, compared with 18.4 for blacks and Latinos from integrated neighborhoods. Even within integrated areas, therefore, minority groups experienced higher rates of violence than whites ($t = 4.7, p < .001$); but exposure to violence in integrated neighborhoods is nothing compared with that in mixed and segregated neighborhoods, where the violence index reaches values of 42.4 and 85.1, respectively. In other words, blacks and Latinos from segregated residential environments experienced 7.3 times more violence growing up than whites ($t = 25.9, p < .001$). As is true with the disorder indices, the violence indexes are generally greater in schools, but once again the ordering is the same: exposure to violence rises monotonically as the focus moves from integrated to mixed to segregated schools. As a result, the exposure of Latinos and African Americans to violence was around 50% greater in segregated schools than in schools typically attended by whites ($t = 12.3, p < .001$).

The bottom panel of the table shows the overall severity of the disorder and violence experienced across schools and neighborhoods while growing up, which we will employ as a summary measure in subsequent analyses. Again, exposure to disorder and violence on this index is roughly the same for whites and Asians as well as African Americans and Latinos who came of age in integrated circumstances, with mean values of 24.3, 25.1, and 27.6, respectively. Exposure to disorder and violence increases steadily as segregation rises, however, with the mean index reaching 38.8 among Latinos and blacks from mixed backgrounds and 54.8 among those growing up under conditions of segregation ($F = 223.2, p < .001$). In short, students who came of age in segregated schools and neighborhoods experienced overall amounts of disorder and violence that were twice as severe, on average, as the amounts experienced by their white, Asian, or integrated minority counterparts ($t = 22.9, p < .001$).

The bottom line of the table presents prima facie evidence of segregation's effect on cognitive skills. The index most commonly used to measure the intellectual abilities of college students is the Scholastic Aptitude Test, and as part of the NLSF students were asked to report their SAT scores. Given the salience of the SAT in the admissions process, students are well aware of their scores and unlikely to forget them. As is well known, performance on the SAT is characterized by a significant majority-minority test score gap that is not eliminated by controlling for socioeconomic status and other background characteristics (Phillips et al. 1998). Research has found that whites and Asians perform better on the SAT than African Americans and Latinos (Jencks and Phillips 1998), and this intergroup differential is replicated in the NLSF.

The bottom line of the table suggests, however, that segregation and its sequelae of disorder and violence might explain part of the test score gap. African Americans and Latinos from integrated backgrounds display a score that is closer to those of Asians and whites than blacks and Latinos from mixed and segregated backgrounds. As segregation increases, however, average black and Latino SAT scores progressively fall, dropping by around 40 points among those from mixed backgrounds and by around 90 points among those from segregated backgrounds ($F = 154.6$, $p < .001$). Thus NLSF minorities who grew up attending segregated schools and living in segregated neighborhoods experienced cognitive adaptations that appear to have depressed their performance on the SAT.

Other Hidden Hazards

The foregoing tabulations indicate a strong empirical correlation between segregation and exposure to disorder and violence within schools and neighborhoods and also between segregation and cognitive skills as measured by the SAT, consistent with the pathway depicted in the top half of figure 6.1. Table 6.3 provides evidence relevant to the pathway depicted in the bottom half of the figure by examining the connection between segregation and negative events experienced within students' interpersonal networks as freshmen and sophomores. Rather than considering schools and neighborhoods separately, as in tables 6.1 and 6.2, here we employ an average measure of segregation experienced across both settings while growing up.

Table 6.3
Experience of stressful life events for whites, Asians, and blacks and Latinos by level of neighborhood segregation experienced in high school

			Latinos and Blacks by Segregation		
	Whites	Asians	Integrated	Mixed	Segregated
Death					
Parent	1.7%	1.2%	1.8%	1.3%	2.4%
Immediate Family	23.6%	21.3%	28.9%	33.8%	34.5%
Extended Family	23.9%	21.0%	24.6%	31.4%	31.9%
Friend	13.6%	8.6%	12.1%	14.5%	17.5%
Any Death	62.8%	52.1%	60.6%	76.5%	85.4%
Mean Number of Deaths	0.60	0.51	0.67	0.79	0.84
Crime in Immediate Family					
Victimization	13.7%	7.7%	14.2%	19.8%	20.2%
Trouble with Law	10.0%	5.2%	10.2%	17.8%	17.8%
Any Crime Problem	23.7%	12.8%	20.2%	34.2%	37.4%
Mean Number Crime Issues	0.29	0.14	0.29	0.47	0.47
Social Problems in Immediate Family					
Had Serious Illness or Disability	16.1%	13.7%	17.9%	23.2%	21.4%
Had Unplanned Pregnancy	2.0%	1.2%	4.0%	5.8%	6.6%
Dropped out of School	3.1%	2.2%	4.1%	7.7%	5.9%
Became Homeless	1.0%	0.3%	2.4%	3.0%	4.2%
Went into Drug/Alcohol Rehab	4.1%	0.9%	4.6%	6.7%	7.7%
Went on Public Assistance	2.0%	1.8%	2.7%	5.6%	5.2%
Divorced or Separated	7.0%	4.0%	7.2%	9.5%	8.9%
Became Unemployed	11.6%	11.3%	13.0%	17.4%	20.7%
Any Social Problem	46.8%	35.4%	45.9%	70.7%	80.1%
Mean Number Social Problems	0.56	0.42	0.66	0.95	0.94
Combined Death, Crime, Social					
Percent with Any Stressful Event	65.4	57.2	70.6	77.4	77.1
Average Number Stressful Events	1.45	1.07	1.62	2.21	2.25
Weighted Social Stress Index	37.3	28.4	40.5	58.6	59.6

The top line of table 6.3 focuses on what is perhaps the greatest shock a student can experience: the death of a parent. Fortunately the frequency of this event is very low. Only 1.7% of whites and 1.2% of Asians experienced the death of a parent. The incidence of parental mortality was about the same among Latinos and African Americans from integrated and mixed backgrounds, at 1.8% and 1.3%, respectively; but the death rate was slightly higher at 2.4% among those from segregated backgrounds. This difference, however, is not statistically significant ($F = 0.9, p = .47$).

Because the death of a parent is a rare event for people aged 18 to 20, the greater mortality risks associated with segregation are difficult to observe among the parents of freshman and sophomore college students. More telling are the rates of death among the students' immediate and extended family members. Whereas no more than 29% of whites, Asians, and minorities from integrated settings experienced the death of an immediate family member, the figure is 34% among minorities from mixed backgrounds and 35% among minorities from segregated backgrounds ($F = 12.8$, $p < .001$). A similar contrast prevails with respect to mortality within extended family networks ($F = 7.4$, $p < .001$). In general, compared with white students, African Americans and Latinos from a segregated background are roughly 45% more likely to have experienced a death in their immediate or extended family network.

People from segregated backgrounds are also more likely to experience a death in their circle of friends. Whereas 18% of those coming from segregated circumstances reported the death of a friend since beginning college, only 12% of those from integrated circumstances did so, compared with 9% among Asians and 14% among whites ($F = 6.4$, $p < .001$). The bottom line of the top panel shows the average number of deaths experienced by students during their first two years of college or university. Whereas whites experienced an average of 0.60 deaths during their freshman and sophomore years, the figure is 0.79 for people who came of age in mixed settings and 0.84 among those who grew up in segregated schools and neighborhoods, a 28% percent differential in personal experience with the stress of bereavement for a friend or relative ($F = 19.6$, $p < .001$). Whereas 85% of black and Latino respondents from segregated circumstances experienced a death in their social networks, only 61% of minorities from integrated circumstances did so.

The second panel of the table considers exposure to negative events associated with crime and criminal justice by ascertaining whether any family member had been criminally victimized or had gotten "in trouble with the law." Once again blacks and Latinos were more exposed to negative circumstances than whites; and, as before, the degree of negative exposure displayed in the table rises as segregation increases. Whereas 14% of white students reported that a member of their immediate family had been criminally victimized and 10% had family members in legal trouble, and whereas the respective figures for blacks and Latinos from integrated backgrounds are roughly the same, among minority students coming from segregated settings, the figures are much higher, at 20% ($F = 15.9$, $p < .001$). In the end, 24% of whites reported having some kind of crime problem in their family compared with 37% of blacks and Latinos from segregated backgrounds. For the former, the mean number of legal issues was 0.29, but it was 0.47 for the latter, a 60% differential ($t = 4.8, p < .001$).

The third panel considers other negative events within the respondent's immediate family, including health problems, unplanned pregnancies, school difficulties, homelessness, drug or alcohol problems, welfare use, divorce or separation, and job loss. The pattern of variation observed across categories generally replicates the one already established. Asians experience the fewest negative events, followed by whites and by African Americans and Latinos from integrated backgrounds. The incidence of negative events is greater among those from mixed backgrounds and greater still among those from segregated backgrounds. Whereas around 46% of the minority respondents who grew up in integrated schools and neighborhoods reported some problem within their immediate family, the figure is 71% among those from mixed circumstances and 80% among those from segregated settings ($F = 24.8, p < .001$). The average number of problems experienced by minorities from segregated circumstances is 0.94 compared with 0.66 among minorities from an integrated background ($t = 8.2$, $p < .001$).

Considering all the problems covered in table 6.3 (in the bottom panel), we observe that 65% of whites and 57% of Asians experienced a stressful event as freshmen or sophomores, along with 71% of blacks and Latinos from integrated backgrounds. In contrast, 77% of blacks and Latinos from a mixed or segregated background experienced a negative event in their social network ($F = 24.8, p < .001$). The average number of stressful events is 1.5 for whites, 1.1 for Asians, and 1.6 for blacks and Latinos from integrated settings, but 2.2 for blacks and Latinos from mixed settings and 2.3 for those from segregated circumstances ($F = 56.3, p < .001$).

These figures understate the contrast between groups, however, for they weight all negative events equally. In the above reckoning, having a parent die has the same relative importance as having a brother drop out of high school. We therefore sought to create an index that would assign different weights to different life events according to the amount of stress they produce. To do so, we used the Holmes-Rahe Social Adjustment Scale (Holmes and Rahe 1967; Holmes and Masuda 1974), matching events on the NLSF inventory of life events to the corresponding analogue on the Holmes-Rahe scale and assigning the relevant number of "life change units." The Holmes-Rahe scale ranges from 11 (the weight assigned minor violations of the law, such as getting a traffic ticket) to 100 (the death of a spouse). We then computed a weighted scale of social stress as follows:

$$SSI = E_i * HRS_i,$$

where SSI is the social stress index, E_i refers to life event i experienced by a respondent, and HRS_i refers to the Holmes-Rahe scale score associated with event i. The resulting index ranges from 0 to 322 with a reliability coefficient of .50 (Cronbach's alpha—see appendix C), and mean values are shown in the last line of table 6.3.

This weighted stress index more clearly reveals the differential exposure of racial-ethnic groups to negative life events by degree of segregation. Asians experienced the least social stress, with a weighted stress index of 28.4. The index for whites is higher at 37.3 (a figure about 30% greater). The stress index for African Americans and Latinos from integrated backgrounds is only slightly higher than that for whites at 40.5, but rises to 58.6 among those from mixed backgrounds and nearly 60 among those from segregated backgrounds. In other words, the average black or Latino student from a segregated background experienced about 60% more life stress during his or her first two years of college than the typical white student, and more than twice the stress experienced by the typical Asian student.

It thus seems clear that, owing to segregation, blacks and Latinos, even those currently inhabiting a very privileged and protected niche in American society, are exposed to much more stress within their social networks than other students, and that the extent of exposure to negative life events rises sharply as the degree of segregation increases. Table 6.4 considers whether this variation in exposure to stress is, in turn, associated with differences in respondents' behavior and their physical and mental well-being.

The top panel of table 6.4 indicates whether respondents sent money to their parents or visited them during the academic year (not counting vacations). We also present the mean amount of money sent and the average number of days spent away from campus. As seen in chapter 4, most students receive money from their families, so it is unsurprising that the vast majority of students in all categories did not send any money to parents. During their freshman and sophomore years, only 4.2% of whites and 5.6% of Asians said they did so. Even though most African Americans and Latinos likewise did not send money home, the figures are higher than for whites or Asians and increase with degree of exposure to segregation. Thus 9.8% of minorities from integrated settings sent money to their parents,

Table 6.4
Potential responses to stressful life events by whites, Asians, and blacks and Latinos during freshman and sophomore years by level of neighborhood segregation experienced in high school

			Latinos and Blacks by Segregation		
	Whites	Asians	Integrated	Mixed	Segregated
Family Involvement					
Sent Money to Parents	4.2%	5.6%	9.8%	11.4%	18.4%
Median Amount Sent	$200	$263	$200	$200	$300
Mean Number of Visits	5.18	6.51	6.22	6.26	7.19
Mean Days Away	6.75	7.74	8.20	8.52	9.72
Sent Money to Other Relatives	4.4%	8.8%	12.3%	16.6%	22.2%
Median Amount Sent	$100	$100	$100	$100	$140
Index of Family Involvement	8.2	9.4	9.6	10.3	11.4
Respondent Health					
Serious Illness or Disability	9.9%	8.2%	7.8%	11.2%	12.0%
Visited Psych Counselor	5.6%	4.4%	5.7%	5.5%	6.9%
Visited Student Health	14.8%	14.0%	17.9%	20.9%	21.7%
Was Lonely or Homesick	12.4%	18.6%	16.1%	18.1%	25.1%
Any Health Problem	28.8%	30.7%	32.8%	36.8%	41.2%
Index of Poor Health	7.4	7.6	8.0	8.6	9.4

compared with around 11.4% of those from mixed backgrounds and 18.4% from segregated backgrounds ($F = 27.0$, $p < .001$). Among those who sent money home, students from segregated circumstances sent the most—a median value of $300 compared with $200 for whites—despite the fact that students in this category are by far the least well-off financially.

Latinos and blacks are also more likely to visit their parents off campus than whites or Asians, and the propensity to visit once again rises with segregation. Thus, the average white student made 5.2 trips and spent around 6.8 days seeing his or her parents, whereas the average black or Latino from an integrated setting made 6.2 trips and spent 8.2 days away from campus, compared with 6.3 trips and 8.5 days among minority students from mixed backgrounds and 7.2 trips and 9.7 days among those from segregated backgrounds. These differences are highly significant in statistical terms. The F-ratio for parental trips is 6.4 and that for days spent away is 21.0 (both well under $p = .001$). In sum, minority freshmen from a segregated background spent three more days away from campus than the average white student.

We also considered financial remittances sent to other family members. As before, blacks and Latinos are more likely to remit money and to send larger quantities when they do so, and both indicators of family involvement rise as segregation increases. Whereas 4.4% of whites sent money to family members, the figure is 12.3% for blacks and Latinos from integrated backgrounds, 16.6% for those from mixed backgrounds, and 22.2% for those from segregated backgrounds ($F = 34.4$, $p < .001$), and the median amount sent was $140 among those from segregated circumstances compared with just $100 for all others.

In order to capture overall differences in family involvement, we created a summary index using the following formula:

$$IFI = PV + OFV + MSP/100 + MSF/100,$$

where *IFI* is the index of family involvement, *PV* is the number of parental visits made, *OFV* is the number of visits to other family members, *MSP* the amount of money sent to parents, and *MSF* is the amount of money sent to other family members. With a range of 0 to 141 and a mean of 9.6 this index is highly skewed, with a few respondents reporting very high degrees of family involvement and most reporting virtually none. The reliability of the scale is also extremely low, however, yielding a Cronbach's alpha of just .13, prompting us to exclude it from subsequent regression analyses.

Despite its low reliability, the scale does succinctly summarize differences in family involvement between different groups of students. Whereas the scale of family involvement averages 8.2 points for whites, 9.4 for Asians, and 12.3 for African Americans and Latinos from integrated backgrounds, it stands at 16.6 among those from mixed circumstances and 22.2 among those from segregated backgrounds. On this admittedly crude scale, in other words, black and Latino students coming from segregated settings are twice as involved as white students with their families.

The bottom panel of figure 6.4 assesses the mental and physical health of respondents by determining whether or not they experienced a serious illness or disability since arriving on campus, visited a psychological counselor, visited student health services, or ever felt "lonely or homesick." Once again the familiar pattern emerges, with blacks and Latinos generally reporting more threats to their well-being than whites or Asians, with a rising incidence of health issues as segregation rises. For example, whereas 15% of whites and 14% of Asians said they had visited student health services,

18% of blacks and Latinos from integrated backgrounds did so, and this share rises to 22% among those who grew up in segregated circumstances ($F = 9.6$, $p < .001$). Across all indicators, the percentage mentioning any health problem rises from 29% among whites to 33% among blacks and Latinos from integrated settings and reaches 41% among those from segregated settings ($F = 2.4$, $p < .05$).

In order to summarize respondent health we created a composite scale by adding together the various elements of the bottom panel in the following fashion:

$$IPH = VPC + VHC + LHF + SID,$$

where *IPH* represents an index of poor health, *VPC* is the frequency of visits to a psychological counselor on a 0 to 10 scale, *VHC* is the frequency of visits to the student health center on a 0 to 10 scale, *LHF* is the frequency of feeling lonely or homesick on a 0 to 10 scale, and *SID* is whether or not the respondent experienced a serious illness or disability (0 to 1 scale). Over two years of college, these indicators yield a scale with a range of 0 to 44, a mean value of 8.1, and a Cronbach's alpha of .36 (again too low for use in later regressions). Nonetheless, on this scale whites achieve a score of 7.4 compared with 7.6 for Asians and 8.0 among blacks and Latinos from integrated backgrounds. In contrast, the scale of poor health rises to 8.6 among those from mixed backgrounds and 9.4 among those from segregated backgrounds. In crude terms, then, the physical and mental well-being of students coming from a segregated background is about 27% worse than that of the typical white student ($F = 10.5$, $p < .001$).

Achievement on the Rocks

According to our theory, the elevated levels of violence and disorder associated with segregation operate indirectly through long-term and short-term pathways to affect academic performance among students at selective colleges and universities. In the long term, exposure to violence and disorder while growing up elevates allostatic load to yield cognitive changes that inhibit scholarly achievement years later. In the short run, violence and disorder mean that black and Latino students experience a surfeit of negative events in their social networks, draining them of time and emotional energy that could otherwise be devoted to studies.

In table 6.5 we document the effect of segregation on these mediating variables by regressing SAT scores and the scale of social stress on two indicators: the average minority proportion a respondent experienced while growing up (our measure of segregation) and the respondent's average exposure to disorder and violence. In doing so, we naturally control for group membership and relevant background characteristics. The left-hand columns present coefficients and standard errors for the SAT regression, and the right-hand columns present these statistics for the stress regression. As hypothesized, segregation has a very strong and significant effect in depressing SAT scores, even after controlling for parental education, socioeconomic status, and individual academic preparation. As seen in the leftmost B column, each point increase in the minority proportion decreases SAT scores by 0.70 points, and each point increase in the scale of disorder and violence decreases SAT performance by about half a point. Given the observed range of each variable, these two effects have the potential of reducing scores on the SAT by 70 points and 90 points, respectively.

The inhibition of cognition associated with exposure to disorder and violence presumably occurs through the long-run influence of allostatic load. The effect of racial and ethnic isolation most likely occurs through linguistic mechanisms. African Americans who come of age in segregated schools and neighborhoods generally do not speak standard American English as their native tongue. Rather, they speak Black English Vernacular, a distinctive language with its own rules of pronunciation, diction, and grammar (see Labov 1972; Baugh 1983; Labov and Harris 1986). For students growing up in segregated inner-city environments, learning to speak the language of the college classroom is equivalent to mastering a second language, with consequent effects on their performance on standardized tests and for their learning.

Once exposure to disorder and violence is controlled statistically, however, racial isolation itself has no effect on stress within social networks. The right-hand columns show estimates for the regression equation predicting social stress. As can be seen, the coefficient for the minority proportion is close to zero and statistically insignificant. As expected, though, exposure to disorder and violence has a powerful and highly significant effect on social stress, dramatically raising the frequency and severity of negative events occurring to people in students' social networks. The observed range of disorder and violence potentially accounts for 123 points on the scale of social stress.

Table 6.5
Effects of ecological segregation, disorder, and violence on academic cognitive skills and family stress

	SAT Score		*Social Stress Index*	
Independent Variables	B	SE	B	SE
Key Indicators				
Group				
Whites	—	—	—	—
Asians	9.900	6.542	−21.096***	3.629
Latinos	−20.511*	8.916	0.555	5.110
Blacks	−64.575***	8.137	7.305	6.391
Ecological Conditions				
Average Minority Proportion	−0.699***	0.106	−0.072	0.109
Exposure to Disorder and Violence	−0.504***	0.158	0.659***	0.092
Control Variables				
Demographic Background				
Male	38.912***	4.468	−4.676	3.497
Foreign-Born Parent	−5.734	9.433	−3.884	4.248
Two-Parent Family	4.481	6.022	−18.874***	4.864
Siblings under 18	−3.387	2.907	−4.516**	1.490
Education of Parents				
No College Degrees	—	—	—	—
One College Degree	13.099†	6.861	−13.211*	5.524
Two College Degrees	30.674**	9.672	−14.088†	7.655
One Advanced Degree	42.042***	6.643	−18.847***	5.269
Two Advanced Degrees	56.898***	8.835	−12.471†	6.706
Economic Status				
Home Value (000)	0.014†	0.015	0.001	0.001
Ever on Welfare	−8.518	8.862	25.488***	5.091
Income > $100,000	−4.301	4.980	−5.261	3.975
Academic Preparation				
AP Courses Taken	22.209***	2.428	−1.152	0.708
High School GPA	96.479***	14.624	−9.221	6.137
Self-rated Preparation	5.489***	0.937	−0.116	0.872
Social Preparation				
Self-efficacy	−1.441	0.960	−0.594	0.735
Self-esteem	0.783	0.601	0.174	0.264
Susceptibility to Peer Influence	3.632***	0.541	1.175**	0.410
Social Distance from Whites	0.503	0.502	0.219	0.332
Intercept	797.259***	55.410	129.363***	32.546
R^2	0.462***		0.119***	
Number of Cases	2,517		2,939	

†$p<.10$ *$p<.05$ **$p<.01$ ***$p<.001$

The regressions in table 6.6 complete the analysis by showing the effect segregation has on grades through the mediating factors of cognitive skills and social stress. The left-hand columns regress the minority proportion and disorder-violence index on GPA earned through the sophomore year while controlling for group membership and background characteristics, but not including measures of cognitive skills and social stress. The right-hand columns estimate a full model that includes these two mediating factors. Again, the B columns contain the regression coefficients and the SE columns their standard errors.

The left-hand columns demonstrate the strong effects that racial isolation and exposure to disorder and violence have on college grade achievement. The greater the representation of minorities in the schools and neighborhoods during childhood, and the greater the violence and disorder respondents were exposed to, the lower the grades they earned during the first two years of college. Once the mediating effects of cognitive skills and social stress are included in the equation (right-hand columns), however, the significant effect of exposure to disorder and violence disappears. In other words, exposure to disorder and violence affects grade achievement entirely through the indirect pathways we have postulated. In the long run, high levels of disorder and violence undermine the accumulation of needed cognitive resources, whereas in the short run they yield an accumulation of negative events occurring to people in the affected students' networks. Even controlling for these mediating effects, however, racial isolation itself retains a significant, though somewhat reduced, effect on the grades earned by students, probably through the linguistic effects noted above. Thus the social isolation implied by segregated schools and neighborhoods has both direct and indirect effects on grade achievement in college.

The Danger below the Surface

Because American schools and neighborhoods remain substantially segregated on the basis of race and ethnicity, a large share of black and Latino college students will necessarily have grown up in a segregated social world characterized by low exposure to people outside their own group and high exposure to social disorder and violence. These experiences are built into the lives of minority students by the structure of American society. Even

Table 6.6
Effects of ecological segregation and its sequelae on academic performance

Independent Variables	*Without Mediating Variables*		*Full Model*	
	B	SE	B	SE
Key Indicators				
Group				
Whites	—	—	—	—
Asians	0.037**	0.012	0.036**	0.012
Latinos	−0.047*	0.019	−0.033†	0.018
Blacks	−0.157***	0.030	−0.129***	0.023
Segregation and Its Sequelae				
Average Minority Proportion	−0.0011***	0.00035	−0.00077*	0.00036
Exposure to Disorder and Violence	−0.0084***	0.00027	−0.00051	0.00035
Mediating Variables				
Cognitive Skills (SAT Score)	—	—	0.00062***	0.00009
Index of Social Stress	—	—	−0.00019*	0.00008
Control Variables				
Difficulty of Courses				
Number of Easy Courses	0.027***	0.004	0.024***	0.004
Number of Hard Courses	−0.005	0.003	−0.007†	0.004
Demographic Background				
Male	−0.053**	0.015	−0.078***	0.015
Foreign-Born Parent	0.014	0.018	0.016	0.018
Two-Parent Family	0.021	0.021	0.019	0.020
Siblings under 18	−0.007	0.008	−0.005	0.008
Education of Parents				
No College Degrees	—	—	—	—
One College Degree	0.023	0.024	0.027	0.022
Two College Degrees	0.089***	0.023	0.072***	0.020
One Advanced Degree	0.083**	0.026	0.062*	0.024
Two Advanced Degrees	0.145***	0.029	0.112***	0.025
Economic Status				
Home Value (000)	0.000	0.000	0.000	0.000
Ever on Welfare	−0.008	0.026	0.006	0.024
Income > $100,000	0.042*	0.020	0.033	0.021
Academic Preparation				
AP Courses Taken	0.016**	0.005	0.003	0.005
High School GPA	0.433***	0.027	0.386***	0.032
Self-rated Preparation	0.028***	0.003	0.024***	0.024
Social Preparation				
Self-efficacy	−0.005*	0.002	−0.005†	0.003
Self-esteem	0.004*	0.002	0.005*	0.002

Table 6.6 *(continued)*

	Without Mediating Variables		*Full Model*	
Independent Variables	B	SE	B	SE
Susceptibility to Peer Influence	0.009***	0.001	0.008***	0.001
Social Distance from Whites	0.002	0.002	0.002	0.002
Intercept	1.189***	0.123	0.66***	0.153
R^2	0.325***		0.360***	
Number of Cases	2,927		2,767	

†*p*<.10 **p*<.05 ***p*<.01 ****p*<.001

black and Latino students interviewed by the NLSF—who inhabit one of the most privileged sectors of American society by virtue of having gained admission to an elite academic institution—are not immune to the stress and consequent damage emanating from the continuing reality of educational and residential segregation throughout the United States.

Some might believe that the use of race-sensitive criteria to ensure the enrollment of underrepresented minorities at elite schools has leveled the playing field. According to those who hold this view, such students have been given a chance for an outstanding education and are free to compete for academic achievement on an equal basis with other students, and worries about disadvantages that minority students might continue to face are simply "excuses" (see McWhorter 2000; Thernstrom and Thernstrom 2003). The analyses presented in this chapter question that view by tracing the long- and short-term implications of segregation for black and Latino students. We show how circumstances in the barrio or the ghetto can reach out to undermine academic achievement even among students who have seemingly escaped the strictures of segregation to take up the privileged life of a student at an elite college or university.

The pathways by which segregation undermines academic achievement are subtle and not readily observable to the casual observer on or off campus. When a black or Latino student tells a professor that a paper deadline was missed because he or she was attending to a personal or family issue, this might seem to be an "excuse." After all, white and Asian students do not invoke this explanation for lack of performance with the same frequency, so something must be "wrong" with Latinos and African Americans. In fact, we have shown that segregation exposes minority students to higher frequencies of negative events within their networks of friends and families. Minority students *must* attend to more personal and family issues in the course of their studies because of the segregated structure of American society.

At the same time, minority students may experience higher rates of learning disabilities. As shown in chapter 2, black and Latino students generally make much heavier use of special services provided by the institution for students with learning issues, such as tutoring, remedial courses, and special advising and counseling. Again, a casual observer on or off campus might observe the higher incidence of learning issues among Latino and black students and conclude they are again making "excuses." What they do not observe, however, is that significant shares of these students grew up in segregated inner-city schools and neighborhoods where they were exposed to very high rates of disorder and violence during critical phases of their cognitive development, and that the inevitable allostatic load compromised mental functioning in ways that now, years later, make it more difficult for them to concentrate, pay attention, apply themselves, and successfully learn.

Because American schools and neighborhoods are highly segregated, and because segregation concentrates poverty to create unusually disordered and disadvantaged social environments, social stress and cognitive limitations will inevitably be expressed at higher rates among black and Latino students. Because the chain of causation that produces these effects is so subtle and so indirect, however, many professors, administrators, and advisers on campus end up blaming the students for their perceived deficiencies, and many students end up blaming themselves. In this sense the effects of segregation constitute submerged rocks waiting to sink the academic performance of unwary students. A racially segregated society perforce cannot be a race-blind society, and students and administrators need to understand this fact in evaluating the academic performance of minority students on campus.

7 The Shoals of Stereotypes

As mentioned in chapter 1, the theory of stereotype threat was originated by Steele (1988, 1992) to account for the apparent academic underperformance of stigmatized social groups. He argued that members of disparaged minority groups are prone to underperform academically because of a fear of living up to negative stereotypes about the intellectual abilities of their group. Even if one rejects the stereotype categorically, virtually everyone in the United States knows about the racist canard that blacks are intellectually inferior to whites. The view that African Americans are genetically less intelligent than others evolved historically in conjunction with slavery and Jim Crow as part of a deliberate effort to dehumanize African Americans and thereby legitimate their economic subjugation in a society otherwise dedicated to universal liberty and human freedom (Frederickson 2002).

Although rooted in the South, the caricature of African Americans as simple, shuffling, and servile spread nationwide and became part of American popular culture, repeated in songs, stories, folklore, minstrel shows, and later on in movies, radio programs, and television shows (see Sweet 2000; Bogle 2003). Some stereotypical images became brand trademarks and were distributed to the kitchens and parlors of homes throughout the United States (see Kern-Foxworth 1994). Such was the low regard of whites for African Americans that substantial majorities nationwide continued to support legal segregation in transportation and education well into the 1940s; and as late as 1963 more than 60% of whites supported laws prohibiting intermarriage (Schuman et al. 1997).

Although a majority of white Americans now reject an explicit racist ideology and stereotypical images have disappeared from popular culture or have been modified to conform to contemporary sensibilities (see Manning 1998), most people are well aware of the stereotypes even if they do not believe them personally. Moreover, even if they do not feel free to say so publicly, some fraction of white Americans still think that African Americans are genetically less intelligent than whites (Bobo 1997; Bobo and Smith 1998). Indeed, several prominent scholars have recently argued this viewpoint forcefully and quite publicly (see Herrnstein and Murray 1994; Rushton 2000).

African Americans, of course, are acutely aware of the historical legacy of racism and the persistence of negative stereotypes about them (Steele 1988, 1992; Crocker and Quinn 1998). Every time black students are called on to perform academically, they well understand that they are at risk of confirming a deeply rooted and very negative stereotype about their group. Stereotypical intimations of intellectual inferiority also extend to Latinos. In the 1996 Multi-City Survey of Urban Inequality, for example, a representative sample of white respondents in Los Angeles rated blacks as 37% less intelligent than whites and Latinos as 45% less intelligent (Charles 2000). In contrast, whites rated Asians to be 9% more intelligent than themselves, and Asians themselves perceived a similar intellectual pecking order. Given this pattern, we would expect the theory of stereotype threat to apply to blacks and Latinos at selective schools but not to whites or Asians.

Failure to perform up to institutionally expected academic standards is psychologically distressing because it implies that the stereotype may, in fact, be true: a poor intellectual performance might convince white observers that black and Latino students indeed *are* intellectually inferior to whites and Asians. Even if minority students do not believe the stereotype themselves, it is nonetheless socially embarrassing to seemingly confirm it before a white and Asian audience. Moreover, if black and Latino students have internalized the negative stereotype themselves, they may adapt psychologically by downplaying the importance of academic success in determining self-worth and put in less effort toward academic achievement, essentially disidentifying from education as a domain of self-evaluation. If they fail, they can always tell themselves that they really did not try hard and that academic success is not that important anyway.

The theory of stereotype threat rests on three basic assumptions. First, it assumes that people are motivated to think well of themselves and have others do the same. Second, it assumes that anxieties about the possibility of performing badly increase the likelihood of performing poorly. Third, it assumes that disidentification—psychological disengagement from the domain in question—stems from the internalization of negative stereotypes over the long term.

Disidentification should not be confused with the related but more general concept of devaluation, which refers to the abstract perception of a domain as unimportant. Disidentification involves the specific removal of intellectual achievement from the domain of self-esteem (Crocker and Major 1989; Crocker and Quinn 1998). It is well documented, for example, that African Americans generally value education—indeed, they value it as much as or more than other racial and ethnic groups (Hochschild 1995). Despite this valuation, African Americans consistently underperform academically but nonetheless have very high levels of self-esteem (Mruk 1999). This occurs because academic performance is not a central domain in which African Americans construct self-esteem: they have disidentified with academic achievement as a metric of self-worth.

The theory of stereotype threat has received strong and consistent support from social psychology experiments conducted in laboratory settings (Steele and Aronson 1995; Aronson, Quinn, and Spencer 1998). Analysis done in *The Source of the River* also found results consistent with its leading hypothesis. Specifically, Massey et al. (1993) found that black and Latino students who harbored doubts about their group's intellectual ability and also identified strongly with mainstream American culture earned significantly lower grades in their first term as freshman. It was assumed that these students were vulnerable to stereotype threat.

In the present chapter we undertake a more systematic and refined test of the theory by constructing explicit indicators of the degree to which negative stereotypes are accepted by minority students (stereotype internalization) and the degree to which they expect people outside the group to evaluate their performance in terms of negative stereotypes (stereotype externalization). We then develop indicators of psychological disidentification and subjective performance burden, relate each of these to the internalization and externalization of stereotypes, and show how all contribute to lowering the grades earned by otherwise qualified black and Latino students.

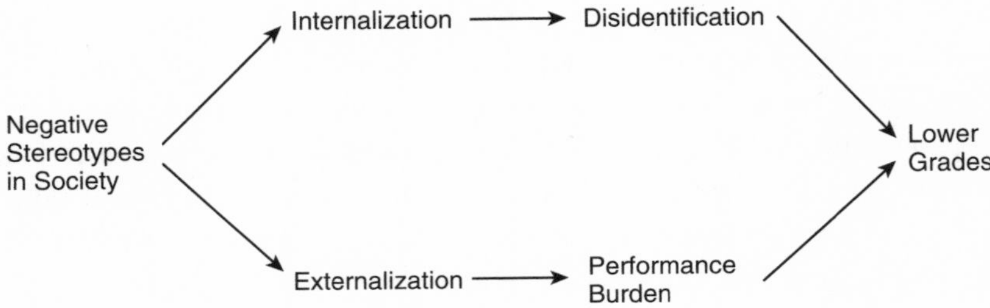

Figure 7.1.
Conceptual model of the effect of stereotype threat on grade point average

Mapping the Shoals

In moving from laboratory to survey research, a crucial step is the specification of a clear model to guide analysis. Figure 7.1 presents a schematic diagram that captures our conceptualization of the process of stereotype threat and how it works in the real world, as opposed to the staged world of the laboratory. Exogenous to any individual are societal stereotypes that exist about various racial and ethnic groups. Simply by living in American society—by participating in its institutions and interacting with its people—minority members become aware of negative stereotypes about themselves and, depending on their position in the social structure, absorb them to a greater or lesser degree.

We hypothesize that stereotypes manifest themselves among individuals in two ways: internally and externally. Stereotypes are internalized when they are wholly or partly adopted by the individual and incorporated into one's social cognition (Fiske and Taylor 1991). This internalization may be conscious or unconscious. Recent work has shown the remarkable degree to which stereotypes are absorbed implicitly, below the level of conscious awareness (see Banaji and Hardin 1996; Dovidio et al. 1997; Bargh 1997). Given the difficulty of measuring unconscious attitudes using a social survey, however, we focus here on the explicit rather than the implicit internalization of negative stereotypes. That is, we measure the degree to which respondents consciously subscribe to negative beliefs about their group's abilities. To the extent that such explicit views represent the tip of a much larger cognitive iceberg, our limited measurement is conservative: if we find any variation at all in the explicit endorsement of negative stereotypes by blacks and Latinos, and to the extent that we find any connection at all between such a variation and academic behavior, it is likely that better measurement would yield even stronger results.

We measure the internalization of negative stereotypes for Latinos and blacks based on responses to three items in the NLSF. Respondents were asked to assess whether their group is intelligent or unintelligent, hard-working or lazy, and whether their group "sticks with it or gives up easily." They rated each on a continuum from strongly disagree to strongly agree, yielding a scale with a hypothetical range of 0 to 18 and a Cronbach's reliability coefficient of .610 (see appendix C). The mean level of internalization on this scale is around 6.6 for both black and Latino students, with an observed range of 0 to 14 and a standard deviation of around 2.3. There is thus considerable variation in the degree to which individual minority students have internalized negative stereotypes about their group.

The externalization of stereotypes occurs when minority members expect others to act on the basis of prejudicial notions when evaluating them. As argued above, most African Americans are well aware of the negative stereotype of black intellectual ability. Indeed, growing up in American society, it is nearly impossible *not* to learn about the stigma of black intellectual inferiority. It is logical to assume, therefore, that many black students *expect* whites, Asians, and others to draw on this stereotype in evaluating their performance on intellectual tasks.

We measured externalization using a scale composed of four items, each rated on a 0 to 10 continuum running from complete disagreement to complete agreement. Respondents were asked whether they expect whites to treat others equally or discriminate, whether they expect Asians to treat others equally or discriminate, whether they expect instructors holding stereotypes to use them in evaluating group members, and whether they think students holding stereotypes will use them in making evaluations. The resulting scale yields a hypothetical range of 0 to 40 and a reliability coefficient of .588 (see appendix C). Externalization is somewhat greater for blacks than for Latinos, with a mean scale value of 22.7 compared with 20.0. The observed range is 0 to 34, and the standard deviation of 6.5 for blacks and 6.2 for Latinos again indicates considerable interpersonal variation with respect to the externalization of negative stereotypes.

Although they are both grounded in the same societal stereotype, internalization and externalization have different behavioral manifestations. On the one hand, internalization—the conscious acceptance of the negative stereotype of intellectual inferiority—over time leads to a process of disidentification, expressed among students by a reduction of their academic work effort. If academic success is removed from the domain of self-esteem, then logically less effort is expended to achieve it. A reduction in effort, of course, yields poorer academic performance and lower grades. We consider two possible measures of disidentification: the subjective rating of each person's own academic effort reported in chapter 2 and his or her estimation of hours spent studying, reported in chapter 3.

On the other hand, externalization—the expectation that others will draw on negative stereotypes in making evaluations of individual performance—creates a psychological burden that increases test anxiety and undermines grade achievement by creating a subjective belief that one's performance reflects on the entire group. African Americans who believe that professors and other students are prejudiced will come to feel as if they are carrying the entire race on their back every time they are asked to compete academically. If they fail to acquit themselves well, it will reflect badly not only on themselves and their family but on the entire race. They will have publicly confirmed the canard of intellectual inferiority.

We measured the subjective performance burden using a nine-item scale that asked subjects to rate the extent of their agreement or disagreement (on a 0 to 10 continuum) with items such as: "if my instructors know my difficulty in class they will think less of me," "if I excel academically it reflects positively on my own group," and "I don't want to look foolish or stupid in class" (see appendix C for the full set of items). The resulting scale has a theoretical range of 0 to 90 and a Cronbach's alpha of .714. Consistent with our line of reasoning, blacks experience the greatest performance burden, evincing a scale score of 31.0, whereas whites experience the least, with a scale score of 22.5. Asians and Latinos are in between with respective scores of 27.8 and 26.8.

Uncharted Dangers

As just argued, we expect the internalization of negative stereotypes to put black and Latino students at academic disadvantage through a process of psychological disidentification, whose behavioral marker is a reduction of academic effort (Steele 1999; Oyserman et al. 2003). The regressions reported in table 7.1 show that internalization indeed has the expected effect on the

Table 7.1
Effects of stereotype internalization on subjective rating of academic effort and hours spent studying by black and Latino students

	Subjective Effort		*Hours Studied*	
Independent Variables	B	SE	B	SE
Key Variables				
Stereotype Internalization				
Internalization Scale	−0.044*	0.017	−0.455**	0.136
Control Variables				
Demographic Background				
Male	−0.373***	0.100	−0.994	0.965
Foreign-Born Parent	0.106	0.121	2.940**	0.933
Two-Parent Family	0.000	0.103	0.496	0.864
Siblings under 18	−0.009	0.040	0.031	0.402
Education of Parents				
No College Degrees	—	—	—	—
One College Degree	0.065	0.108	−1.755	1.148
Two College Degrees	0.201	0.138	−0.814	1.100
One Advanced Degree	0.271†	0.146	−0.410	1.217
Two Advanced Degrees	0.439**	0.144	0.297	1.068
Economic Status				
Home Value (000)	0.000	0.001	0.002	0.002
Ever on Welfare	−0.335**	0.119	−0.112	0.826
Income > $100,000	−0.221†	0.120	−1.401	1.001
Academic Preparation				
AP Courses Taken	0.004	0.028	0.538**	0.162
High School GPA	0.491**	0.158	6.690***	0.924
Self-rated Preparation	0.036*	0.014	−0.024	0.129
SAT Score (00)	−0.124**	0.041	−0.002	0.003
Social Preparation				
Self-efficacy	0.003	0.014	0.090	0.142
Self-esteem	0.022*	0.008	−0.024	0.129
Susceptibility to Peer Influence	0.014	0.011	0.057	0.079
Social Distance from Whites	−0.004	0.010	0.073	0.073
Intercept	5.680***	0.558	4.540	5.526
R^2	0.055		0.070	
Number of Cases	1,401		1,401	

†$p<.10$ *$p<.05$ **$p<.01$ ***$p<.001$

effort that black and Latino students put into their schoolwork, controlling for a variety of background factors; and the effect holds whether one considers subjective or objective indicators of effort. The greater the internalization of negative group stereotypes, the lower the subjective work effort reported by students and the fewer the hours they spent studying. Of the two measures, the objective report of hours studied is most strongly and significantly affected by stereotype internalization.

We thus find clear and unambiguous support for the process of disidentification hypothesized by Steele and others—as black and Latino students display a stronger internalization of negative stereotypes about themselves and their group they systematically reduce their effort, both subjectively in terms of self-perceived effort and objectively in terms of the number of hours they spend studying per week. Specifically, we estimate that minority students reduce their weekly study time by almost one-half hour for each point increase in the internalization score. Given that the internalization index has an observed range of 0 to 14, moving from the lowest to the highest level essentially subtracts seven hours of weekly study time from the students' work efforts, a rather sizable effect.

Our second hypothesis is that the externalization of stereotypes—the belief that whites, Asians, and academic authority figures hold negative views about black and Latino intellectual capacities and draw on these stereotypes in making evaluations—will exacerbate the performance burden felt by black and Latino students. To test this idea we regressed our indicator of externalization on the subjective performance burden rating provided by students, controlling for background characteristics. The externalization index measures the degree to which respondents expect others around them to engage in racial discrimination and stereotyping, whereas the performance burden index measures how sensitive they are to the perception of others and the degree to which they think their behavior reflects positively or negatively on their group. The former rests on a respondent's assessment of the behavior of others, whereas the latter rests on a respondent's assessment of his or her own feelings. The OLS estimates shown in table 7.2 again offer clear support for the hypothesis. Each point increase in the externalization scale is associated with a 0.12-point increase in the perceived performance burden. With a respondents evincing a range of 0 to 34 on the 40-point externalization scale, this means that moving from minimum to maximum externalization shifts the performance burden by 4.8 points on its 90-point scale.

Table 7.2
Effects of stereotype threat on subjective performance burden experienced by black and Latino students

Independent Variables	*Outcome: Performance Burden*		
	B	SE	*P* Value
Key Variables			
Stereotype Threat			
Externalization Scale	0.119*	0.056	0.045
Control Variables			
Demographic Background			
Male	1.689*	0.806	0.046
Foreign-Born Parent	1.847†	0.917	0.054
Two-Parent Family	1.707*	0.698	0.022
Siblings under 18	0.106	0.376	0.779
Education of Parents			
No College Degrees	—	—	—
One College Degree	−0.167	1.279	0.897
Two College Degrees	−0.417	1.199	0.731
One Advanced Degree	0.418	1.106	0.709
Two Advanced Degrees	−0.588	1.226	0.635
Economic Status			
Home Value (000)	0.000	0.001	0.693
Ever on Welfare	1.923*	0.742	0.015
Income > $100,000	−0.016	1.130	0.989
Academic Preparation			
AP Courses Taken	0.581**	0.188	0.005
High School GPA	1.824†	0.953	0.067
Self-rated Preparation	−0.084	0.126	0.510
SAT Score (00)	1.179*	0.444	0.013
Social Preparation			
Self-efficacy	−0.446*	0.180	0.020
Self-esteem	−0.310***	0.085	0.001
Susceptibility to Peer Influence	0.712***	0.099	0.000
Social Distance from Whites	−0.097	0.089	0.286
Intercept	49.136***	7.663	0.000
R^2	0.137		
Number of Cases	1,335		

†$p<.10$ *$p<.05$ **$p<.01$ ***$p<.001$

The ultimate importance of the foregoing processes—internalization and externalization, disidentification and heightened performance burden—is the degree to which the intervening variables translate into differential rates of academic success. Table 7.3 contains OLS regression results from an equation that we estimated to predict the GPA earned by students through their freshman and sophomore years from indexes corresponding to each of the foregoing psychological constructs. The left-hand columns predict GPA from measures of the internalization and externalization by themselves, whereas the right-hand columns add in the intervening variables of subjective effort, hours studied, and performance burden.

In order to assess the effect of stereotype threat in accounting for intergroup differentials in grade performance, we estimate the equation including whites and Asians, with stereotype internalization and externalization indexes coded as zero for them. Although the successive addition of explanatory variables to models of grade determination in prior chapters has been successful in eliminating the GPA gap between whites and Latinos, so far the black-white gap has been stubbornly resistant to elimination by statistical controls. With no controls at all, black students earn an average GPA that is 0.35 points lower than that of their white counterparts—roughly a third of a grade point. As shown in chapter 2, simply controlling for socioeconomic background factors reduced the gap to around 0.19 points, but adding additional controls for academic variables did virtually nothing to reduce the gap further; and when controls were introduced for social factors (chapter 3), the apparent gap actually increased slightly to 0.21. Likewise, the introduction of controls for financial and budgetary factors (chapter 4) yielded an estimated GPA gap of 0.23 points.

It was only when we began to introduce factors that are specific to race and ethnicity that the black-white gap began to decline. Introducing controls for the various social undercurrents in chapter 5 reduced the gap to 0.14, whereas controlling for segregation and its sequelae in chapter 6 yielded an estimated gap of 0.13. In the present chapter we find that the simple introduction of measures of stereotype internalization and externalization reduces the estimated grade gap to 0.10, its lowest level yet. In the final chapter, we will observe what happens when all these sets of factors are controlled simultaneously.

Introducing measures for the intervening variables of academic effort and performance burden does raise the black coefficient back up to −0.115,

Table 7.3
Effects of stereotype threat on GPA earned through sophomore year

	Without Intervening Variables		*With Intervening Variables*	
Independent Variables	B	SE	B	SE
Key Variables				
Group				
Whites	—	—	—	—
Asians	0.015	0.012	0.018	0.011
Latinos	−0.008	0.026	−0.021	0.030
Blacks	−0.101***	0.033	−0.115***	0.033
Stereotype Threat				
Internalization Scale	0.002	0.004	0.003	0.003
Externalization Scale	−0.004*	0.001	−0.004**	0.001
Intervening Variables				
Subjective Effort	—	—	0.033***	0.005
Hours Studied (00)	—	—	0.246***	0.048
Performance Burden (00)	—	—	−0.112***	0.041
Control Variables				
Difficulty of Courses				
Number of Easy Courses	0.023***	0.003	0.022***	0.002
Number of Hard Courses	−0.006†	0.004	−0.009*	0.003
Demographic Background				
Male	−0.076***	0.016	−0.046**	0.013
Foreign-Born Parent	0.015	0.017	0.015	0.019
Two-Parent Family	0.022	0.019	0.028	0.022
Siblings under 18	−0.008	0.009	−0.007	0.023
Education of Parents				
No College Degrees	—	—	—	—
One College Degree	0.033	0.021	0.025	0.023
Two College Degrees	0.079***	0.017	0.057***	0.016
One Advanced Degree	0.070***	0.021	0.055**	0.019
Two Advanced Degrees	0.118***	0.021	0.102***	0.023
Economic Status				
Home Value (000)	0.000	0.000	0.000	0.000
Ever on Welfare	−0.004	0.020	0.014	0.018
Income > $100,000	0.038†	0.021	0.037†	0.020
Academic Preparation				
AP Courses Taken	0.003	0.005	0.002	0.005
High School GPA	0.387***	0.032	0.348	0.029
Self-rated Preparation	0.025***	0.004	0.022***	0.003
SAT Score (00)	0.064***	0.009	0.070***	0.009

(continued)

Table 7.3 *(continued)*

	Without Intervening Variables		*With Intervening Variables*	
Independent Variables	B	SE	B	SE
Social Preparation				
Self-efficacy	−0.004	0.003	−0.003	0.002
Self-esteem	0.004*	0.002	0.003	0.002
Susceptibility to Peer Influence	0.008***	0.001	0.008***	0.001
Social Distance from Whites	0.001	0.002	0.002	0.002
Intercept	0.597***	0.160	0.476*	0.189
R^2	0.358***		0.395	
Number of Cases	2,751		2,631	

†$p<.10$ *$p<.05$ **$p<.01$ ***$p<.001$

suggesting that some of the GPA differential occurs through mediating factors. Indeed, comparing the two sets of estimates reveals that internalization has no direct effect on grades at all—its effect is entirely through disidentification, or the reduction in work effort. Externalization, in contrast, has both direct and indirect effects. Across both equations, the coefficient for stereotype internalization is near zero and nowhere close to statistical significance, meaning that internalization operates only through the mediating effects of work effort, measured both objectively and subjectively. These effects of objective and subjective effort are shown in the right-hand columns of table 7.3. Both self-rated academic effort and the number of hours spent studying per week have strong and highly significant positive effects on GPA. Even though the internalization of stereotypes itself has no direct effect on grades earned, therefore, by reducing the total effort put into studies it substantially reduces overall grade performance, as predicted by the disidentification hypothesis of stereotype threat.

At the same time, the externalization of stereotypes has effects on grades earned that are independent of those of internalization. Believing that others will act on the basis of negative stereotypes in evaluating individual performance increases the subjective burden that respondents feel when they are called on to perform academically, and a higher subjective performance burden, in turn, yields lower grades. Even holding this effect constant, however, the externalization appears to affect grade achievement directly, in ways that are not captured by subjective performance burden alone. Even if minority students do not feel a psychological burden when performing academically, if they believe their professors and fellow students are evaluating them prejudicially no matter what, it could well undermine their motivation to excel, thus lowering grades.

Sinking Achievement

In this chapter we have systematically tested the theory of stereotype threat by specifying a structural model of the phenomenon and estimating its effect using data from a large population of students attending twenty-eight different institutions of higher education. We posited that the negative stereotype of black and Latino intellectual inferiority would manifest itself psychologically in two ways. On the one hand, some minority students, by virtue of their experiences in society, will have internalized negative stereotypes to some extent and come believe in the intellectual inferiority of black and Latino students. On the other hand, some minority students will have externalized negative stereotypes, coming to believe that whites and Asians will necessarily draw on the stigma of intellectual inferiority in evaluating black and Latino students. The internalization of stereotypes was hypothesized to lead to a disidentification with academic success and a subsequent reduction of work effort that translates into lower grades. The externalization of stereotypes was hypothesized to yield a performance burden that also lowers grade achievement.

Statistical estimates of structural equations specified to represent the foregoing model were generally consistent with the theory of stereotype threat. We found considerable variation in the degree to which black and Latino students have internalized the stereotype of minority intellectual inferiority. Other work has shown that this variation is rooted in students' social origins (Massey and Fischer 2005). Those most at risk of internalizing negative stereotypes appear to be black and Latino males from affluent families who made few in-group friends while growing up and who consequently developed a weak racial/ethnic identity.

We also uncovered significant variation in the degree to which blacks and Latinos expect others to draw on negative stereotypes in making evaluations. Other work has also shown that those most prone to externalize stereotypes are black and Latino females from a disrupted but well-educated family background who grew up under integrated circumstances but with a strong in-group identity and a high social distance from whites.

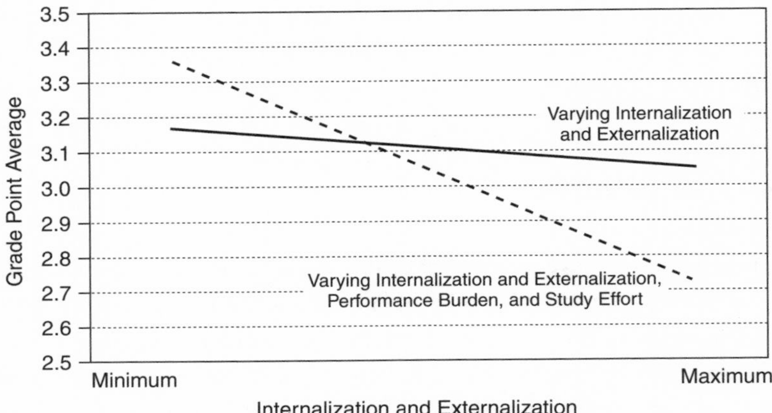

Figure 7.2.
Effects of stereotype internalization and externalization on grade point averages of black students

Dark-skinned minority respondents generally expect more stereotyping than those with light complexions (Massey and Fischer 2005).

Consistent with the laboratory work pioneered by Steele and colleagues, we found that internalization of negative stereotypes has a very strong effect in reducing academic work effort, assessed both subjectively using self-ratings of scholarly effort and objectively using reported hours of study, suggesting a clear process of disidentification. Also consistent with prior work in social psychology, we found that externalization of negative stereotypes is generally associated with a higher subjective performance burden. Minority students who expect others to evaluate them in terms of negative stereotypes feel their performance reflects not just on themselves but on all members of their racial or ethnic group.

When considered together, self-rated effort, reported hours of study, and the subjective performance burden felt by respondents had strong and significant effects on grades earned during the freshman and sophomore years, holding constant parental education, economic status, academic preparation, demographic background, and social preparation. The potential for negative stereotypes to undermine grade achievement is suggested by figure 7.2, which shows the GPA predicted for black students as the various components of the stereotype process range from their minimum to maximum observed values.

The solid line shows what happens to black GPAs if the internalization and externalization scales range from their minimums to their maximums and are allowed to determine academic effort and performance burden, which in turn determine grade point average. Allowing stereotypes by themselves to do their work, black GPA falls from 3.17 when stereotypes are neither internalized nor externalized to 3.05 when they reach their respective maximum observed values. The dotted line varies the indicators of study effort and performance burden also from their minimum to maximum values rather than letting them be predetermined by levels of internalization and externalization. This exercise takes a black student from the best case to the worst case to observe the effect on grades.

The best case is when the hypothetical African American has neither internalized nor externalized stereotypes, puts in the maximum observed effort, and experiences the minimum observed performance burden. Under these optimal circumstances, the student would be expected to earn a GPA of 3.36. The worst case is when the hypothetical black student has internalized and externalized stereotypes to the maximum extent and also cuts back effort to the minimum while experiencing the highest observable performance burden. Under these very negative circumstances, the hypothetical student's GPA falls to 2.73, holding all other factors constant. In other words, as Steele (1997, 1998) so aptly put it, influences seemingly as intangible as "a threat in the air" can have significant effects on the academic achievement of minority students.

8 The Wake from Affirmative Action

Until the 1970s, most of the institutions included in the NLSF had very few black or Latino students. Prior to the civil rights era, they were excluded by a variety of subtle and not so subtle mechanisms, and the very presence of both groups on the campuses of elite institutions is the result of deliberate actions taken to overcome a legacy of past discrimination. Colleges and universities now work sincerely to comply with relevant civil rights legislation and no longer consciously practice racial or ethnic discrimination in recruitment or admissions; but most institutions have gone beyond the simple elimination of discriminatory barriers and taken a variety of affirmative steps to ensure the representation on campus of formerly excluded groups. The mix of "affirmative actions" taken to achieve racial and ethnic diversity on campus varies from institution to institution, but since their inception early in the post–civil rights era, the programs have been quite controversial.

Over the years, critics have leveled three basic charges against the use of race-sensitive criteria in college admissions: (1) affirmative action constitutes reverse discrimination that lowers the odds of admission for other, better-qualified nonminority students; (2) affirmative action creates a mismatch between the skills of minority students and the abilities required for success at selective institutions, setting them up for academic problems; and (3) affirmative action stigmatizes members of the target group as less than fully qualified, which results in demoralization and substandard performance by students in the favored group who may, in fact, be very well qualified.

The first criticism—that affirmative action constitutes reverse discrimination (see Glazer 1976)—has not stood up to empirical scrutiny. Studies show that minority affirmative action generally has small and insignificant effects on the admission prospects of white students (Wilson 1995; Dickens and Kane 1999). In legal terms, moreover, the Supreme Court recently held that using race as one of *several* factors in college admissions is indeed constitutional and allowable under federal law (see Gratz v. Bollinger 2003; Grutter v. Bollinger 2003). In light of this decision, and owing to a lack of appropriate data from the NLSF to test it, we will not consider the reverse discrimination hypothesis further in this chapter.

The second hypothesis, which argues that affirmative action sets up minority students for failure by placing them in academic settings where they are underprepared, has been called *the mismatch hypothesis* because it posits a disconnect between the skills minority students possess and those they need for success at competitive institutions of higher education (Sowell 2004; Thernstrom and Thernstrom 1999). Although this hypothesis makes intuitive sense, it likewise has not been supported empirically (see Holzer and Neumark 2000; Kane 1998). Bowen and Bok (1998), for example, found that blacks who attended selective institutions were *more likely* to graduate than their counterparts at less-selective institutions. Likewise, Alon and Tienda (2004) found that minority students generally thrive at selective institutions, whatever their origins. Selectivity, however, has little do with how much is actually learned in college (Pascarella and Terenzini 2005).

A third argument against affirmative action is that, at a collective level, it stigmatizes minority group members as intellectually inferior (see Thernstrom and Thernstrom 1999). We label this proposition the *social stigma hypothesis* because it claims that affirmative action underscores the belief that minority students, especially African Americans, are less intelligent and would not be on campus except for a relaxation of academic standards under affirmative action. If white students believe that many of their black peers would not be there were it not for a "lowering" of standards under affirmative action and, more important, if black students *perceive whites* to believe this (see Torres and Charles 2004), then affirmative action may indeed undermine minorities' academic performance by heightening the social stigma they already experience because of race or ethnicity.

In addition to the foregoing hypotheses posed by critics of affirmative action, Fischer and Massey (2005) and Massey and Mooney (2007) offer a fourth possibility, which they labeled the *stereotype threat hypothesis*: the

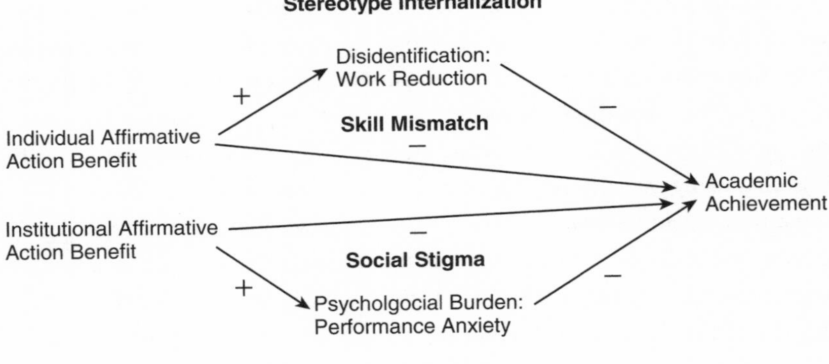

Figure 8.1.
Conceptual model of affirmative action's effects on academic achievement

idea that affirmative action exacerbates the psychological burdens associated with stereotype threat. For minority students who feel threatened because they have internalized negative beliefs about their group, that threat will be all the greater if they themselves fall below the institutional norm for SAT performance. Likewise, for those who feel they are representing the race every time they are called on to perform academically, their performance burden is heightened in contexts where their group's average SAT is known to be well below that of other students at the institution.

Our conceptual model is summarized in figure 8.1. For students entering a selective college or university, whether they themselves received an affirmative action benefit and whether their institution makes extensive use of affirmative action criteria are exogenous factors over which they have no control. They either received an individual admissions benefit or they did not, and they are entering a school that practices affirmative action for certain groups of students or does not. Of course, they do not know either fact with absolute certainty—they are simply making informed guesses based on knowledge of their own and their group's SAT scores and other admissions criteria.

Building on the allegations of affirmative action's critics, we posit that individual-level race-sensitive admissions affect grade achievement indirectly by exacerbating the process of disidentification, especially among those who have internalized negative stereotypes, and by heightening the performance burden, especially among those prone to stereotype externalization. While the stereotype threat hypothesis argues that affirmative action affects performance *indirectly* through its effect on disidentification and performance burden, the skills mismatch hypothesis posits a *direct* effect at the individual level. Members of targeted groups who benefit from a relaxing of admissions standards under affirmative action are set up for academic trouble later on because they are less prepared than other students for the rigors of competition on elite campuses. A second direct effect is the social stigma hypothesis. If a group is perceived to be on campus "illegitimately," such perceptions could produce a tense social atmosphere characterized by intergroup disputes that poison relations on campus and make life difficult for members of the targeted group, yielding social pressures that undermine academic performance.

Assessing the Wake

To gauge the effects of affirmative action on academic performance, one must devise some operational measure by which students from extremely diverse backgrounds can be compared. For this reason, debates about affirmative action intersect with broader debates about the value and appropriateness of standardized testing in college admission (Lemann 1999; Owen 1999; Zwick 2002). Most attention has focused on the SAT, which has been shown to be an imperfect predictor of college performance, especially among minorities (Bowen and Bok 1998; Fleming 2002; Fleming and Garcia 1998). Despite vocal criticisms, however (see Gould 1981; Taylor 1980), the SAT remains a staple of the college admissions process, though it may be less important at selective private institutions, which generally cast a wider net in their search for meritorious students by taking into account a variety of skills, talents, and accomplishments in addition to grades and test scores (see Steinberg 2002; Springer and Franck 2005).

Wherever they apply to college, however, students and parents display an obsessive concern with SAT scores, and this test continues to signify to the general public how "well qualified" a student is to attend a prestigious institution of higher education, as evidenced by the prominence of SAT scores in the annual college and university ratings published by *U.S. News and World Report* (see U.S. News and World Report 2005). When critics of affirmative action speak out against race-sensitive admissions, moreover, the evidence they most often cite to document the "unfairness" of race-sensitive admissions is the large black-white test score gaps (see Jencks and Phillips 1998; Thernstrom and Thernstrom 1999).

For these reasons, when Espenshade, Chung, and Walling (2004) sought to quantify the admissions advantage granted to affirmatively targeted groups, they did so in terms of an SAT score "bonus." We likewise use SAT scores to measure affirmative action, not because they are ideal, but because they offer a practical method that can be applied across groups and schools, in addition to occupying center stage in the affirmative action debate. In essence, we take the critics at their word and reason that if admissions standards have indeed been "loosened" to facilitate the entry of underrepresented minorities, then we would expect to observe a gap in SAT scores between minority group members and other students on campus.

The effects of affirmative action are theoretically observable at both the individual and the institutional level. At the individual level some minority group members will have SAT scores that are unusually low by the usual standards of their academic institution. To measure affirmative action at the individual level, we computed the difference between the SAT score earned by specific black and Latino students and the institutional average. For students with SAT scores that equaled or exceeded the institutional average we coded the variable as 0, and for those with scores below the institutional average we took the absolute value of the difference to indicate the relative likelihood that the student received an affirmative action benefit. The greater the value of this index, we argue, the greater the odds that the student in question received an affirmative action "bonus" in the admissions process.

In essence, this operationalization of affirmative action assumes that minority SAT scores fall below the institutional average because admissions officers trade off test scores against other criteria associated with their desire to recruit more minority students—the essence of affirmative action. If the mismatch hypothesis is correct, then the larger the magnitude of the index, the lower the grades the students will earn in college, other things equal. According to our calculations, 84% of black students had test scores that were below the institutional average, compared with around 66% of Hispanics. Among the former, the size of the discrepancy ranged from 0 to 515 points and averaged 131 points across all students, and among the latter the range went from 0 to 510 points and averaged 76 points.

Given the plethora of guides publishing institutional average SAT scores (see College Board 2005a; Fiske 2005; Meltzer et al. 2005; Yale Daily

News 2005; U.S. News and World Report 2005), an individual from a targeted group with a low SAT score in either verbal or math skills or both will likely be well aware that his or her score is below the usual level for the institution. In addition, whatever one's own SAT scores might be, students in theory can observe a gap between members of a targeted group and students in general, either directly because the data are published (online or by a college rating service) or indirectly because group differences in performance are apparent in classrooms and members of targeted groups concentrate in what are perceived to be "easy" classes.

At the institutional level as well, trading off test scores against other indicators of merit in order to achieve diversity will tend to produce average SAT scores for Latinos and African Americans that are as a whole lower than usual for a particular campus. To measure affirmative action at the institutional level, we took the difference between the average SAT score earned by blacks or Hispanics on campus and that earned by all students at the particular institution. We hypothesize that the larger this gap, the more an institution used criteria other than test scores to determine minority admissions. Among the twenty-eight schools in our sample, *none* displayed mean black and Latino SAT scores that were above the institutional average, suggesting that all institutions practiced some form of affirmative action. The average difference between black and total SAT scores across institutions ranged from 43 to 194 and averaged 122 points. For Hispanics, the average difference was 61 points with a range that went from 56 to 139.

Swamping the Boat

In table 8.1 we regress students' subjective estimates of their academic effort on our index of affirmative action and on our index of internalization to test one version of the stereotype threat hypothesis. As documented in the prior chapter, the internalization of stereotypes is negatively related to academic work effort. But the interactive model presented in the right-hand columns provides no evidence that this basic effect is in any way exacerbated by being a likely beneficiary of affirmative action; nor does individual affirmative action have any direct effect on subjective effort, thus disconfirming the hypothesis that affirmative action heightens the effect of stereotype threat through the internalization of negative beliefs about one's group.

Table 8.1
Effects of three affirmative action variables on subjective effort put forth by black and Latino students in the National Longitudinal Survey of Freshmen

	Main Effects Only		*Interactive Model*	
Independent Variables	B	SE	B	SE
Key Predictors				
Affirmative Action				
Individual	−0.001	0.001	0.001	0.001
Internalization	−0.046**	0.017	−0.018	0.029
Individual × Internalization	—	—	0.000	0.000
Control Variables				
Difficulty of Courses				
Number of Easy Courses	0.022	0.016	0.022	0.016
Number of Hard Courses	0.031†	0.016	0.032†	0.016
Demographic Background				
Male	−0.371**	0.109	−0.378**	0.110
Foreign-Born Parent	0.085	0.122	0.083	0.119
Two-Parent Family	0.004	0.102	0.006	0.103
Siblings under 18	−0.010	0.040	−0.013	0.039
Education of Parents				
No College Degrees	—	—	—	—
One College Degree	0.070	0.109	0.073	0.109
Two College Degrees	0.193	0.133	0.185	0.132
One Advanced Degree	0.263†	0.144	0.260†	0.144
Two Advanced Degrees	0.433**	0.143	0.430**	0.144
Economic Status				
Home Value (000)	0.000	0.000	0.000	0.000
Ever on Welfare	−0.315**	0.116	−0.309*	0.115
Income > $100,000	−0.224†	0.122	−0.219†	0.122
Academic Preparation				
AP Courses Taken	0.008	0.028	0.009	0.027
High School GPA	0.489**	0.158	0.477	0.156
Self-rated Preparation	0.036*	0.015	0.034*	0.015
SAT Score (00)	−0.175**	0.055	−0.172**	0.055
Social Preparation				
Self-efficacy	0.003	0.014	0.003	0.015
Self-esteem	0.021*	0.008	0.021*	0.008
Susceptibility to Peer Influence	0.014	0.011	0.014	0.011
Social Distance from Whites	−0.003	0.010	−0.003	0.010
Intercept	6.250***	0.600	6.071***	0.617
R^2	0.059		0.060	
Number of Cases	1,401		1,401	

†*p*<.10 **p*<.05 ***p*<.01 ****p*<.001

Table 8.2 moves on to consider the effects of individual affirmative action and internalization on objective effort as measured by hours studied per week. Again we see the familiar effect of disidentification documented in the last chapter, with the internalization of stereotypes negatively predicting hours studied. But as before there is no evidence that this disidentification is in any way intensified among individuals who are beneficiaries of affirmative action, nor does individual affirmative action influence objective effort directly. Taken together, therefore, these two analyses fail to sustain the disidentification version of the stereotype threat hypothesis. Individual affirmative action does not appear to heighten the internalization of stereotypes to exacerbate disidentification and thereby promote poor academic performance among black and Latino students.

Table 8.3 tests whether or not affirmative action measured at the institutional level functions to exacerbate the subjective performance burden experienced by black and Latino students, either by itself or through interaction with the externalization of stereotypes. In this case the results are mixed. Although we do not find a significant interaction between institutional affirmative action and stereotype externalization, we do find that institutional affirmative action itself has a significant direct effect on the psychological burden experienced by minority students. That is, the larger the gap between the average SAT scores of minority students on campus and the overall average at the institution, the heavier the subjective performance burden experienced by African Americans and Latinos when they are called on to perform academically. In other words, the use of affirmative action by an institution does appear to heighten the subjective performance burden experienced by black and Latino students because of stereotype externalization.

Because we already know from prior work that a higher subjective performance burden leads to lower grades, the former conclusion implies that institutional affirmative action indeed undermines grade performance indirectly by heightening the performance burden experienced by minority students. The regression estimates in table 8.4 complete our analysis by testing whether affirmative action has any direct effects on grade achievement, as specified by the mismatch and social stigma hypotheses. The left-hand columns of the table estimate the effects of individual and institutional affirmative action on the GPAs earned by black and Latino students, holding constant the effects of hours studied, subjective effort, performance burden, and other background characteristics.

Table 8.2
Effects of three affirmative action variables on hours studied per week by black and Latino students in the National Longitudinal Survey of Freshmen

	Main Effects Only		*Interactive Model*	
Independent Variables	B	SE	B	SE
Key Predictors				
Affirmative Action				
Individual	0.008	0.007	−0.004	0.011
Internalization	−0.459**	0.133	−0.672**	0.198
Individual × Internalization	—	—	0.002	0.002
Control Variables				
Difficulty of Courses				
Number of Easy Courses	−0.488**	0.142	−0.493**	0.143
Number of Hard Courses	0.236	0.141	0.235	0.141
Demographic Background				
Male	−1.464	1.015	−1.413	0.998
Foreign-Born Parent	2.712**	0.948	2.727**	0.941
Two-Parent Family	0.270	0.877	0.252	0.882
Siblings under 18	−0.027	0.401	−0.008	0.409
Education of Parents				
No College Degrees	—	—	—	—
One College Degree	−1.677	1.095	−1.703	1.114
Two College Degrees	−0.977	1.110	−0.914	1.095
One Advanced Degree	−0.398	1.219	−0.376	1.213
Two Advanced Degrees	0.119	1.042	0.138	1.049
Economic Status				
Home Value (000)	0.001	0.002	0.001	0.002
Ever on Welfare	−0.157	0.825	−0.210	0.825
Income > $100,000	−1.443	1.010	−1.487	0.987
Academic Preparation				
AP Courses Taken	0.415*	0.190	0.410*	0.188
High School GPA	6.058***	1.063	6.147***	1.060
Self-rated Preparation	0.000	0.132	0.011	0.134
SAT Score (00)	0.373	0.581	0.353	0.578
Social Preparation				
Self-efficacy	0.082	0.139	0.086	0.139
Self-esteem	−0.001	0.072	−0.006	0.072
Susceptibility to Peer Influence	0.073	0.084	0.071	0.084
Social Distance from Whites	0.070	0.071	0.072	0.072
Intercept	−0.527	7.655	0.831	7.643
R^2	0.083		0.084	
Number of Cases	1,401		1,401	

$^*p<.05$ $^{**}p<.01$ $^{***}p<.001$

Table 8.3
Effects of three affirmative action variables on subjective performance burden felt by black and Latino students in the National Longitudinal Survey of Freshmen

	Main Effects Only		*Interactive Model*	
Independent Variables	B	SE	B	SE
Key Predictors				
Affirmative Action				
Institutional	0.022**	0.007	0.038	0.025
Externalization	0.109†	0.059	0.175	0.120
Institutional × Externalization	—	—	−0.001	0.001
Control Variables				
Difficulty of Courses				
Number of Easy Courses	−0.108	0.139	−0.108	0.140
Number of Hard Courses	0.273	0.166	0.272	0.166
Demographic Background				
Male	1.481†	0.757	1.486†	0.753
Foreign-Born Parent	2.003*	0.937	1.976*	0.932
Two-Parent Family	1.798**	0.672	1.800*	0.672
Siblings under 18	0.099	0.363	0.100	0.362
Education of Parents				
No College Degrees	—	—	—	—
One College Degree	−0.163	1.324	−0.182	1.334
Two College Degrees	−0.689	1.185	−0.698	1.195
One Advanced Degree	0.195	1.099	0.191	1.102
Two Advanced Degrees	−0.941	1.173	−0.944	1.180
Economic Status				
Home Value (000)	0.001	0.002	0.001	0.002
Ever on Welfare	1.857*	0.727	1.869*	0.725
Income > $100,000	−0.014	1.118	−0.025	1.119
Academic Preparation				
AP Courses Taken	0.469*	0.183	0.476*	0.184
High School GPA	1.488	0.935	1.475	0.941
Self-rated Preparation	−0.079	0.122	−0.077	0.122
SAT Score (00)	−1.053*	0.458	−1.054*	0.460
Social Preparation				
Self-efficacy	−0.432*	0.182	−0.429*	0.183
Self-esteem	−0.340***	0.085	−0.341***	0.085
Susceptibility to Peer Influence	0.695***	0.102	0.694***	0.101
Social Distance from Whites	−0.132	0.089	−0.131	0.090
Intercept	47.833***	7.805	46.379***	8.188
R^2	0.145***		0.146***	
Number of Cases	1,335		1,335	

†$p<.10$ *$p<.05$ **$p<.01$ ***$p<.001$

Table 8.4
Effect of selected variables on GPA earned through the sophomore year by students in the National Longitudinal Survey of Freshmen

	Black and Latino Students		*All Students*	
Independent Variables	B	SE	B	SE
Key Predictors				
Group				
Whites	—	—	—	—
Asians	—	—	0.019	0.014
Latinos	—	—	−0.016	0.023
Blacks	—	—	−0.041	0.043
Affirmative Action				
Individual	0.000	0.000	0.000	0.000
Institutional	−0.001***	0.0002	−0.001**	0.0003
Mediating Factors				
Subjective Effort	0.033***	0.006	0.032***	0.005
Hours Studied	0.002***	0.001	0.002***	0.0003
Performance Burden	−0.001	0.001	−0.001*	0.0004
Control Variables				
Difficulty of Courses				
Number of Easy Courses	0.030***	0.003	0.022***	0.003
Number of Hard Courses	−0.017**	0.005	−0.010**	0.003
Demographic Background				
Male	−0.062***	0.020	−0.045***	0.013
Foreign-Born Parent	0.032	0.029	0.010	0.021
Two-Parent Family	0.041	0.029	0.029	0.021
Siblings under 18	0.001	0.013	−0.007	0.008
Education of Parents				
No College Degrees	—	—	—	—
One College Degree	0.047*	0.022	0.029	0.022
Two College Degrees	0.091**	0.026	0.059**	0.017
One Advanced Degree	0.058*	0.026	0.059**	0.021
Two Advanced Degrees	0.121***	0.030	0.105***	0.025
Economic Status				
Home Value (000)	0.000	0.000	0.000	0.000
Ever on Welfare	0.025	0.030	0.018	0.020
Income > $100,000	0.030	0.023	0.035	0.020
Academic Preparation				
AP Courses Taken	0.008	0.007	0.003	0.005
High School GPA	0.280***	0.032	0.357***	0.029
Self-rated Preparation	0.017**	0.005	0.022***	0.003
SAT Score (00)	0.102***	0.022	0.072***	0.012

Table 8.4 *(continued)*

Independent Variables	*Black and Latino Students*		*All Students*	
	B	SE	B	SE
Social Preparation				
Self-efficacy	−0.004	0.004	−0.004	0.003
Self-esteem	0.005†	0.002	0.003†	0.002
Susceptibility to Peer Influence	0.010***	0.002	0.008***	0.001
Social Distance from Whites	0.001	0.002	0.001	0.001
Intercept	0.202	0.268	0.423**	0.183
R^2	0.340***		0.396***	
Number of Cases	1,333		2,661	

†$p < .10$ *$p < .05$ **$p < .01$ ***$p < .001$

This regression provides no empirical support for the mismatch hypothesis. Black and Latino students with relatively low SAT scores do no better or worse than their counterparts who scored at or above the average for their institution. Thus affirmative action does not appear to set individual students up for failure by creating a mismatch between cognitive skills and academic demands at competitive colleges and universities. Other things equal, individual affirmative action beneficiaries earn the same grades as other students on campus.

We do find a significant effect of *institutional* affirmative action on the grade performance of black and Latino students, however. The greater the discrepancy in SAT scores between minority students and others on a particular campus, the lower the grades earned by individual black and Latino students at the same campus. Thus, a sizable minority-majority test score gap within any institution appears to create a social context that makes it more difficult for minority students to perform academically, thus lowering the grades they earn, an outcome consistent with the social stigma hypothesis.

The right-hand columns of table 8.4 estimate the effect of affirmative action on the academic performance of minority students relative to all students on campus. White and Asian students by definition receive no affirmative action benefit and thus receive scores of zero. As with other race-related variables we have examined, the introduction of affirmative action indicators has a significant effect in reducing the black-white achievement gap. Indeed, for the first time in any of our models the GPA differential is reduced to statistical insignificance. According to the regression estimate, once institutional affirmative action is included as a predictor, African

Americans earn grades that are roughly equal to those of whites—just 0.03 points lower, a difference that is far from the threshold of statistical significance. In substantive terms, institutional affirmative action is found to have a very significant negative effect on grade achievement, net of other factors in the model, suggesting that institutional affirmative action may indeed undermine academic achievement by exacerbating stereotype threat, stigmatizing minority group members as unqualified, and thus increasing the subjective performance burden they experience.

Steering Clear of the Shoals

Our statistical analyses of the academic effects of affirmative action have produced results that no doubt simultaneously reassure and challenge the supporters of affirmative action in higher education. On the one hand, we find no evidence to support the mismatch hypothesis, which argues that minority students are set up for poor grade performance because affirmative action creates a gap between their abilities and those required for success at very competitive and demanding academic institutions. We also find no evidence that affirmative action exacerbates the basic process of disidentification for individual minority students. The receipt of an affirmative action bonus by black and Latino students does not bring about a reduction of objective or subjective work effort on the part of students, either by itself or through interaction with stereotype internalization.

On the other hand, we did uncover evidence that affirmative action functions at the institutional level to undermine the grades earned by black and Latino students. The extensive use of race-sensitive criteria under affirmative action, when it produces a large test score gap between minority and other students on campus, appears to lower minority achievement in two ways. Directly, a large test score gap creates a stigmatizing social context within which black and Latino students find it more difficult to perform, and indirectly a large test score gap heightens the subjective performance burden experienced by minority students because of stereotype threat. We thus confirm both the social stigma hypothesis and the performance burden version of the stereotype threat hypothesis.

After the strong evidence in support of the theory of stereotype threat presented in the prior chapter, this result should not be surprising. If stereotype threat is a real phenomenon with significant effects on intellectual performance—as scores of laboratory studies and now our analysis of survey data suggest—then it stands to reason that any institutional policy that, however inadvertently, highlights the poorer performance of minority students on a very visible and widely discussed benchmark of academic qualification stands a good chance of exacerbating, however unintentionally, the performance burden experienced by black and Latino students because of stereotype threat and stigmatizing group members as people whose academic qualifications are indeed suspect.

This result does not mean that minority affirmative action in college admissions is necessarily detrimental to the academic interests of minority students and should be abandoned. Rather, it implies that as currently administered by selective institutions in the United States, the application of race-sensitive admissions criteria appears to create a stigmatizing setting that undermines minority academic performance in direct and indirect ways. If there is one thing proven about social stigma and stereotype threat, it is that they are quite malleable and sensitive to external manipulation (Perry, Steele, and Hilliard 2004). If the way affirmative action is administered and framed on campus can be changed so as to mitigate the stigma now being created, its negative academic effects will, in theory, disappear.

At the center of the debate on affirmative action has been the University of Michigan, one of the "elite public" institutions included in the NLSF. There, as on the campuses of other selective colleges and universities, black students had a long-established track record of academic underperformance. In that setting Steele and colleagues (2009) intervened to test his hypothesis that "wise" interventions could not only mitigate the effects of stereotype threat but produce superior performance.

For Steele, wise interventions are actions taken and programs implemented by faculty and staff to negate stigma, defuse the power of negative stereotypes, and overcome subjective performance burden (Steele 1997). Specific elements of a wise program intervention include: (1) optimistic faculty-student relationships, in which instructors communicate expectations of exceptional rather than poor performance and offer critical feedback in the context of an encouraging relationship; (2) an emphasis on challenge rather than remediation in learning, which conveys to students their potential for growth rather than their accumulated deficiencies; (3) a stress on the expandability of intelligence through incremental experience, training, and effort rather than framing intellect as a fixed and limited resource; (4) affirmation of the minority students' belonging on campus and their routine acceptance as members of the scholarly community; (5) validation of multiple approaches and perspectives in addressing academic issues, which communicates to students that the campus is an environment within which stereotypes are not likely to be used or welcomed.

Thus Steele and colleagues initiated a special program for African American students at the University of Michigan, but rather than stigmatizing students by labeling the program as remedial or compensatory, they were told that as Michigan students they had survived a very competitive selection program and that their assignment to the "21st century program" was intended to maximize their strong potential. In this way, university officials acknowledged their worth as scholars, communicated their high expectations for these students, and explicitly labeled the program as nonremedial. Once in the program, students were offered the "opportunity" to join a "challenge" workshop on one of several difficult subjects and participated in weekly discussion groups centered on assigned readings that allowed them to talk about adjustment-related academic, social, and even personal experiences.

A systematic analysis of program participants' academic progress showed that black students who participated in the 21st century program lived up to their academic potential whereas comparable students who were assigned to remedial programs did not. No matter what their SAT scores, black students in programs that were labeled compensatory earned a mediocre GPA of 2.5. Grades were the same whether the student scored two standard deviations below or above the mean. In contrast, among those participating in the 21st century program grade performance was strongly linked to SAT test scores. Those who were two standard deviations below the mean did not perform any worse than the students in the remedial group; but those at and above the mean performed much better: as well as white students assigned to the same program and better than white students in an unassigned control group. Thus, whereas black students in the program who scored two standard deviations below the mean SAT earned around a 2.5 GPA, those at the mean earned around a 2.9 and those two standard deviations above the mean earned a GPA of nearly 3.4 (Steele 1997; Steele et al. 2007).

The Michigan field experiment confirms that stereotype threat is indeed quite malleable and amenable to influence by programs and policies. Massey and Fischer (2005) showed that increasing the presence of minority faculty in the classroom caused the minority performance burden to be eliminated; and as Massey and Mooney (2007) point out, selective colleges and universities have long been running two other "affirmative action" programs without creating social stigma or raising the performance burden of participants: one for students with athletic skills and the other for children of alumni. In their study of three private universities, Espenshade, Chung, and Walling (2004) found that 50% of legacy applicants were admitted compared with 49% of athletes, 39% of African Americans, 32% of Latinos, and just 25% of applicants in general. Thus affirmative action for "legacy" students and athletes is even more extensive than for minorities, yet Massey and Mooney found no evidence of an enhanced performance burden among them. Indeed, the only significant statistical effect they found was for athletes, and for them the effect of institutional affirmative action was negative, acting to reduce anxieties about academic performance.

These findings suggest that if minority students were welcomed and supported at selective institutions in the same way that star athletes and legacy students routinely are, the grade performance of black and Latino students might improve markedly. If anything, elite colleges and universities presently seem to be doing the opposite of wisely intervening in support of minority students. When they arrive on campus, black and Latino students are often singled out for special treatment in ways that typically imply a need for "remediation." As noted in chapter 2, black and Latino students were far more likely than whites or Asians to report the receipt of special instruction in reading, writing, mathematics, test taking, and study skills, and were much more likely to report using a tutor. Overall, black students were more than twice as likely as white students to receive institutional help.

The worst possible situation is for minority students to be typically selected into remedial programs on the basis of race and ethnicity rather than ability or level of preparation, thus communicating the tacit assumption that all black and Latino students are of suspect intellectual quality no matter what their class or educational background. Under this policy, minority students who have two professionally employed parents and who attended an elite prep school and scored highly on the SAT receive the same message of suspected deficiency and low expectations as those who come from a single-parent, welfare-dependent household and who attended inner-city public schools and scored much lower on the SAT. Tellingly, Steele (1997) found that high-ability black students who were assigned to remedial groups not only failed to realize the same intellectual potential as those assigned to the 21st century program but actually performed worse than black students in an unassigned control group of regular students. Perhaps for this reason, we found in chapter 2 that students who made more frequent use of special institutional programs earned significantly lower grades than other students, holding constant academic preparation and other factors.

In the end, our finding that the affirmative programs administered to the 1999 cohort of freshmen at selective colleges and universities undermined grade performance by stigmatizing students and increasing the subjective performance burden tells us less about the inherent weaknesses of affirmative action than about the poor fashion in which the programs are implemented and the failure of college administrators to appreciate the continuing power of stereotype threat. Affirmative actions taken to ensure the inclusion of athletes and legacies have been run for decades without stigmatizing either the children of alumni or football players, and without creating debilitating performance burdens. There is no good reason that affirmative action programs for minorities cannot be run in the same way.

9 College at Midstream

At this point in our journey downstream we have undertaken a series of very detailed analyses of students' academic choices, living conditions, financial circumstances, and social behavior during the first two years of college, extending the research that Massey et al. (2003) began in *The Source of the River*, which documented differences in the social backgrounds of students attending America's selective colleges and universities. Here we have focused on emergent similarities and differences among students expressed in the course of their freshman and sophomore years, and we have paused along the way to consider the influence of each set of factors on grades earned over the course of these two years of college.

The main lesson learned to this point is that adjusting to college is challenging for all students, in academic, financial, and social terms, and that adaptations in these domains carry a price in terms of grade achievement. The more pressures that students face, the worse their grades. All students confront common academic, financial, and social challenges in adapting to college, of course, but the pressures are generally more intense for minority groups; and the greater severity of these "normal" challenges partly explains the lower performance of African Americans and Latinos relative to whites and Asians.

In addition to these universal sources of student angst, however, black and Latino students face other, unique pressures that rarely, if ever, come up for whites or Asians. Indeed, white students, faculty, and administrators may have a hard time even visualizing these minority-specific challenges. Most whites, for example, are probably blissfully unaware of the racial and ethnic undercurrents that bedevil minority students on campus, and few can likely relate to the onus of stereotype threat or appreciate the stigma of a heightened performance burden from affirmative action programs. In the preceding chapters, we have delved into all these factors in considerable depth and detail.

To this point, however, we have considered the effect of students' academic and social situations on only one indicator of academic success—grade achievement—but a successful college career involves more than earning good grades. In addition to maintaining a decent grade point average, students need to accumulate a suitable number of course credits for graduation. Moreover, neither grades nor credits will be of much use if students leave school before attaining a degree; and always, of course, there is the issue of personal happiness and satisfaction. It would be a Pyrrhic victory for universities if minority students were able to compile an academic record that allowed them to graduate but experienced such torment and misery along the way that they left campus angry, embittered, and unwilling to support the institution as it endeavors to educate future generations of minority students.

In this final chapter, therefore, we consider the college experience more broadly by examining subjective indicators of satisfaction as well as the objective outcome of GPA. At the same time, we expand the analysis to include other objective outcomes, such as accumulating course credits and departing prematurely from the institution. In considering the latter outcome, moreover, we measure the influence of academic performance and college satisfaction as predetermined variables conditioning the odds of leaving school. Finally, rather than considering the influence of academic, social, financial, and minority-related pressures separately in one-by-one analyses, we specify a single comprehensive model to estimate their separate, independent effects on various outcomes while controlling for relevant background factors, essentially our attempt to model the complex relationships summarized in figure 1.1.

The View at Midstream

Toward the end of the sophomore year, NLSF respondents were asked to reflect on their college experiences by answering three basic questions: How

Table 9.1
Indicators of attachment to college at the end of the sophomore year

Indicator of Attachment	Whites	Asians	Latinos	Blacks
Subjective Indicators				
Academic Satisfaction	3.44	3.30	3.39	3.31
Social Satisfaction	3.34	3.17	3.26	3.03
College Experience So Far	3.02	2.82	2.85	2.64
Satisfaction Scale	3.26	3.09	3.16	2.99
Objective Indicators				
Grade Point Average	3.35	3.34	3.13	3.00
Course Credits Accumulated	15.62	15.85	14.81	14.33
Percentage Leaving Institution	9.90	8.12	10.85	11.51

satisfied are you with your intellectual development since enrolling in your college or university? How satisfied are you with your social life since enrolling? And, considering everything, how would your rate your experience so far? Students responded on a simple five-choice continuum of satisfaction: very dissatisfied, somewhat dissatisfied, neither satisfied nor dissatisfied, somewhat satisfied, or very satisfied. We coded these responses ordinally from 0 to 4, and averages of the resulting scales are presented by group in the top panel of table 9.1.

On the 4-point scale of satisfaction with intellectual development at college, most students pronounced themselves well satisfied, with ratings in the range of 3.30 to 3.44. And why not? They were attending some of the best schools in the country. Nonetheless, Asians and African Americans appear slightly less satisfied than whites and Latinos, and the differences are statistically significant ($F = 5.9$, $p < .001$). On the social satisfaction scale, more variation appears. Although the average degree of satisfaction is still quite high, the range of 3.03 to 3.34 is twice that observed for satisfaction with intellectual development. Although the numerical averages generally fall at the interface between somewhat satisfied and very satisfied, Asians and blacks nonetheless lag behind whites and Latinos in satisfaction with their social lives ($F = 16.7$, $p < .001$).

When students were asked to consider everything in thinking about their college experience, they responded with average ratings that fall further on the satisfaction scale, into the range of 2.64 to 3.02, with whites once again at the top and African Americans at the bottom ($F = 28.5$, $p < .001$). Although students were generally satisfied with their academic progress, therefore, they were somewhat less happy with their social lives and even more negative when they considered their overall collegiate experience. Moreover, across all satisfaction indexes black and white students fall at opposite ends of the continuum: whites are always the most satisfied and blacks always the least satisfied, no matter what aspect of college life is considered and the gap between highest and lowest average ratings. Asians and Latinos fall in between, but Latinos are generally more optimistic and upbeat than Asians.

The last line in the top panel of the table shows average values for a summated rating scale created by combining scores across these three satisfaction items to create a single index of student satisfaction (Cronbach's alpha .67—see appendix C). In terms of overall satisfaction, whites pronounced themselves most content at the end of the sophomore year, with a scale score of 3.26. They are followed by Latinos at 3.16, Asians at 3.09, and African Americans at 2.99. The range of scale scores is not great, but the intergroup differences are nevertheless significant statistically ($F = 24.1$, $p < .001$).

The bottom panel shows various indicators of academic performance through the end of the sophomore year. As already noted, the GPAs of whites and Asians are nearly the same at 3.35 and 3.34, respectively. Latinos fall significantly behind at 3.13, and African Americans are lowest at 3.00 ($F = 146.4$, $p < .001$). This ordering had changed little in either relative or absolute terms since the beginning of the freshman year (cf. Massey et al. 2003). However, given black students' higher aspirations for graduate and professional education compared with whites, the relative deficit in grade performance represents potentially a more serious problem for them, indicating a larger gap between expectations and achievement midway through college.

In keeping with these differentials in grade achievement, whites and Asians generally had completed more courses by the end of the sophomore year than African Americans or Latinos. Whereas whites reported an average of 15.6 course credits and Asians around 15.9 credits, the figures for Latinos and blacks are 14.8 and 14.3, respectively ($F = 6.4$, $p < .001$). Fortunately, intergroup differentials in the likelihood of leaving school are much smaller. By the spring of the sophomore year, only 8.1% of Asians had left the institution in which they had originally enrolled, compared with 9.9% of whites, 10.9% of Latinos, and 11.5% of African Americans, a limited range that does not attain statistical significance ($F = 1.8$, $p = .140$).

Downstream toward Graduation

To this point we have considered a variety of potential influences on student success while endeavoring to control for background differences known from earlier work to be important in predicting academic performance. Table 9.2 draws on analyses carried out in chapters 2 through 8 to assemble a comprehensive list of factors whose influence on academic progress we have investigated to this point. More than seventy-five indicators are grouped under eight general rubrics, including curricular factors, social factors, financial issues, social undercurrents, ecological factors, stereotype threat, and affirmative action.

Under curricular factors we propose to investigate the effects of several of the specific measures considered in chapter 2: declared major, relative number of easy versus hard courses taken, subjective perceptions of effort and difficulty, degree to which academic assistance was sought from different sources, and aspirations for education beyond the bachelor's degree. We also propose to investigate a variety of social factors weighed in chapter 3, including kind of housing, exposure to distractions, peer culture, involvement in selected organizations and activities, and the allocation of time among competing uses. The financial factors from chapter 4 that we investigate include the relative cost of college, the relative debt incurred for schooling, sources of financial support, and the reported frequency of financial aid problems.

Moving away from these universal challenges to academic success and turning to minority-specific issues, we consider a variety of indicators to capture the social undercurrents identified in chapter 5: the racial-ethnic composition of college classes, whether or not the student ever had a nonwhite professor, the amount of support received from close social contacts, degree of involvement in majority and minority organizations, dating behavior, and various measures of the campus racial climate.

Under the heading of ecological factors, which were covered in chapter 6, we measure various sequelae of segregation, including exposure to disorder and violence, family stress, and cognitive skills. The influence of stereotype threat, investigated in chapter 7, is assessed using the measures we developed for stereotype internalization, stereotype externalization, subjective effort, and performance burden, as well as hours studied. The potential effects of affirmative action just discussed in the last chapter are captured using individual and institutional measures of affirmative action,

Table 9.2
List of independent variables used in initial models predicting satisfaction, grade point average, failing a course, and departure from school

Curricular Factors

Major
- None Declared
- Biological-Physical Sciences
- Math–Comp Sci–Engineering
- Social-Behavioral Sciences
- Humanities
- Professions
- Other

Difficulty of Courses
- Number of Easy Courses
- Number of Hard Courses

Subjective Perceptions
- Difficulty of Courses
- Degree of Effort

Academic Assistance
- Institutional Help
- Professorial Help
- Peer Help

Academic Aspirations
- M.A, or Equivalent
- Ph.D. or Equivalent

Social Factors

Kind of Housing
- Always in Dormitory
- Ever in Apartment
- Ever in Fraternity/Sorority
- Ever with Relatives

Distractions
- Frequency of Distraction
- Frequency of Evasive Action

Peer Culture
- Support for Academics
- Support for Social Life

Involvement in Activities
- Career Development
- Varsity or Junior Varsity Sports
- Intramural Sports
- Fraternity or Sorority
- Religious Group
- Environmental or Political Group
- Community Group

Social Factors

Time allocation
- Academic
- Extracurricular
- Recreational
- Work
- Maintenance
- Sleep
- Time Stress Index

Financial Issues

Relative Cost per Child
- Family Cost/Income
- Family Cost/Home Value

Relative Debt per child
- Debt/Income
- Debt/Home Value

Sources of Support
- Hours Worked/Hours Studied
- Money from Family
- Credit Card from Family

Financial Aid Problems
- Frequency of Problems

Social Undercurrents

Diversity of First Class
- % Asian
- % Latino
- % Black

Diversity of Faculty
- Had Asian Professor
- Had Latino Professor
- Had Black Professor

Diversity of Friends
- # Asian Friends
- # Latino Friends
- # Black Friends

Social Support
- Social Support Scale

Group Involvement
- In Majority-White Group
- In Majority-Asian Group
- In Majority-Latino Group
- In Majority-Black Group

Social Undercurrents

Romantic Behavior
- No Date or Partner
- Dated outside Group
- Partner outside Group

Campus Racial Climate
- Negative Reaction In-group
- Negative Reaction Out-group
- Negative Climate Scale

Ecological Factors

Segregation
- Minority Proportion

Sequelae of Segregation
- Disorder-Violence Index
- Family Stress Index
- Cognitive Skills (SAT)

Stereotype Threat

Awareness of Stereotypes
- Internalization Scale
- Externalization Scale

Mediating Variables
- Subjective Effort
- Hours Studied
- Performance Burden

Affirmative Action
- Individual Index
- Institutional Index

Plus Controls For:
- Demographic Background
- Education of Parents
- Economic Status
- Academic Preparation
- Social Preparation

measuring the degree to which an individual minority group member is likely to have benefited from affirmative action and the degree to which affirmative action is likely practiced in a college or university's admissions.

The analytic strategy we employ is to regress all the foregoing indicators, along with background controls and group dummies, on four outcomes relevant to assessing academic progress at midstream: overall satisfaction with the collegiate experience, grade point average, accumulated course credits, and departure from the institution in question. In each case, we inspect the resulting regression estimates and select those variables from table 9.2 whose coefficients are significant at least at the 10% threshold. We include these variables and the controls in a second-round estimation and present the resulting coefficients as a final model to identify key determinants of each academic outcome.

Getting Good Grades

The left-hand columns in table 9.3 show the results of this stepwise estimation procedure to reveal key determinants of grade achievement through the sophomore year. In general, grade point average is more strongly linked to academic than social circumstances. The choice of major, for example, appears to make a significant difference in grades earned. Those majoring in a profession generally earned the highest grades, followed by majors in the humanities, those in the biological sciences, those in the social sciences, and finally those in math–computer science–engineering. As a rule, students who had not yet selected a major by the end of the sophomore year earned the lowest grades of all, though their GPA is not significantly different from those in the residual category of "other" majors.

As one would expect, GPA is significantly higher among those taking a larger number of "easy" classes and lower among those taking more "hard" courses. Whatever the objective difficulty of courses, moreover, students who subjectively *perceived* their course work to be more difficult in fact earned systematically lower grades than others. Higher grades are also linked to greater effort on the part of students, more contact with faculty, and to aspirations for postgraduate doctoral work. Students who earned high grades in college also tended to be those who had earned good grades in high school; and they assessed their preparation for college to be strong and reported high SAT scores. As noted before, grade achievement is strongly related to parental education: the more postsecondary degrees

Table 9.3
Effects of selected variables on GPA and scale of college satisfaction at end of sophomore year

	Grade Point Average		*College Satisfaction*	
Predictor Variable	B	SE	B	SE
Group				
White	—	—	—	—
Asian	−0.001	0.021	−0.080*	0.037
Latino	0.013	0.023	−0.015	0.051
Black	−0.044	0.047	−0.067	0.043
Academic Outcomes				
Freshman-Sophomore GPA	—	—	0.101*	0.041
Curricular Factors				
Major				
None Declared (Reference)	—	—	—	—
Biological-Physical Sciences	0.074*	0.023	0.024	0.040
Math–Comp Sci–Engineering	0.035†	0.020	0.024	0.046
Social-Behavioral Sciences	0.053**	0.019	0.035	0.035
Humanities	0.080***	0.016	−0.003	0.049
Professions	0.133***	0.019	0.109**	0.041
Other	0.046	0.061	0.193*	0.087
Measured Difficulty of Courses				
Number of "Easy" Courses	0.018***	0.003	0.005	0.004
Number of "Hard" Courses	−0.009**	0.003	−0.005	0.004
Subjective Perceptions				
Difficulty of Courses	−0.025**	0.009	—	—
Degree of Effort	0.047***	0.007	0.027**	0.007
Academic Assistance				
Institutional Help	−0.002***	0.0005	—	—
Professorial Help	0.002***	0.0005	—	—
Peer Help	−0.003**	0.0009	0.004**	0.001
Academic Aspirations				
No More than B.A. (Reference)	—	—	—	—
M.A. or Equivalent	0.001	0.022	—	—
Ph.D. or Equivalent	0.049*	0.023	—	—
Social Life				
Kind of Housing				
Always in Dormitory (Reference)	—	—	—	—
Ever in Apartment	−0.008	0.021	−0.009	0.028
Ever in Fraternity/Sorority	−0.062*	0.029	−0.137**	0.047
Ever with Relatives	−0.059†	0.032	−0.208*	0.097

Table 9.3 *(continued)*

Predictor Variable	*Grade Point Average* B	SE	*College Satisfaction* B	SE
Social Life, Cont.				
Peer Culture				
Support for Social Life	—	—	0.004	0.003
Involvement in Activities				
Career Development Group	0.053**	0.019	—	—
Foreign-Language Group	0.047*	0.023	—	—
Fraternity or Sorority	—	—	0.058*	0.026
Intramural Sports	0.038*	0.015	—	—
Environmental-Political Group	—	—	0.100**	0.029
Community Group	0.039*	0.014	0.039†	0.020
Time Allocation				
Recreational	−0.0007**	0.0002	—	—
Sleep	—	—	−0.001	0.001
Financial Issues				
Relative Cost				
Cost/Home Value per Child (000)	0.0002**	0.0001	—	—
Financial Aid Problems				
Frequency of Problems	—	—	−0.006**	0.002
Social Undercurrents				
Diversity or First Class				
% Asian	0.001*	0.0005	—	—
Faculty Diversity				
Had Latino Professor	0.024*	0.011	—	—
Had Black Professor	—	—	0.098***	0.020
Friends' Diversity				
# Asian Friends	0.006	0.004	—	—
# Latino Friends	−0.024**	0.007	—	—
# Black Friends	−0.005	0.004	—	—
Social Support				
Scale of Social Support	0.002*	0.001	−0.012***	0.002
Group Involvement				
In Majority-White Group	—	—	0.069***	0.023
In Majority-Asian Group	—	—	0.060*	0.030
Racial Climate on Campus				
Negative Climate Scale	0.003	0.003	−0.035***	0.007
Ecological Factors				
Childhood Segregation				
Proportion Minority	—	—	0.001	0.001

(continued)

Table 9.3 *(continued)*

Predictor Variable	*Grade Point Average* B	SE	*College Satisfaction* B	SE
Ecological Factors, Cont.				
Sequelae of Segregation				
Family Stress Index (00)	−0.026**	0.008	—	—
Cognitive Skills (SAT) (00)	0.075***	0.010	—	—
Stereotype Threat				
Intervening Variables				
Performance Burden (00)	−0.097*	0.046	—	—
Affirmative Action				
Individual (00)	0.035**	0.012	−0.042**	0.014
Institutional (00)	−0.1031**	0.035	—	—
Control Variables				
Demographic Background				
Male	−0.056***	0.014	0.095***	0.026
Foreign-Born Parent	0.019	0.016	−0.031	0.034
Two-Parent Family	0.032	0.021	−0.007	0.031
Siblings under 18	0.004	0.009	−0.008	0.017
Education of Parents				
No College Degrees (Reference)	—	—	—	—
One College Degree	0.020	0.022	0.043	0.051
Two College Degrees	0.063**	0.020	0.011	0.050
One Advanced Degree	0.060*	0.025	0.008	0.046
Two Advanced Degrees	0.096**	0.030	−0.004	0.050
Economic Status				
Home Value (000)	−0.0001**	0.00005	0.000	0.000
Ever on Welfare	0.026	0.024	0.042	0.039
Income > $100,000	0.041†	0.021	0.002	0.033
Academic Preparation				
AP Courses Taken	−0.001	0.005	−0.002	0.007
High School GPA	0.334***	0.032	0.153**	0.045
Self-rated Preparation	0.018**	0.004	0.002	0.006
Social Preparation				
Self-efficacy	−0.007*	0.003	0.019**	0.005
Self-esteem	0.004*	0.002	0.009**	0.005
Susceptibility to Peer Influence	0.005**	0.001	−0.012***	0.004
Social Distance from Whites	0.002	0.0014	−0.009***	0.002
Intercept	0.564***	0.193	1.700***	0.256
R^2	0.447***		0.226***	
Number of Cases	2,426		2,205	

†$p < .10$ *$p < .05$ **$p < .01$ ***$p < .001$

that parents have among them, the higher the grades earned by their children in college. That this strong effect persists even after the application of extensive statistical controls underscores the critical role played by parents in children's human capital formation (see Lareau 2000, 2003).

To the extent that social factors influence grade achievement at all, they tend mostly to be negative. Students earn lower grades if they study frequently with peers, belong to a fraternity or sorority, spend more time on recreational activities, and have a larger number of Latino friends. Alone among social factors, receiving support from close contacts is positively associated to grades. Factors specific to the minority experience also generally reduce grade achievement. The higher family stress and lower SAT scores associated with a segregated upbringing contribute significantly to lower grades, as does a higher performance burden emanating from stereotype threat.

Students who used institutional services for remedial support were especially prone to low grades, though this could represent reverse causality—students who are earning low grades turn to the institution for help. It could also indicate the stigmatizing effect of well-intentioned institutional policies. Consistent with this interpretation, the indicator of institutional affirmative action is strongly significant in the negative direction—the more an institution is likely to have applied affirmative action in minority admissions, the lower the grades earned by minority students on campus. Although individual affirmative action also has a significant effect on grade performance, it is opposite that predicted by critical advocates of the mismatch hypothesis. Individuals likely to have been affirmative action beneficiaries actually did *better* than other students, a finding that replicates earlier results obtained by Fischer and Massey (2007) using a different analytic specification.

Once all the foregoing effects are taken into consideration, white, Asian, Latino, and black students are all found to perform at the same GPA level, as indicated by the small and insignificant group coefficients. According to the final model, therefore, the student earning the highest grades is the daughter of well-educated parents, who earned good grades in high school, scored well on the SAT, has high self-esteem, and aspires to a doctoral degree or its equivalent. By the end of her sophomore year she has already selected a professional major and by her own account is putting considerable effort into her studies. Nonetheless she has still taken a significant number of "easy" courses and cultivated interactions with her professors, has avoided sororities to live on campus in a dorm or apartment, minimizes recreational time, and makes friends with Asian students. She works on her studies independently without relying on the institution or peers for academic assistance and has taken a course from a Latino professor.

In contrast, the profile of a student who is struggling academically is that of a male neither of whose parents went to college, who earned low grades in high school, scored poorly on the SAT, has low self-esteem, and feels unprepared for college. By the end of the sophomore year he has not yet settled on a major and is making heavy use of institutional services and relying on peers for academic support. He is quite sensitive to the opinions of others and cannot depend on close contacts for emotional support. Although the student in question is likely to be a minority group member, the low grades are not attributable to race or ethnicity per se but more to greater family stress and depressed cognitive skills linked to a segregated upbringing, along with greater psychological burdens associated with stereotype threat, which is exacerbated by the way his institution administers its affirmative action policies.

Sources of Satisfaction

The right-hand columns of table 9.3 present estimates showing the social and academic determinants of college satisfaction, which we measure using the rating scale described above. As in the prior analysis, the model was specified first by estimating a comprehensive model with all the variables listed in table 9.2 and then eliminating those that proved insignificant at the 10% level before undertaking a final estimation. We also add freshman-sophomore GPA as a determinant of satisfaction expressed at the end of the sophomore year. The top panel reveals that after the inclusion of comprehensive controls intergroup differences in satisfaction are mostly eliminated. Other things equal, only Asians stand out clearly for having lower levels of satisfaction than whites, though the negative coefficient for black students approaches significance at the 10% level ($p = .13$).

In contrast to grade achievement, college satisfaction is more a social and psychological than an academic process. Satisfaction is strongly determined by personality, of course. Higher levels of self-efficacy and self-esteem are strongly associated with college satisfaction, whereas susceptibility to peer influence and a greater perceived social distance from whites are linked to lower contentment. Apart from these individual psychological factors, satisfaction is most strongly influenced by a student's social circumstances.

Involvement in a fraternity or sorority, membership in an environmental or political group on campus, and participation in a community organization are all positively related to student satisfaction in college. Interestingly, however, while being a *member* of a fraternity or sorority is positively related to satisfaction, actually *living in* a Greek house is negatively related to satisfaction, illustrating the ambivalent influence of Greek life. Turning to peers for academic assistance is strongly associated with satisfaction, as is involvement with majority-white and majority-Asian groups on campus. Satisfaction is also higher among students who report having taken a freshman class with a black professor, suggesting the benefits of faculty diversity for all students. Whereas satisfaction may be low among those living in fraternities or sororities, it is lower still among those living off campus with relatives.

The receipt of more frequent social support from close personal contacts is, somewhat surprisingly, associated with lower levels of satisfaction; but this probably reflects reverse causality: those with personal problems tend to rely more on social contacts for support. Aside from living with family members and living in a fraternity or sorority, the main social predictors of satisfaction—all quite negative—are experiencing financial aid difficulties, perceiving a negative racial climate on campus, and being a likely beneficiary of individual affirmative action, once again underscoring the unique difficulties faced by minority students at selective schools.

In contrast to the large role played by social factors in determining college satisfaction, academic considerations have a relatively minor influence. Students earning higher grades are, unsurprisingly, more satisfied with college, but this effect, though significant, is not among the strongest in the model. Likewise, although students with professional and other majors stand out as more satisfied, beyond these two choices the selection of a major does not influence satisfaction much, nor does the relative number of easy versus hard courses, nor the subjective perception of course difficulty, nor aspirations for postundergraduate education. Likewise, neither cognitive skills as measured by the SAT nor academic preparation as measured by advanced placement courses and self-assessed college preparation play any detectable role in determining student satisfaction. Besides college grades, the only academic factors that influence satisfaction appear to be subjective academic effort and grades earned in high school. Those students who reported putting in more effort and who earned good grades in high school generally reported themselves to be more satisfied at college.

According to our statistical estimates, therefore, the most dissatisfied college student is an Asian male with low self-esteem and limited feelings of self-efficacy who perhaps benefited from affirmative action in admissions but earned relatively low grades in high school. He is sensitive to peer influences and cares how others perceive him but nonetheless perceives a large social distance between himself and whites on campus. He lives off campus with other family members from whom he receives most of his social support. On campus he experiences problems with financial aid and perceives a negative racial climate. Not surprisingly, therefore, he belongs to few majority-dominant campus groups and does not participate in campus groups or community organizations.

In contrast, the most satisfied student is a self-confident and efficacious white or Hispanic female who earned high grades in high school and lives in a dorm or apartment with roommates while studying hard, majoring in a profession, playing intramural supports, and joining campus religious organizations. She has no real financial problems, belongs to majority-white as well as majority-Asian organizations, and receives positive feedback from peers for social activities. These profiles would seem to describe the alienated male and the popular coed.

Accumulating Credits

Table 9.4 shows the effects of social and academic factors on two indicators of college persistence: the number of course credits accumulated and the likelihood of leaving school by the end of the sophomore year. The left-hand columns show the results for the prediction of accumulated course credits, inserting college GPA and college satisfaction as predetermined variables along with the factors specified in table 9.2. Once these statistical controls are applied, there are no significant differences between groups in terms of credits accumulated. Other things equal, whites, Asians, Latinos, and African Americans all appear to be moving down the curricular river at the same pace.

Like grade achievement, the accumulation of course credits is more an academic than a social process. Not surprisingly, students who earn high grades as freshmen and sophomores are much more likely than others to accumulate course credits, as are students who have declared a major by

Table 9.4
Effects of selected variables on likelihood of number of course credits accumulated and whether or not the student left school by end of sophomore year

	Credits Accumulated		*Left School*	
Predictor Variable	B	SE	B	SE
Group				
White	—	—	—	—
Asian	−0.287	0.273	−0.430†	0.262
Latino	0.170	0.263	0.303	0.308
Black	−0.430	0.301	−0.107	0.471
Academic Outcomes				
Freshman-Sophomore GPA	1.784***	0.324	0.775**	0.304
Satisfaction with College	0.258†	0.146	−1.306***	0.191
Course Credits Accumulated	—	—	−0.320***	0.047
Curricular Factors				
Major				
None Declared	—	—	—	—
Biological-Physical Sciences	0.591	0.353	0.995**	0.364
Math–Comp Sci–Engineering	1.190**	0.369	1.095*	0.517
Social-Behavioral Sciences	0.124**	0.432	0.528	0.371
Humanities	1.4901**	0.448	0.164	0.506
Professions	2.506***	0.421	1.151**	0.392
Other	0.975*	0.479	1.176***	0.359
Measured Difficulty of Courses				
Number of Easy Courses	0.498***	0.060	−0.006	0.081
Number of Hard Courses	0.569**	0.057	0.027	0.044
Subjective Perceptions				
Difficulty of Courses	—	—	−0.088	0.110
Degree of Effort	—	—	−0.045	0.090
Academic Assistance				
Peer Help	—	—	−0.021†	0.013
Academic Aspirations				
No More than B.A.	—	—	—	—
M.A. or Equivalent	—	—	0.376	0.243
Ph.D. or Equivalent	−0.539**	0.181	0.621*	0.295
Social Life				
Kind of Housing				
Ever in Apartment	−0.782*	0.335	—	—
Ever with Family	−2.246***	0.521	—	—
Distractions				
Frequency of Evasive Action	—	—	0.027*	0.013

(continued)

Table 9.4 *(continued)*

Predictor Variable	*Credits Accumulated* B	*Credits Accumulated* SE	*Left School* B	*Left School* SE
Social Life, Cont.				
Peer Culture				
Peer Support for Social Life	—	—	−0.028†	0.016
Involvement in Activities				
Career Development	—	—	−0.418	0.453
Varsity or Junior Varsity Sports	—	—	−1.481***	0.217
Intramural Sports	—	—	−1.059†	0.633
Fraternity or Sorority	—	—	−1.431*	0.632
Religious Group	—	—	−2.080*	0.940
Environmental or Political Group	—	—	−1.080	0.700
Community Group	—	—	−1.328***	0.274
Time Allocation				
Academic	0.006	0.005	—	—
Recreational	−0.007*	0.002	0.005	0.004
Budget Constraints				
Relative Cost				
Cost/Home Value per Child (000)	—	—	−0.004*	0.002
Relative Debt				
Debt/Income per Child	—	—	−0.391†	0.229
Debt/Home Value per Child (000)	−0.035*	0.017	—	—
Sources of Support				
Money Received from Family (000)	0.005	0.004	−0.046	0.040
Financial Aid Problems				
Frequency of Problems	—	—	0.011	0.011
Social Undercurrents				
Diversity of First Class				
% Asian	−0.035**	0.012	—	—
% Black	—	—	0.017*	0.007
Faculty Diversity				
Had Black Professor	—	—	−0.078	0.154
Friends' Diversity				
# Black Friends	—	—	0.050	0.039
# Asian Friends	−0.099*	0.044	—	—
Romantic Behavior				
Dated outside Group	—	—	0.276	0.272
Racial Climate on Campus				
Negative Climate Scale	−0.050*	0.021	—	—

Table 9.4 *(continued)*

Predictor Variable	*Credits Accumulated* B	SE	*Left School* B	SE
Ecological Factors				
Sequelae of Segregation				
Family Stress Index	−0.002**	0.0006	—	—
Cognitive Skills (SAT) (00)	0.002	0.002	—	—
Affirmative Action				
Institutional	—	—	−0.003	0.004
Control Variable				
Demographic Background				
Male	0.005	0.169	0.039	0.205
Foreign-Born Parent	0.211	0.196	−0.509†	0.266
Two-Parent Family	−0.037	0.165	0.094	0.214
Siblings under 18	−0.053	0.049	−0.044	0.149
Education of Parents				
No College Degrees	—	—	—	—
One College Degree	0.001	0.291	−0.057	0.406
Two College Degrees	0.018	0.311	0.409	0.332
One Advanced Degree	−0.126	0.209	0.152	0.307
Two Advanced Degrees	−0.253	0.311	0.178	0.340
Economic Status				
Home Value (000)	0.000	0.000	0.002†	0.001
Ever on Welfare	−0.089	0.173	0.040	0.335
Income > $100,000	0.078	0.146	0.062	0.190
Academic Preparation				
AP Courses Taken	0.091	0.056	−0.053	0.067
High School GPA	0.016	0.409	−1.211**	0.392
Self-rated Preparation	−0.004	0.027	0.053	0.037
Social Preparation				
Self-efficacy	−0.023	0.028	−0.004	0.045
Self-esteem	0.005	0.019	−0.003	0.023
Susceptibility to Peer Influence	−0.024	0.029	0.008	0.026
Social Distance from Whites	−0.017	0.016	−0.023	0.024
Intercept	4.549***	2.270	9.156***	2.037
R^2	0.371		0.461***	
Number of Cases	2,521		2,328	

†$p<.10$ *$p<.05$ **$p<.01$ ***$p<.001$

the end of the sophomore year. Among majors, those in the professions and "other" subjects accumulate the most credits, followed by those in math–computer science–engineering and the biological-physical sciences. The numbers of "easy" and "hard" courses taken are both associated with the accumulation of credits, which simply confirms the obvious fact that people who take more courses accumulate more credits. Having aspirations to earn a Ph.D. seems to reduce the accumulation of credits, however.

College satisfaction is only marginally influential in determining the number of course credits accumulated by sophomores ($p = .09$), and the total number of credits is not affected in any way by membership in campus or community organizations. Most of the social influences on credit accumulation are negative. Living off campus in an apartment or with family members is associated with a significantly lower rate of credit accumulation; and as one might expect, the more time respondents devote to recreational activities, the fewer credits they earn. Likewise, the greater the relative amount of debt a students assumes, the lower the number of credits compiled. Attending a first class with a higher percentage of Asians and having Asian friends are both associated with the accumulation of fewer credits as well. Although stereotype threat and affirmative action do not influence the accumulation of credits, the number of credits earned is significantly reduced by a negative racial climate and by high levels of family stress. None of the socioeconomic or demographic controls has any real influence on the number of credits earned by the end of the sophomore year.

In summary, the profile of a student on a fast track to accumulating credits for graduation is someone who takes lots of courses and has selected a major in the professions, sciences, mathematics, engineering, or some "other" field; who aspires to earn no more than a B.A., minimizes recreational time, lives on campus, and accumulates little debt; who attends classes with relatively few Asians and does not have Asian friends; and who comes from an integrated background that yields low levels of family stress.

In contrast, the profile of a student falling behind in the accumulation of credits toward graduation is someone who has not chosen a major by the end of the sophomore year or who has selected a major in the social sciences or humanities; who aspires to earn a Ph.D. or equivalent but nonetheless devotes substantial time to recreation; who lives off campus in an apartment or with relatives and hangs out with Asian friends while taking courses with relatively large shares of Asian students; who experiences significant family stress and has accumulated a relatively large amount of educational debt.

Determinants of Departure

The last analysis we perform, shown in the right-hand columns of table 9.4, predicts the likelihood, by the end of the sophomore year, of leaving the college or university in which the student enrolled as a freshman—contingent on college GPA, college satisfaction, course credits, and significant variables from table 9.2. As illustrated in figure 1.1, we follow Tinto (1993) in arguing that college attrition stems from a lack of integration on campus, social as well as academic, and our findings generally support this view. On the social side, departure from college is negatively associated with college satisfaction, peer support for social life, studying with peers, and membership in campus or community organizations. On the academic side, the likelihood of departure is reduced by a higher accumulation of course credits and having a living situation that is conducive to studying (one that does not require evasive action such as going to the library to get work done).

Academically, leaving school is also strongly predicted by grade point average, the choice of major, and aspirations for postgraduate study, but the direction of these effects is opposite what one might initially expect. Earning higher grades and picking certain majors will *increase,* rather than decrease, the odds of departure. Majors in the professions, natural sciences, math–computer sciences–engineering, and "other" fields, in particular, are associated with a *higher* likelihood of leaving school, as is the aspiration to earn a doctoral degree. Rising educational costs and greater family debt, however, seem to tie students to the institution.

These results suggest two very different kinds of school leavers. The first category includes students who are dissatisfied with their collegiate experience so far, who have accumulated relatively few credits, who find little peer support on campus, and who have joined no campus or community organizations. This group would seem to include social isolates who simply have not managed to connect with others on campus. The second category is made up of ambitious students who seek to earn a Ph.D., have maintained a high grade point average, have declared a major in science, math, or the professions, and who have not yet accumulated many credits toward completing their choices of major. This group would seem to comprise high achievers who have not yet gone very far in their academic career, whose aspirations cannot be satisfied at the institution, and who therefore seek to move elsewhere. These profiles are not mutually exclusive, of course, making the person most likely to leave someone who is both socially detached and academically disaffected, especially if the person is not very indebted financially and finds himself or herself frustrated by frequently having to leave his or her dorm room or apartment to get work done.

Managing the Collegiate Crosscurrents

At the halfway point on the river to college graduation, our results suggest that success in college arises from a complex blend of academic and social processes. Earning good grades is substantially an academic process that depends on selecting an appropriate major, choosing the right blend of easy and hard courses, making a strong academic effort, minimizing recreational time, seeking out contact with faculty, joining career development or foreign-language groups, having high academic aspirations, and having prepared in high school for the intellectual demands of an elite college education. Apart from these academic circumstances, which are at least partly under the control of students themselves, being blessed with highly educated parents through the accident of birth also confers a large scholastic advantage in the competition for grades.

Although the process of earning good grades may be fundamentally academic, the foregoing academic precursors of grade achievement may be enhanced or undermined by social circumstances on campus. All students benefit from living on campus in dormitories where friendships can form and from receiving support from close social connections. Living off campus with relatives or in a fraternity or sorority is generally associated with lower grade achievement. In addition to these universal social contingencies, however, minority students face unique social challenges to earning a high GPA. Given the prevalence of segregation in American society, minority students often have social networks that extend back into disadvantaged schools and neighborhoods with high rates of crime and social disorder, which yield high levels of family stress that undermine grade performance. Minority students also earn lower grades because of performance burdens that stem from the well-documented phenomenon of stereotype threat, burdens that are often exacerbated by the stigmatizing way institutions administer affirmative action on campus.

Although it also has academic determinants, student satisfaction with college is more a social than an academic process. Getting good grades and putting in a good academic effort are important in generating satisfaction, of course, but so is living with others in campus housing, participating in campus-based voluntary groups, joining mainstream campus organizations, and studying with peers. Satisfaction is not strongly related to choice of major, the distribution of easy and hard courses, the perceived difficulty of course work, the amount of time spent studying, interaction with faculty, or involvement in career development groups on campus. As with grades, however, minority students face special challenges to achieving satisfaction, especially if they are low income. Satisfaction is undermined by frequent problems with financial aid, by a lack of exposure to black faculty, and by having an SAT score below the institutional average and thus being a likely beneficiary of affirmative action. Satisfaction is unrelated to the absolute value of the SAT.

Earning high grades and being satisfied with one's college experience are both important in moving students down the collegiate river toward graduation. In terms of the accumulation of credits, a high college GPA is more strongly predictive than satisfaction, and the progression toward graduation on this dimension appears to be linked more strongly to academic than to social factors. The accumulation of credits is strongly associated with the selection of a major by the sophomore year, with the taking of numerous courses, both easy and hard, and with aspirations for an advanced degree. As with grades, these academic precursors may be helped or hindered by social circumstances. Living off campus in an apartment or with relatives, devoting excessive time to recreation, incurring large debts, and, somewhat surprising, having Asian friends and classmates are negatively associated with the accumulation of course credits. Once again, minority students experience special challenges, with credit accumulation being significantly undermined by the perception of a negative racial climate on campus and by family stress linked to ongoing segregation.

In terms of persistence, departure from a college or university appears to reflect a relatively balanced combination of social and academic processes. Socially, the likelihood of departure is lowered by high levels of student satisfaction, by involvement in campus and community organizations, by the perception of strong peer support for social life, and by the presence of black classmates. Academically, the odds of departure are reduced by the accumulation of course credits, the selection of a major by the sophomore year, especially in science, engineering, or the professions, and a living situation that is conducive to studying at home. Ironically the likelihood of departure is increased by aspiring to a doctoral degree and earning high grades, but this pattern is presumably less about dropping out and more about moving to improved academic circumstances. Fortunately, the various minority-specific processes that undermine grade performance, satisfaction, and credit accumulation do not appear to play a significant role in leaving school. We found no evidence that persistence through the sophomore year was in any way influenced by racial undercurrents, segregation, stereotype threat, or affirmative action.

The foregoing results suggest the existence of two parallel processes at work among students attending selective colleges and universities in the United States: a mostly *social process of persistence* by which students derive satisfaction and become attached to the institution, and a mostly *academic process of achievement* whereby students earn good grades and steadily accumulate course credits. Both are obviously important in considering a student's academic success. Staying in school is essential, since unless one is enrolled one cannot accumulate the course credits required for graduation. Getting good grades is also important, not only because failing courses precludes the accumulation of needed credits, but also because high grades are important to students who aspire to graduate or professional education after college—and a majority of students in all groups expect to go on for either a master's, a Ph.D., or some professional degree after completing their undergraduate work.

The twin outcomes of persistence and achievement stem from very different processes with only partly overlapping sets of determinants. Persistence depends more on a student's individual satisfaction and social integration and less on academic matters. Indeed, academic achievement may at times necessitate that a student leave the institution in question. As we have seen, those earning higher grades, selecting certain scientific and technical majors, and aspiring to advanced degrees are more likely than others to depart. Good grades, in contrast, depend less on social integration and more on how academic preparation and social background interact with a particular institutional environment to encourage or discourage academic effort. Since the causes of leaving school and academic underperformance are so different, the policies necessary to address them should also be distinct.

First and foremost, student retention should be seen as more a social than an academic issue, one that reflects two interconnected and mutually reinforcing components: satisfaction and integration. Satisfaction stems from engagement, which is partly a matter of temperament and personality, of course. Students who are self-confident, comfortable with themselves, independent, and hardworking tend to be engaged and satisfied with college; and given the fact that temperament varies by gender, it is also true that, other things equal, males are more satisfied than females.

There is probably not much college officials can do to influence the personality of 18-year-olds; and sex change operations are not recommended to address female dissatisfaction. College officials *can* pay attention to personality characteristics in the admissions process, however, to select students with personalities and temperaments predictive of engagement; and they *can* be sensitive to the fact that female students will be at higher risk of dissatisfaction than their male counterparts and do more to encourage female engagement. Indeed, persistence can be enhanced for both males and females by the creation of institutionalized opportunities for engagement. Our results show that students who live in dorms or apartments with roommates, study with friends, and participate in student organizations are more satisfied. Putting students in anonymous high-rise dormitories, assigning them to single-person units, and cutting back on campus organizational activities thus contribute to isolation and alienation, which lead to dissatisfaction and leaving school.

Building a system of college houses that interweave living, learning, and teaching to foster community; creating theme dorms around common social or academic interests; supporting intramural team sports; and encouraging team projects as a regular part of the curriculum will foster engagement to lower the risk of leaving school. Finally, offering a welcoming environment on campus for religious organizations is more than about being tolerant and open-minded; it is also a practical way to foster engagement and raise rates of student retention. Encouraging clubs and programs of special interest to women would be a simple way of compensating for their greater risk of disaffection.

Race and ethnicity inevitably come into play when considering student satisfaction. Minority students who perceive a large social distance between themselves and whites are more prone to dissatisfaction, and although a negative racial climate on campus has a strong effect on the satisfaction on all students, it is especially relevant for groups that have historically been excluded from elite settings. It is thus critically important that institutions maintain an atmosphere of tolerance, acceptance, respect, and appreciation for diversity when it comes to race and ethnicity. Doing so is not about being "politically correct" but about enhancing students' connection to the institution and the learning it dispenses, which is something of great benefit to whites as well as Asians, Latinos, and African Americans.

Institutions also need to be careful in how they implement affirmative action programs and how they publicly frame their taking into account of racial and ethnic criteria in the admissions process. Our results show that students who are likely beneficiaries of affirmative action are less satisfied with college than others and that those attending schools that practice more extensive affirmative action earn lower grades. These effects likely reflect the inadvertent creation of stigma by college officials. Institutional efforts to maintain racial and ethnic diversity among students should never be presented as involving a lowering of the bar, a bending of rules, a making of exceptions, or a loosening of standards to accommodate students who are somehow lacking, deficient, or challenged on some important dimension.

Administrators at selective colleges and universities should take a cue from the other two affirmative action programs they currently run—for the children of alumni and for people with athletic talent—and present minority affirmative action in an equally positive and affirmative light. With respect to admissions, institutions should present themselves as looking for manifestations of excellence and achievement in a variety of domains, of which test-taking ability is just one, and a narrow one at that. Framed in this way, each student is presumed to be outstanding and accomplished in some important way, giving faculty the right to expect great things rather than anticipating deficiencies.

Although student retention is partly about satisfaction, and satisfaction stems from social engagement, staying in school is also about social integration in ways that are independent of those involved in promoting satisfaction. Integration is about participating in specific groups and organizations on campus. What the group does or stands for is less important than the fact that it exists for students to join. As far as we can tell, being a member of just about *any* campus organization increases the odds of satisfaction and lowers the odds of leaving school. When institutions provide resources, facilities, and moral support for student-run organizations, in a very real and direct way they are acting to promote student retention and to reduce the dropout rate. The policy of universities should therefore be to encourage the formation of whatever groups and organizations students are interested in, as long as their goals and purpose are consistent with the principles of tolerance, openness, civility, and mutual respect that constitute the foundations of intellectual freedom on campus.

The one note of caution in the blanket call for support of student organizations concerns fraternities and sororities, which offer something of a double-edged sword for academic achievement and integration. Like other collective organizations, they act strongly to increase satisfaction and reduce the odds of leaving school. But unlike other organizations, fraternities and sororities also appear to have a downside, for in addition to increasing the odds of leaving school, we found that actually *living in* a Greek house also reduces both satisfaction and grade attainment. Moreover, to the extent that fraternities and sororities provide venues for parties and other recreational activities, they constitute a repository for students' time that not only detracts from that spent studying but also itself has an independent negative effect on grade achievement. Although the Greek system may provide fellowship that lowers dropout rates, if left to run amok it can also promote low academic achievement and undermine student satisfaction.

Earning good grades involves a complex interplay of factors that go well beyond satisfaction and integration. To a large extent, of course, grade achievement depends very strongly on social and academic preparation, as well as family background, things over which the institution has no control once the admissions decision has been made. The higher the grades earned in high school, the more students feel prepared for college-level work, the better their scores on the SAT, and the higher their aspirations for earning academic degrees, the better their grades in college. Moreover, the higher their self-esteem and the more they care about how others perceive them, the better they do academically as college freshmen and sophomores. Even holding these indicators of social and academic preparation constant, moreover, the greater the education of their parents, the better students' grades in college. As the number of degrees held by a student's mother and father increases, so does grade performance. There is clearly something—probably many things—about growing up in a household with well-educated parents that promotes learning later in life.

Once a student's educational background is held constant, economic factors do not play a central role in conditioning academic achievement. Far more important is how background and preparation interact with the institutional setting to influence grades. At one level, this interaction is fairly straightforward. Grades depend fundamentally on the academic choices students make from among the array of options at institution: when to declare a major, which major to declare, how many easy versus hard courses to take, how much effort to expend in academic pursuits, how much time to spend studying versus partying, how much contact to seek with faculty, and so on. In general, students who earn high grades are those who put in a lot of academic effort, devote a lot of time to schoolwork, decide early on a major, pick a major in the professions, sciences, or engineering, and who interact with professors.

These results seem quite obvious, and to improve academic outcomes the logical actions for universities would be to reduce student-faculty ratios, create opportunities for student-faculty interaction, and provide students with sufficient guidance and appropriate academic advising so that they choose majors suitable to their interests and abilities. Such recommendations hardly constitute rocket science. But owing to the structural organization of American society with respect to race, class, and ethnicity, student choices and academic outcomes play out in unique and distinctive ways for black and Latino students. As we have shown, social undercurrents—the ongoing effects of segregation, stereotype threat, and even affirmative action—come into play in subtle ways that strongly condition minority students' grade achievement.

Although many Americans would like to believe the United States has become a "race-blind" society, our results suggest otherwise. Patterns of personal association are highly structured along racial lines, whether we consider patterns of friendship, dating, partnering, or organizational participation. Given the numerical dominance of whites on most campuses, we would expect extensive association with whites on the part of Asians, Latinos, and African Americans in the absence of social mechanisms that specifically promote homogamy, and this is generally what we find for Asians and Latinos, but not for African Americans. Given their small numbers on most college campuses, the high degree of racial homogeneity in friendship, dating, partnering, and organizational participation among blacks provides strong evidence that highly racialized social mechanisms are indeed extant on the campuses of selective colleges and universities.

We provided evidence that one such mechanism—social sanctioning—is more common than many would care to admit and that it is very much a two-way street, with whites and blacks both policing a campus color line. Nearly half of all black men reported being harassed by black friends or acquaintances for crossing that line with a date or romantic partner, whereas 42% reported negative reactions from black strangers and 39% from strangers in their partner's group. Although the friends of black women are somewhat more accepting of out-group dating than those of their male counterparts, nearly half of the female African American respondents reported harassment from black strangers for having an interracial relationship, and 43% reported harassment from strangers in their partner's group.

These reports clearly indicate the existence of a racialized social environment on campus, a conclusion that is confirmed by other reports. In general, this racialization stems from the actions of the students themselves rather than faculty or other authorities. Very few African Americans said they had been made to feel uncomfortable by faculty or been discouraged by professors because of race, and the frequency with which black students were stopped and asked for identification by campus police was no different than that reported by whites and Latinos. However, nearly a third said they had been made to feel self-conscious because of their race by classmates, and nearly a quarter reported hearing derogatory remarks from other students.

These findings point to the fact that even in the post–civil rights era, when formal racial barriers and overt discrimination have largely been eliminated from institutional settings such as colleges and universities, African American students are nonetheless required to perform academically in a highly charged, very racialized social context. We have already noted that the perception of a negative racial environment has a strong, direct, and very adverse effect on student satisfaction and in this way contributes higher rates of leaving school.

We also found that the racialized environment on campus influences academic achievement indirectly through the process of stereotype threat. Specifically, whenever black students are called on to perform academically, they see themselves as being at risk of confirming the negative stereotype of black intellectual inferiority. To the extent they believe that the perceptions of white students and professors are influenced by this racist canard, they experience a psychological performance burden that other students never face. They feel it is not just themselves who are being judged intellectually but the entire group, and this extra psychological pressure undermines grade achievement. To the extent that they have internalized negative stereotypes about their group—integrating them into their social cognition at some level—they solve the internal conflict by disidentifying with education as a domain of self-worth, which is manifested behaviorally by reduced effort and study time, which then translates into lower grades.

Ironically, the negative effect of stereotype threat can be heightened by a program that is intended to benefit underrepresented minorities. Affirmative action, at least as currently framed and administered at selective colleges and universities, appears to exacerbate stereotype threat and confer on black students a social stigma that contributes to lower academic performance. Individuals who are likely to have benefited from affirmative action experience a higher performance burden than others, and minorities at institutions where affirmative action is more extensively practiced earn lower grades. We therefore underscore the importance of framing the use of race-sensitive criteria in admissions not as a lowering of standards to compensate for student deficits but rather as an effort to attract students who are talented across a variety of domains.

Unfortunately, the actions of many universities to provide remedial or compensatory supports for minority students achieve precisely the opposite result, signaling to students and faculty on campus that something important is indeed lacking among African American and Latino students. As discussed in chapter 7, institutional interventions must be "wise" if they are to be successful. We found that students making use of remedial classes, special compensatory courses, and academic tutors actually do worse than other students. Likewise, Steele et al. (2009) found that black students given "remedial" instruction actually did worse than those who experienced no intervention at all. A wise intervention is one that challenges students, communicates expectations of achievement and success, and labels students as promising and exceptional rather than deficient.

A serious problem with many remedial programs is that too often they are extended to students on the basis of race and ethnicity, ignoring differences in class and family background as well as differences in the degree of academic preparation. A key finding in *The Source of the River* was that the black and Latino student populations are extremely diverse. When a professor, administrator, or counselor interacts with someone of African origin, it is a serious and damaging error to immediately assume he or she comes from a poor, inner-city background and attended a disadvantaged public school. At selective colleges and universities, especially, this assumption will be incorrect in a majority of cases. Black and Latino students should not be sent into special immersion or remedial training programs simply because they are black or Latino. Doing so only stigmatizes well-prepared students from well-educated families and exacerbates the performance burden that all minority students must confront because of stereotype threat.

A key factor structuring the diversity of black and Latino students is segregation. Because high levels of segregation continue to characterize American schools and neighborhoods, significant numbers of minority students have grown up in a segregated social world, and most will have friends and family members that inhabit segregated neighborhoods. This fundamental fact, which is built into the very fabric of American society and has prevailed for more than a century, has significant implications for minority students even after they have decamped to the safe and privileged confines of a prestigious and highly selective college or university.

Because the social networks of most black and Latino students extend back into segregated ghettos and barrios, and given the elevated rates of social disorder and violence that characterize those settings, negative events are much more likely to happen to the friends and relatives of African Americans and Latinos than to those of whites and Asians. As a result, all minority students, but especially those from a segregated background, end up devoting more time, energy, and resources than others to family issues. Although students make their own decisions about how much time and how many resources to devote to various activities, these choices are always constrained, and because of the continuing reality of segregation in the United States, they are constrained for black and Latino students in ways that rarely occur for whites and Asians. Black and Latino students are generally under greater time pressure than other students, and they are frequently called on to deal with social stresses that other students hardly ever face.

Segregation also has long-term implications for academic performance because of how it shapes human cognition. The human brain is a remarkably plastic and malleable organ that is very sensitive to the social environment it experiences, especially during critical phases of cognitive growth and development before age 18. Growing up in a racially isolated social world characterized by high levels of disorder and violence inevitably leaves a mark on development, shaping cognition in distinctive ways that affect academic performance years later. We have shown how the sociolinguistic isolation that accompanies segregation, and the violence and disorder that accompany the concentration of poverty experienced by children while growing up, significantly lower performance on the SAT test at age 18, and that the resulting test score gap translates into lower grades. It is not because black students are genetically less intelligent that their scores are lower, but because a large fraction of them came of age in a disadvantaged social environment that most white Americans never have to face.

Again, there is not much a college or university can do to change the cognitive adaptations of people who grew up under conditions of intense segregation. Although lower SAT scores are indeed associated, on average, with lower grades, there are many paths to learning, and many other factors in these students' backgrounds that predict high grade achievement. The task is to harness those talents and abilities and to communicate to students that intelligence is not a fixed quantity that one carries for life, but a resource that can be built incrementally through individual initiative, effort, and hard work.

Although selective colleges and universities are in many ways oases of freedom, equality, and tolerance in a social world still characterized by prejudice, ignorance, and inequality, they are still a part of American society and are not immune from the forces of racial and ethnic stratification that continue to bedevil it. Selective colleges and universities may not be able to end racial segregation, halt discrimination, or eliminate prejudice all by themselves; but because they are always training the next generation of social, economic, and political leaders, they are in a better position than most institutions to make a good start.

Appendix A
Questionnaire Used in Spring of Freshman Year

Survey of College Life and Experience: Second Wave Instrument

Courses and Grades

Thank you for agreeing to speak with us again. When we first spoke with you last Fall we asked a lot of questions about how you grew up—your family background, the neighborhoods where you lived, and the schools you attended. This interview will be much shorter and will focus on your experiences since coming to college. To begin with, I'd like to ask about your course work and grades so far.

1. Is (Student's University) on a quarter or semester system?

   Quarter _____ Semester _____

2. About what was the date that classes began at (Student's University)?

   Date __________

3. About what date did classes end?

   Date __________

4. At the beginning of Fall term, how many courses did you register for? Include each course in which you originally registered, even if you later dropped it.

   Number of courses _____

5. Could you please tell me the department, number, and title for each course you registered in last Fall? In each case, please indicate whether you eventually dropped it, and if you completed it what your final grade was.

Department	Number	Title	Dropped?	Grade
1.				
2.				
3.				
4.				
5.				
6.				

6. *Quarter System Only:* At the beginning of Winter term, how many courses did you register for? Include each course in which you originally registered, even if you later dropped it.

   Number of courses: _____

7. *Quarter System Only:* Could you please tell me the department, number, and title of each course you registered in during Winter term? In each case, please indicate whether you eventually dropped it, and if you completed it what your final grade was.

Department	Number	Title	Dropped?	Grade
1.				
2.				
3.				
4.				
5.				
6.				

8. At the beginning of Spring term, how many courses did you register for? Include each course in which you originally registered, even if you later dropped it.

   Number of courses _____

9. Could you please tell me the department, number, and title for each course you registered in last Fall? In each case, please indicate whether you are still registered and what grade you expect to earn.

Department	Number	Title	Still Registered?	Expected Grade
1.				
2.				
3.				
4.				
5.				
6.				

10. Have you declared a major yet?

    If yes, what major? ______________________

Living Arrangements

11. In which of the following do you presently live:

    On campus dormitory?

    On campus apartment?

    Off campus apartment?

    Fraternity or sorority?

    Off campus house?

    With parents or other relative?

    Other _______________

12. With how many others do you share your dorm, apartment, or house?
13. Do you have a separate bedroom?
14. Do you share a bathroom with others?
15. Is there someplace in your dorm, apartment, or house where you can be alone to read or study?
16. In the dorm, apartment, or house where you now live, indicate on a scale of 0 to 10 how often the following things have occurred, where

0 indicates they never happened and 10 indicate they happened virtually every day:

	Never 0	Every day 10
I was trying to study but was distracted by talking or conversation		
I was trying to study but was distracted by someone playing a stereo		
I was trying to study but was distracted by someone watching TV		
I was trying to study but was distracted by friends partying		
I was trying to study but friends talked me into going out		
I had to leave home to get my schoolwork done		
I stayed late at the library to avoid going home		
I felt lonely and homesick		
I felt like I just wanted to get away from campus for a while		

17. During the Fall term, how many times did you visit your mother or father?

    How many total days did you spend away from campus on these visits?

18. About how much do you pay a month to live in your dorm, apartment, or house?

19. About how much does it cost you each month to eat regular daily meals?

Work, Study, and Social Habits

20. I want you to think back to the most recent Tuesday on which school was in session. Beginning at the time you awakened, could you please tell me what you did during each hour of the day until you retired for the night. On that Tuesday, what time did you awake? At what time did you retire for the evening to go to sleep?

    Exact Time Awakened _X_ Exact Time Went to Bed _Y_

For simplicity, let's classify your activities into a few general categories:

Grooming

Eating

Sleeping

Attending class

Playing sports

Studying

Working for pay

Socializing

Relaxing

Doing volunteer work

Other

Beginning at (next whole hour from X), take me through that most recent Tuesday when school was in session and account for your time. During the first hour, from X to X + 1, were you mostly grooming yourself, eating, sleeping, attending class, studying, socializing, or relaxing?

How about from X + 1 to X + 2? What was your principal activity then?

Continue hour by hour from X + 2 to Y.

21. Now I want you to consider the last week, from Monday through Friday, on which classes were held at (Student's University). Could you please estimate the total number of hours that you spent:

Attending class or lab?

Studying?

Doing extracurricular activities?

Watching television?

Listening to music?

Working for pay?

Doing volunteer work in community?

Playing or practicing sports?

Attending a sporting event?

Attending parties?

Socializing with friends (besides at parties)?

Sleeping?

Other ____________________

22. Now, let's think about the most recent weekend between two weeks when classes were being held and you were on campus. Beginning on Saturday morning and continuing through Sunday night, about how many hours did you spend:

Attending class or lab?

Studying?

Doing extracurricular activities?

Watching television?

Listening to music?

Working for pay?

Doing volunteer work in community?

Playing or practicing sports?

Attending a sporting event?

Attending parties?

Socializing with friends (besides at parties)?

Sleeping?

Other ______________

23. On a scale of 0 to 10, where 0 indicates you never engage in a behavior and 10 indicates you always do it, please indicate the frequency with which you:

	Never 0	Always 10
Ask professors questions in class		
Raise your hand during a lecture when you don't understand something		
Approach professors after class to ask a question		

Meet with professors in their offices to ask about material you don't understand

Meet with professors in their offices to talk about other matters

Study in library

Look for a book or article in the library

Use campus computer lab

Use the Internet for course-related research

Study with other students

Study by yourself

Organize study groups with friends or classmates

Seek help from a formal tutor

Use services available for disabled students

Seek help from a friend or classmate

Take special instruction to improve writing skills

Take special instruction to improve reading skills

Take special instruction to improve mathematical skills

Take special instruction to improve test-taking skills

Take special instruction to improve study skills

Used the college career placement service

Visit an academic adviser to discuss your progress

Speak to a financial aid counselor about money matters

Visit the student health clinic about a physical problem

Visit a counselor about a psychological issue

Interfering Problems

25. Lots of things may happen in families to affect young people. In the last two years, have any of the following happened within your family? (Mark All That Apply)

My parent or guardian moved to a new home

One of my parents got married or remarried

My parents got divorced or separated

A parent lost a job (which one?)

A parent started a new job (which one?)

I became seriously ill or disabled

An unmarried sister got pregnant

A brother or sister dropped out of school

A parent went on public assistance

Another member of my immediate family went on public assistance

A member of my immediate family used illegal drugs

A member of my immediate family spent time in a drug/alcohol rehabilitation program

A member of my immediate family was the victim of crime

A member of my immediate family got into trouble with the law

A member of my immediate family became seriously ill or disabled

A member of my immediate family became homeless for a period of time

A parent died (which one?)

Another close relative died

Financial Matters

26. About how much money do you think you will need to attend college this academic year, including tuition, academic fees, room and board, and your daily expenses for living and entertainment?

    Amount Needed __________

27. Of this total amount, how much will be funded from each of the following sources?

    Parental contributions:

    Contributions from other family members:

    Grant or fellowship from university:

Grant or fellowship from other funding agency:

Student loan:

Personal savings:

Earnings from work/study job:

Earnings from other work:

Other source:

28. At any time during the current academic year have you held a job on which you worked for pay?

    a. If yes: Since the day that classes began last Fall, about how many weeks have your worked in total?

    b. If yes: During that time, about how many hours per week did you work, on average?

    c. If yes: How much do you earn per hour working at your job?

    d. If yes: What kind of work did you do for pay on your most recent job (Interviewer codes into categories)?

       Fast food worker

       Waiter or waitress

       Store clerk, salesperson

       Office or clerical worker

       Library worker

       Babysitting or child care

       Hospital or health worker

       Other

    e. If yes: Are you required to work as part of your school's financial aid package?

    f. If yes: Apart from financial aid requirements, do *you* feel it is necessary to work to finance your college education?

29. Other than birthday or holiday gifts, have you received any money from family members since you have been at college?

    If yes: Amount? From whom?

    ______ ________

    ______ ________

    ______ ________

    ______ ________

30. Other than birthday or holiday gifts, have you *sent* any money to family members since you have been at college?

    If yes: Amount? To whom?

    ______ ________

    ______ ________

    ______ ________

    ______ ________

31. Do you have access to a credit card that you can use while you are at college?

    If yes: About how much, in total, did you charge during the past 30 days?

    If yes: Who typically makes payments on your credit card bills?

    Respondent ______

    Parent(s) ______

    Other family member: ______

    Other person ______

Respondent's Attitudes toward College

32. On a scale of 0 to 10, where 0 indicates total disagreement and 10 indicates complete agreement, how much do you agree or disagree with each of the following statements about college?

	Total Disagreement 0	Total Agreement 10
I am doing less well in college than I would like.		

I am having problems with my financial aid.

I am having problems at home with a family member.

I have too little time to do schoolwork.

I have too little time to do things at home or in the community.

My high school prepared me well for college work.

I am afraid of failing out of college.

33. Using the same scale, how much do you agree or disagree with the following statements?

	Total Disagreement 0	Total Agreement 10
My test scores in class are an accurate indicator of my academic abilities.		
My course grades are an accurate indicator of my academic abilities.		
If I am having trouble with course material, other students probably are as well.		
If I let my instructors know that I am having difficulty in class, they will think less of me.		
If I let other students know that I am having difficulty in class, they will think less of me.		
If instructors hold negative stereotypes about certain groups, it will not affect their evaluations of individual students from that group.		
If other students hold negative stereotypes about certain groups, it will not affect their evaluations of individual students from that group.		
If I excel academically, it reflects positively on my racial or ethnic group.		
If do poorly academically, it reflects negatively on my racial or ethnic group.		

34. On a scale of 0 to 10, where 0 indicates no effort at all and 10 indicates the maximum possible effort, how hard would you say you have been trying during this past year of college?

    Effort rating ______

35. Measuring the degree of difficulty on a scale of 0 to 10, where 0 is not difficult at all and 10 is extremely difficult, how hard were each of the following subjects for you?

	Not Difficult at All 0	Extremely Difficult 10
English		
History		
Mathematics		
Natural Sciences		
Social Studies		
Foreign Languages		

36. In thinking about how hard to try in your college studies, how important for you is each of the following considerations? Use a scale of 0 to 10, where 0 indicates no importance whatsoever and 10 indicates the utmost importance.

	Completely Unimportant 0	Extremely Important 10
I want to make my parents proud of me.		
I don't want to embarrass my family.		
My family is making sacrifices for my education.		
I want to learn the material.		
I need the grades to get into graduate/ professional school.		
Graduating from college will help me get a job.		
I want to keep up with my friends.		
My teachers expect me to do well.		
My teachers encourage me to work hard.		

I don't want to look foolish or stupid in class.

If I don't do well, people will look down on others like me.

Attitudes of Parents and Peers

37. Once again using a scale of importance that goes from 0 to 10, how important is it to your *parents* (or guardian) that you:

	Completely Unimportant 0	Extremely Important 10
Attend (Student's College)?		
Work hard in college?		
Get good grades in college?		
Graduate from college?		
Play sports in college?		
Go on to graduate or professional school?		
Study something "practical"?		
Study whatever interests me?		

38. Considering the views of your friends and close acquaintances here at (Student's College), how important is it to them to:

	Completely Unimportant 0	Extremely Important 10
Attend classes regularly?		
Study hard?		
Play sports?		
Get good grades?		
Be popular/well-liked by students?		
Graduate from college?		
Have a steady boyfriend/girlfriend?		
Spend time with friends just "hanging out"?		
Be willing to party, get wild?		

Go on to graduate or professional school?

Participate in religious activities?

Be happy and personally satisfied?

Do community work or volunteer?

Have a part time job to pay for school?

Study something "practical"?

Study something interesting and creative?

Perceptions of Prejudice

39. In your college classes, have other students ever made you feel uncomfortable or self-conscious because of your race or ethnicity?

    If yes: How often? Rarely, Sometimes, Often, or Very Often?

40. In your college classes, have any of your professors ever made you feel uncomfortable or self-conscious because of your race or ethnicity?

    If yes: How often? Rarely, Sometimes, Often, or Very Often?

41. Walking around campus, have you ever been made to feel uncomfortable or self-conscious because of your race or ethnicity?

    If yes: How often? Rarely, Sometimes, Often, or Very Often?

42. Have the campus police ever asked you to present identification?

    If yes: How often? Rarely, Sometimes, Often, or Very Often?

    If yes: Did you feel the requests were justified? Yes / No

43. Have you ever heard derogatory remarks made about your racial or ethnic group by fellow students?

    If yes: How often? Rarely, Sometimes, Often, or Very Often?

44. Have you ever heard derogatory remarks made about your racial or ethnic group by professors?

    If yes: How often? Rarely, Sometimes, Often, or Very Often?

45. Have you ever heard derogatory remarks made about your racial or ethnic group by other college staff?

    If yes: How often? Rarely, Sometimes, Often, or Very Often?

46. Have you ever experienced any other form of harassment on campus simply because of your race or ethnicity?

    If yes: How often? Rarely, Sometimes, Often, or Very Often?

47. Have you ever experienced harassment from members of your own racial or ethnic group because you interacted or associated with members of some other group?

    If yes: How often? Rarely, Sometimes, Often, or Very Often?

48. Have you ever felt you were given a bad grade by a professor because of your race or ethnicity?

    If yes: How often? Rarely, Sometimes, Often, or Very Often?

49. Have you ever felt you were discouraged by a professor from speaking out in class because of your race or ethnicity?

    If yes: How often? Rarely, Sometimes, Often, or Very Often?

50. Have you ever been discouraged from a course of study by your adviser or professor?

    If yes: How often? Rarely, Sometimes, Often, or Very Often?

51. In the courses you have taken so far this year, how many of your professors have been:

    Female?

    Black?

    Hispanic?

    Asian?

52. Thinking back to the very first class you attended at (College or University), roughly what percentage of the students were:

    Female?

    Black?

    Hispanic?

    Asian?

53. Considering the 10 closest friends you have made since coming to college, how many are:

    Female?

    White?

    Black?

    Hispanic?

    Asian?

Romantic Relationships

54. Since the beginning of the Fall term have you had any steady romantic relationships?

    If yes: How many steady relationships have you had?

    For each relationship: Is this someone you met at college, someone you knew from before, or someone you met off campus?

55. Since the beginning of the Fall term have you engaged in sexual intercourse?

56. Have you ever shared a household with anyone as part of a romantic relationship?

    If yes: Are you currently living with someone?

    If yes: What is the duration of time you lived with this person, in months?

57. Have you ever dated anyone from a racial or ethnic group different from your own?

    If yes, what other group members have you dated?

    Whites?

    Blacks?

    Hispanics?

    Asians?

58. Have you ever been married?

    If yes: Are you currently married?

    If yes: How long have you been married?

59. For women: Have you ever given birth to any children?

    For men: Have you ever fathered any children?

    If yes: How many children have you borne?

    If yes: Have you given any of these children up for adoption?

    If yes: How many children currently live with you?

    If yes: Who has legal custody of your child(ren)?

60. If respondent reports children living with him/her:

    On Monday through Friday, how many hours per day do you typically spend caring for your child(ren)?

    On a typical weekend, how many hours per day do you spend caring for your child(ren)?

    In a typical month, how many school days do you miss because of child care duties?

    How often do child care responsibilities interfere with studying? Never, Sometimes, Frequently, or Very Frequently?

Appendix B
Questionnaire Used in Spring of Sophomore Year

National Longitudinal Survey of Freshmen: Third Wave Instrument

Thank you for agreeing to speak with us again. When we first interviewed you last Fall we asked a lot of questions about how you grew up—your family background, the neighborhoods where you lived, and the schools you attended. During the telephone re-interview we did last Spring we asked about your social and academic experiences as a college freshman. Now we'd like to catch up on your life since we last talked to you. As with the interview last Spring, this conversation will be much shorter than the original Fall survey. Naturally, you are free to stop the interview at any time and can refuse to answer any question. May I proceed? Then let's start with the basics.

1. Are you still enrolled as a student (full- or part-time) at (*name of college or university*)?

   No (Answer Questions 2–6)

   Yes (Go to Question 7)

For Respondents Not Currently Enrolled at Same Institution

2. How important were the following factors in your deciding to leave (*college or university*)? Very unimportant, somewhat unimportant, somewhat important, or very important?

   High cost of education

   Too much debt

   Poor grades

Courses too difficult

Not enough course credits

Poor teaching

Classes too large

Lack of interest

Lack of effort

Lack of friends

Didn't fit in

Family unsupportive

Friends unsupportive

Family responsibilities

Campus racial/ethnic climate

3. Could you please tell me the department, number, title, and grade for each course you took during your last completed term at (*name of college or university*)? List term: Fall 1999, Winter 2000, or Spring 2000.

Department	Number	Title	Final Grade
1.			
2.			
3.			
4.			
5.			
6.			

4. Are you currently enrolled in another college or university?

   Yes (specify) ______________________________ Go to Question 7

5. What is the likelihood that you will re-enroll at some college or university in the next two years?

   Very Unlikely

   Somewhat Unlikely

Somewhat Likely

Very Likely

6. Are you currently working at a paid job?

No (Skip to 75)

Yes:

a. What is your current job? ____________________

b. What is your hourly wage? ____________________

c. How many hours per week? ____________________

Academic Progress at Current Institution

7. During your final term as a freshman last year, how many courses did you register for? Include each course in which you originally registered, even if you later dropped it.

Number of courses ____

8. Could you please tell me the department, number, and title for each course in which you registered during that term? In each case, please indicate whether you eventually dropped it, and if you completed it what your final grade was.

Department	Number	Title	Dropped?	Grade
1.				
2.				
3.				
4.				
5.				
6.				

9. Is (*current college or university*) on a quarter or semester system?

Quarter ___ Semester ___

10. About what was the date that classes began at (*college or university*) in the Fall of 2000?

Date __________

11. At the beginning of Fall term 2000, how many courses did you register for? Include each course in which you originally registered, even if you later dropped it.

    Number of courses _____

12. Could you please tell me the department, number, and title for each course you registered in last Fall? In each case, please indicate whether you eventually dropped it, and if you completed it what your final grade was.

Department	Number	Title	Dropped?	Grade
1.				
2.				
3.				
4.				
5.				
6.				

13. *Quarter System Only:* At the beginning of Winter term, how many courses did you register for? Include each course in which you originally registered, even if you later dropped it.

    Number of courses _____

14. *Quarter System Only:* Could you please tell me the department, number, and title of each course you registered in during Winter term? In each case, please indicate whether you eventually dropped it, and if you completed it what your final grade was.

Department	Number	Title	Dropped?	Grade
1.				
2.				
3.				
4.				
5.				
6.				

15. At the beginning of Spring term, how many courses did you register for? Include each course in which you originally registered, even if you later dropped it.

    Number of courses _____

16. Could you please tell me the department, number, and title for each course you registered in last Fall? In each case, please indicate whether you are still registered and what grade you expect to earn.

Department	Number	Title	Still Registered?	Expected Grade
1.				
2.				
3.				
4.				
5.				
6.				

17. Have you declared a major yet?

    If yes, what major? ______________________

18. At this point in your college career, what is the highest degree you expect to obtain?

    Less Than BA or BS

    BA or BS

    MA or Equivalent (MBA, MPH, MSW, etc.)

    Ph.D., MD, LLD, or Equivalent

19. When you were applying to college or university, how many applications did you send out?

20. To how many schools were you admitted as a freshman?

21. In terms of your preferences, what rank was (*name of college or university*) among those to which you applied?

22. How confident are you that you made the right choice in coming to (*name of college or university*)? Not at all confident, somewhat unconfident, somewhat confident, or very confident?

23. How important is it for you to graduate from (*name of college or university*)? Very unimportant, somewhat unimportant, neither important nor unimportant, somewhat important, or very important?

24. How satisfied are you with your intellectual development since enrolling in (*name of college or university*)? Very dissatisfied, somewhat dissatisfied, neither satisfied nor dissatisfied, somewhat satisfied, very satisfied?

25. How satisfied are you with your social life since enrolling in (*name of college or university*)? Very dissatisfied, somewhat dissatisfied, neither satisfied nor dissatisfied, somewhat satisfied, very satisfied?

26. Considering everything, how would your rate your experience so far at (*name of college or university*)? Extremely negative, very negative, somewhat negative, neither positive nor negative, somewhat positive, very positive, or extremely positive?

27. Did you take the SAT or the ACT test when you were applying to colleges and universities for your freshman year?

    If SAT: Do you happen to recall the verbal score? ___
    The quantitative score? ___

    IF ACT: Do you happen to recall the composite score? _____

Living Arrangements

28. In which of the following do you presently live:

    On campus dormitory?

    On campus apartment?

    Off campus apartment?

    Fraternity or sorority?

    Off campus house?

    With parents or other relative?

    Other ______________

29. Do you presently live in a "theme" dorm or apartment, such as one devoted to a foreign language or cultural orientation?

    If yes: What is the theme or orientation? _________________

30. With how many others do you share your dorm, apartment, or house?

    Total Number ____

    How many are white? ____

    How many are Asian? ____

    How many are Black?: ____

    How many are Latino? ____

31. Do you have a separate bedroom?

32. Do you share a bathroom with others?

33. Is there someplace in your dorm, apartment, or house where you can be alone to read or study?

34. In the dorm, apartment, or house where you now live, how often have the following things occurred? Never, sometimes, often, or very often?

    I was trying to study but was distracted by talking or conversation

    I was trying to study but was distracted by someone playing a stereo

    I was trying to study but was distracted by someone watching TV

    I was trying to study but was distracted by friends partying

    I was trying to study but friends talked me into going out

    I had to leave home to get my schoolwork done

    I stayed late at the library to avoid going home

    I felt lonely and homesick

    I felt like I just wanted to get away from campus for a while

35. About how much do you pay a month to live in your dorm, apartment, or house?

36. About how much does it cost you each month to eat regular daily meals?

37. Between the start of school in the Fall and the beginning of Christmas vacation, how many times did you visit your mother or father?

    How many total days did you spend away from campus on these visits?

38. Between the start of school in the Fall and the beginning of Christmas vacation, how many other trips away from campus did you take?

    How many total days did you spend on these visits?

Use of Time

39. Now I want you to consider the last week, from Monday through Friday, on which classes were held at (*college or university*). Could you please estimate the total number of hours that you spent:

    Attending class or lab?

    Studying?

    Doing extracurricular activities?

    Watching television?

    Listening to music?

    Working for pay?

    Doing volunteer work in community?

    Playing or practicing sports?

    Attending a sporting event?

    Attending parties?

    Socializing with friends (besides at parties)?

    Sleeping?

    Other ____________________

40. Now, let's think about the most recent weekend between two weeks when classes were being held and you were on campus. Beginning on Saturday morning and continuing through Sunday night, about how many hours did you spend:

    Attending class or lab?

    Studying?

    Doing extracurricular activities?

    Watching television?

Listening to music?

Working for pay?

Doing volunteer work in community?

Playing or practicing sports?

Attending a sporting event?

Attending parties?

Socializing with friends (besides at parties)?

Sleeping?

Other _____________

41. How often during the most recent week of classes did you do each of the following things? Never, sometimes, often, or very often?

    Ask professors questions in class

    Raise your hand during a lecture when you don't understand something

    Approach professors after class to ask a question

    Meet with professors in their offices to ask about material you don't understand

    Meet with professors in their offices to talk about other matters

    Study in library

    Look for a book or article in the library

    Use campus computer lab

    Use the Internet for course-related research

    Study with other students

    Organize study groups with friends or classmates

    Seek help from a formal tutor

    Seek help from a friend or classmate

    Used the college career placement service

    Visit an academic adviser to discuss your progress

    Speak to a financial aid counselor about money matters

Visit the student health clinic about a physical problem

Visit a counselor about a psychological issue

Life on Campus

42. In which of the following groups are you currently involved? For those in which you are involved, which have members who are predominantly of your own ethnic or racial group?

    A varsity or junior varsity sports team?

    An intramural sports team?

    A sports club?

    A foreign language group?

    A sorority or fraternity?

    A political group?

    An environmental group?

    A career development group?

    A religious group?

    A music, arts, or theater group?

    Other voluntary group?

43. How much do you agree or disagree with each of the following statements about college? Do you strongly disagree, disagree somewhat, neither agree nor disagree, agree somewhat, or strongly agree?

    I am doing less well in college than I would like.

    I am having problems with my financial aid.

    I am having problems at home with a family member.

    I have too little time to do schoolwork.

    I have too little time to do things at home or in the community.

    My high school prepared me well for college work.

    I am afraid of failing out of college.

44. Using the same scale, how much do you agree or disagree with the following statements? Do you strongly disagree, disagree somewhat, neither agree nor disagree, agree somewhat, or strongly agree?

    My test scores in class are an accurate indicator of my academic abilities.

    My course grades are an accurate indicator of my academic abilities.

    If I am having trouble with course material, other students probably are as well.

    If I let my instructors know that I am having difficulty in class, they will think less of me.

    If I let other students know that I am having difficulty in class, they will think less of me.

    If instructors hold negative stereotypes about certain groups, it affects their evaluations of individual students from that group.

    If other students hold negative stereotypes about certain groups, it affects their evaluations of individual students from that group.

    If I excel academically, it reflects positively on my racial or ethnic group.

    If do poorly academically, it reflects negatively on my racial or ethnic group.

45. On a scale of 0 to 10, where 0 indicates no effort at all and 10 indicates the maximum possible effort, how hard would you say you have been trying to succeed academically during the current year of college?

    Effort rating ______

46. Using the same scale, how hard were you trying in each of the following subjects for you?

    English

    History

    Mathematics

    Natural Sciences

    Social Studies

    Foreign Languages

47. In thinking about your college studies, how important for you is each of the following considerations? Very unimportant, somewhat unimportant, somewhat important, or very important?

    Graduating from college

    Making parents proud of me

    Not embarrassing my family

    Learning course material

    Getting good grades

    Getting into graduate or professional school

    Getting a good job

    Keeping up with my friends

    Meeting professors' expectations

    Not looking foolish or stupid in class

    Not having people look down on me

48. What is the level of faculty interest in students at (*name of college or university*)? Very low, somewhat low, neither low nor high, somewhat high, very high?

49. How would you rate the overall quality of the faculty you have interacted with so far? Awful, very poor, somewhat poor, neither poor nor good, somewhat good, very good, or excellent?

Social Networks

50. Please give the first names of the six people you consider to be closest to you. These are people that you talk to about things going on in your life, do things with, etc.

    Person 1 _________ Person 2 _________ Person 3 _________

    Person 4 _________ Person 5 _________ Person 6 _________

51. Do for Person 1 to Person 4

    a. What is the race/ethnicity of Person X?

    b. What is the gender of Person X?

c. How old is Person X?

d. What is Person X's relationship to you? (can list more than one)

Classmate or coworker

Friend

Teacher

Romantic partner

Family friend

Brother or sister

Parent

Spouse

Other relative

e. What is Person X's level of education?

Less than high school

High school graduate

Currently in same college or university

Currently in other college or university

College graduate

Graduate/professional degree

f. How long have you known Person X?

<1 year $= 0$

No. of years

g. How often to you interact with Person X, by telephone, email, letters, or in-person?

Daily

A few times a week

Once a week

Once a month

A few times a year

Once a year

h. How much do you go to this person for advice?

Always

Often

Sometimes

Rarely

Never

i. How much does this person accept you no matter what you do?

Always

Often

Sometimes

Rarely

Never

j. How much does this person understand what you are really like?

Always

Often

Sometimes

Rarely

Never

k. How much do you share your inner feelings with this person?

Always

Often

Sometimes

Rarely

Never

l. In what situations do you make contact with Person X (check all that apply?

Studying

On campus leisure activities

Telephone

Email

Off campus leisure activities

On campus extracurricular activities

On or off campus work

m. How supportive is Person X of your educational goals?

Very unsupportive

Somewhat unsupportive

Neither supportive nor unsupportive

Somewhat supportive

Very supportive

Interfering Problems

53. Lots of things may happen in families to affect young people. Since we interviewed you last year, have any of the following happened within your family? (Indicate All That Apply)

My parent or guardian moved to a new home

One of my parents got married or remarried

My parents got divorced or separated

A parent lost a job (which one?)

A parent started a new job (which one?)

I became seriously ill or disabled

An unmarried sister got pregnant

A brother or sister dropped out of school

A member of my immediate family went on public assistance

A member of my immediate family used illegal drugs

A member of my immediate family spent time in a drug/alcohol rehabilitation program

A member of my immediate family was the victim of crime

A member of my immediate family got into trouble with the law

A member of my immediate family became seriously ill or disabled

A member of my immediate family became homeless for a period of time

A parent died (which one?)

Another member of my immediate family died

A member of my extended family died

A friend died

Financial Matters

54. About how much money do you think you will need to attend college this academic year, including tuition, academic fees, room and board, and your daily expenses for living and entertainment?

    Tuition

    Academic fees

    Room and board

    Daily expenses

    Total needed:

55. Of this total amount, how much will be funded from each of the following sources?

    Parental contributions:

    Contributions from other family members:

    Grant or fellowship from university:

    Grant or fellowship from other funding agency:

    Student loan:

    Personal savings:

Earnings from work/study job:

Earnings from other work:

Other source:

56. At any time during the current academic year have you held a job on which you worked for pay?

    a. If yes: Since the day that classes began last Fall, about how many weeks have your worked in total?

    b. If yes: During that time, about how many hours per week did you work, on average?

    c. If yes: How much do you earn per hour working at your job?

    d. If yes: Are you required to work as part of your school's financial aid package?

    e. If yes: Apart from financial aid requirements, do *you* feel it is necessary to work to finance your college education?

57. Other than birthday or holiday gifts, have you received any money from family members since you have been at college?

    If yes: Amount? From whom?

Amount?	From whom?
______	________
______	________
______	________
______	________

58. Other than birthday or holiday gifts, have you *sent* any money to family members since you have been at college?

    If yes: Amount? To whom?

Amount?	To whom?
______	________
______	________
______	________
______	________

59. Do you have access to a credit card that you can use while you are at college?

    If yes: About how much, in total, did you charge during the past 30 days?

    If yes: Who typically makes payments on your credit card bills?

    Respondent ______

    Parent(s) ______

    Other family member ______

    Other person ______

Perceptions of Prejudice

Now I would like to ask you a few questions about your perceptions of race relations on campus during the current academic year. Since the beginning of the Fall term:

60. Have other students ever made you feel uncomfortable or self-conscious in your classes because of your race or ethnicity? Never, rarely, sometimes, often, or very often?

61. Have any of your professors ever made you feel uncomfortable or self-conscious in your classes because of your race or ethnicity? Never, rarely, sometimes, often, or very often?

62. Have you ever been made to feel uncomfortable or self-conscious walking around campus because of your race or ethnicity? Never, rarely, sometimes, often, or very often?

63. Have the campus police ever asked you to present identification? Never, rarely, sometimes, often, or very often?

64. Have you ever heard derogatory remarks made about your racial or ethnic group by fellow students? Never, rarely, sometimes, often, or very often?

65. Have you ever heard derogatory remarks made about your racial or ethnic group by professors? Never, rarely, sometimes, often, or very often?

66. Have you ever heard derogatory remarks made about your racial or ethnic group by other college staff? Never, rarely, sometimes, often, or very often?

67. Have you ever experienced harassment from members of your own racial or ethnic group because you interacted or associated with members of some other group? Never, rarely, sometimes, often, or very often?

68. Have you ever felt you were given a bad grade by a professor because of your race or ethnicity? Never, rarely, sometimes, often, or very often?

69. Have you ever felt you were discouraged by a professor from speaking out in class because of your race or ethnicity? Never, rarely, sometimes, often, or very often?

70. Have you ever been discouraged from a course of study by your adviser or professor? Never, rarely, sometimes, often, or very often?

71. In the courses you have taken so far this academic year, how many of your professors have been:

    Female?

    Black?

    Hispanic?

    Asian?

Romantic Relationships

72. Have been on any dates since the school year began?
    If yes, what other group members have you dated?

    Whites?

    Blacks?

    Hispanics?

    Asians?

    Other? Specify ______________

73. If R reports dates with a partner in another group: have you suffered negative reactions because you dated another racial or ethnic group? Never, sometimes, often, or very often?

    From friends or acquaintances in your own group?

    From family members?

    From strangers of own group?

    From strangers in partner's group?

    From other strangers?

74. Do you currently have a steady romantic partner?

    If yes, what is your partner's race or ethnicity?

    White?

    Black?

    Hispanic?

    Asian?

    Other? Specify ________________

Tracking Information

In closing, we would like to update your contact information.

75. What is your current telephone number?
76. What is the name, address, and phone number of your mother?
77. Did she attend (*name of college or university*)?
78. What is the name, address, and phone number of your father?
79. Did he attend (*name of college or univesity*)?
80. Could you please give the name and phone number of at least three other people who would always know how to contact you?

Name	Relationship	Phone Number
Person 1:		
Person 2:		
Person 3:		

81. How supportive is (Person 1) of your educational goals? Very unsupportive, somewhat unsupportive, neither supportive nor unsupportive, somewhat supportive, or very supportive?

    Person 2?

82. Finally, we would like to update the information on your family's socioeconomic status. What is your parent or guardian's household income? In thinking about household income you should include the wages and salaries of all household members, plus any self-employment income they may

have had, along with interest, dividends, alimony payments, social security, and pensions.

<$20,0000

$20,000–$24,999

$25,000–$34,999

$35,000–$49,999

$50,000–$74,999

$75,000–$99,999

$100,000–$124,999

$125,000–$149,999

$150,000–$174,999

$175,000–$199,999

>$200,000

Appendix C
Construction of Social Scales

	Minimum		Maximum
Degree of Academic Effort			
How hard respondent has been trying . . .			
During freshman year	0		10
During sophomore year	0		10
In English as sophomore	0		10
In history as sophomore	0		10
In mathematics as sophomore	0		10
In natural sciences as sophomore	0		10
In social studies as sophomore	0		10
In foreign language as sophomore	0		10
Range of scale	0		10
Cronbach's alpha		.82	
Perceived Difficulty of Courses			
How hard were each of the following subjects . . .			
English	0		10
History	0		10
Mathematics	0		10
Natural Sciences	0		10
Social Studies	0		10
Foreign Languages	0		10
Range of scale (averaged)	0		10
Cronbach's alpha		.75	

	Minimum		Maximum
Use of Institutional Services			
Frequency with which respondent . . .			
Sought help from formal tutor as freshman	0		10
Sought help from formal tutor as sophomore	0		10
Visited academic adviser as freshman	0		10
Visited academic adviser as sophomore	0		10
Used services for disabled as freshman	0		10
Took instruction to improve writing as freshman	0		10
Took instruction to improve reading as freshman	0		10
Took instruction to improve math as freshman	0		10
Took instruction to improve test taking as freshman	0		10
Took instruction to improve study skills as freshman	0		10
Used career placement service as freshman	0		10
Used career placement service as sophomore	0		10
Range of scale	0		120
Cronbach's alpha		.86	
Seeking Faculty Help			
Frequency with which respondent . . .			
Asked professors questions in class as freshman	0		10
Asked professors questions in class as sophomore	0		10
Raised hand during lecture as freshman	0		10
Raised hand during lecture as sophomore	0		10
Approached professors after class as freshman	0		10
Approached professors after class as sophomore	0		10
Met professors about course material as freshman	0		10
Met professors about course material as sophomore	0		10
Met professors about other matters as freshman	0		10
Met professors about other matters as sophomore	0		10
Range of scale	0		100
Cronbach's alpha		.86	
Reliance on Peer Support			
Frequency with which respondent . . .			
Studied with other students as freshman	0		10
Studied with other students as sophomore	0		10
Organized study groups as freshman	0		10

	Minimum		Maximum
Organized study groups as sophomore	0		10
Sought help from classmate as freshman	0		10
Sought help from classmate as sophomore	0		10
Range of scale	0		80
Cronbach's alpha		.77	

Use of Library and Laboratory

Frequency with which respondent . . .			
Studied in library as freshman	0		10
Studied in library as sophomore	0		10
Looked for material in library as freshman	0		10
Looked for material in library as sophomore	0		10
Used campus computer lab as freshman	0		10
Used campus computer lab as sophomore	0		10
Used Internet for course research as freshman	0		10
Used Internet for course research as sophomore	0		10
Range of scale	0		80
Cronbach's alpha		.63	

Frequency of Distraction

How often respondent was distracted by . . .			
Talking or conversation: freshman year	0		10
Someone playing stereo: freshman year	0		10
Someone watching TV: freshman year	0		10
Friends partying: freshman year	0		10
Talked into going out: freshman year	0		10
Talking or conversation: sophomore year	0		10
Someone playing Stereo: sophomore year	0		10
Someone watching TV: sophomore year	0		10
Friends partying: sophomore year	0		10
Talked into going out: sophomore year	0		10
Range of scale	0		100
Cronbach's alpha		.77	

Frequency of Evasive Action

How often respondent had to			
Leave home to do schoolwork: freshman year	0		10
Stay late at library: freshman year	0		10

	Minimum		Maximum
Leave home to do schoolwork: sophomore year	0		10
Stay late at library: sophomore year	0		10
Range of scale	0		40
Cronbach's alpha		.71	

Support for Academics

How important among friends was it to . . .			
Attend class regularly	0		10
Study hard	0		10
Get good grades	0		10
Go to graduate or professional school	0		10
Range of scale	0		40
Cronbach's alpha		.76	

Support for Social Life

How important among friends was it to . . .			
Be willing to party	0		10
Be popular	0		10
Hang out with friends	0		10
Range of scale	0		30
Cronbach's alpha		.41	

Stereotype Internalization

Degree to which respondent sees own group as . . .			
Unintelligent	0		6
Lazy	0		6
Giving up easily	0		6
Range of scale	0		18
Cronbach's alpha		.61	

Stereotype Externalization

Expect out-group (whites/Latinos) to discriminate	0		10
Expect out-group (Asians/ blacks) to discriminate	0		10
If instructors hold stereotypes will affect evaluation	0		10
If students hold stereotypes will affect evaluation	0		10
Range of scale	0		40
Cronbach's alpha		.59	

	Minimum		Maximum
Performance Burden			
If instructors know difficulty will think less of R	0		10
If students know difficulty will think less of R	0		10
If R excels academically reflects positively on group	0		10
If R does poorly academically reflects negatively on group	0		10
R does not want to look foolish or stupid in class	0		10
If R does not do well, people look down on others like R	0		10
How conscious of out-group (white/Latino) perceptions	0		10
How conscious of out-group (Asian/black) perceptions	0		10
How conscious of how teachers perceive you	0		10
Range of scale	0		90
Cronbach's alpha		.71	
Social Support from Four Closest Friends			
How often goes to friend for advice	0		4
How often friend accepts no matter what	0		4
How often friend understands what R is really like	0		4
How often shares inner feelings with friend	0		4
Range of scale (across 4 contacts)	0		64
Cronbach's alpha		.85	
Negative Reactions from In-group			
From friends for intergroup dating	0		4
From family for intergroup dating	0		4
From strangers for intergroup dating	0		4
Harassment from in group for association w/ out-group	0		4
Range of scale	0		16
Cronbach's alpha		.68	

	Minimum		Maximum
Negative Reactions from Out-group			
From strangers in partner's group for intergroup dating	0		4
From other strangers for intergroup dating	0		4
Range of scale	0		8
Cronbach's alpha		.78	
Campus Racial Climate			
Made to feel self-conscious by classmates	0		4
Made to feel self-conscious by professors	0		4
Made to feel self-conscious just walking around	0		4
Heard derogatory remarks from students	0		4
Heard derogatory remarks from professors	0		4
Heard derogatory remarks from others	0		4
Professor discouraged from speaking in class	0		4
Professor or adviser discouraged from course of study	0		4
Professor gave unfair grade because of race	0		4
Range of scale	0		36
Cronbach's alpha		.800	
Satisfaction with College			
Satisfaction with intellectual development	0		4
Satisfaction with social life	0		4
Experience so far	0		4
Range of scale (averaged)	0		4
Cronbach's alpha		.673	

References

Adelman, Clifford. 1999. *Answers in the Tool Box: Academic Intensity, Attendance Patterns, and Bachelor's Degree Attainment*. Washington, DC: Office of Educational Research and Improvement, U.S. Department of Education.

Allen, Walter R., Edgar G. Epps, and Nesha Z. Haniff. 1991. *College in Black and White: African American Studies in Predominantly White and in Historically Black Universities*. Albany: State University of New York Press.

Alon, Sigal, and Marta Tienda. 2004. "Assessing the 'Mismatch' Hypothesis: Differentials in College Graduation Rates by Institutional Selectivity." Working Paper, Office of Population Research, Princeton University.

Anaya, Guadalupe. 1992. "Cognitive Development among College Undergraduates." Doctoral Dissertation, Graduate School of Education and Information Studies, University of California at Los Angeles.

———. 1996. "College Experiences and Student Learning: The Influence of Active Learning, College Environments, and Cocurricular Activities." *Journal of College Student Development* 37:611–22.

Anderson, James, and Dara N. Byrne. 2004. *The Unfinished Agenda of Brown v. Board of Education*. New York: John Wiley and Sons.

Angoff, William H., and Eugene G. Johnson. 1990. "The Differential Impact of Curriculum on Aptitude Test Scores." *Journal of Educational Measurement* 27:291–305.

Arnold, James C., George D. Kuh, Nicholas Vesper, and John H. Schuh. 1993. "Student Age and Enrollment Status as Determinants of Learning and Personal Development and Metropolitan Institutions." *Journal of College Student Development* 34:11–16.

Aronson, Joshua, Diane M. Quinn, and Steven J. Spencer. 1998. "Stereotype Threat and the Academic Under-performance of Minorities and Women."

In Janet K. Swim and Charles Stangor, eds., *Prejudice: The Target's Perspective*. San Diego: Academic Press.

Astin, Alexander W. 1993. *What Matters in College? Four Critical Years Revisited*. San Francisco: Jossey-Bass.

Astin, Alexander W., and Linda J. Sax. 1998. "How Undergraduates Are Affected by Service Participation." *Journal of College Student Development* 39:251–63.

Banaji, Mahzarin, and Christopher D. Hardin. 1996. "Automatic Stereotyping." *Psychological Science* 7:136–41.

Bargh, John A. 1997. "The Automaticity of Everyday Life." Pp. 1–61 in Robert S. Wyer, ed., *The Automaticity of Everyday Life: Advances in Social Cognition*, volume 10. Mahwah, NJ: Lawrence Erlbaum.

Baugh, John. 1983. *Black Street Speech: Its History, Structure, and Survival*. Austin: University of Texas Press.

Becker, Gary S., and H. Gregg Lewis. 1973. "On the Interaction between the Quantity and Quality of Children." *Journal of Political Economy* 81: S279–S288.

Beeson, Melisa J., and Roger D. Wessel. 2002. "The Impact of Working on Campus on the Academic Persistence of Freshmen. *Journal of Student Financial Aid* 32:37–45.

Bobo, Lawrence. 1997. "Race, Public Opinion, and the Social Sphere." *Public Opinion Quarterly* 61:1–15.

Bobo, Lawrence, and Ryan A. Smith. 1998. "From Jim Crow Racism to Laissez-Faire Racism: The Transformation of Racial Attitudes in America." Pp. 182–220 in Wendy Katkin, Ned Landsman, and Andrea Tyree, eds., *Beyond Pluralism: Essays on the Conception of Groups and Group Identities in America*. Urbana: University of Illinois Press.

Bogle, Donald. 2003. *Toms, Coons, Mulattoes, Mammies & Bucks: An Interpretive History of Blacks in American Films*. 4th edition. New York: Continuum International Publishing.

Bohr, Louise, Amaury Nora, and Patrick T. Terenzini. 1995. "Do Black Students Learn More at Historical Black or Predominantly White Colleges?" *Journal of College Student Development* 36:75–85.

Bowen, William G., and Derek Bok. 1998. *The Shape of the River: Long-Term Consequences of Considering Race in College and University Admissions*. Princeton, NJ: Princeton University Press.

Bowen, William G., Martin A. Kurzweil, Eugene M. Tobin, and Susanne C. Pichler. 2005. *Equity and Excellence in American Higher Education*. Charlottesville: University of Virginia Press.

Bowen, William G., and Sarah A. Levin. 2003. *Reclaiming the Game: College Sports and Educational Values*. Princeton, NJ: Princeton University Press.

Bowles, Samuel, and Herbert Gintis. 1976. *Schooling in Capitalist America: Educational Reform and the Contradictions of Economic Life*. New York: Basic Books.

Bremner, J. Douglas. 2002. *Does Stress Damage the Brain? Understanding Trauma-Related Disorders from a Neurological Perspective*. New York: Norton.

Brufee, Kenneth A. 1993. *Collaborative Learning: Higher Education Interdependence and the Authority of Knowledge*. Baltimore: Johns Hopkins University Press.

Cameron, Stephen V., and James J. Heckman. 1999. "Can Tuition Combat Rising Wage Inequality?" Pp. 76–124 in Marvin H. Kosters, ed., *Financial College Tuition: Government Policies and Educational Priorities*. Washington, DC: American Enterprise Institute.

Carter, Rita. 1999. *Mapping the Mind*. Berkeley: University of California Press.

Charles, Camille Z. 2000. "Residential Segregation in Los Angeles." Pp. 167–219 in Lawrence D. Bobo, Melvin L. Oliver, James H. Johnson, Jr., and Abel Valenzuela, Jr., eds., *Prismatic Metropolis: Inequality in Los Angeles*. New York: Russell Sage Foundation.

———. 2001. "Processes of Residential Segregation." Pp. 217–71 in Alice O'Connor, Chris Tilly, and Lawrence Bobo, eds., *Urban Inequality: Evidence from Four Cities*. New York: Russell Sage Foundation.

———. 2003. "The Dynamics of Racial Residential Segregation." *Annual Review of Sociology* 29:67–207.

Charles, Camille Z., Douglas S. Massey, and Gniesha Dinwiddie. 2004. "The Continuing Consequences of Segregation." *Social Science Quarterly* 85:1353–74.

Charles, Camille Z., Kimberly C. Torres, and Rachelle J. Brunn. 2008. "Black Like Who? Exploring the Diverse Identities and Experiences of Black College Students." *Social Forces*, forthcoming.

Chávez, Lydia. 1998. *The Color Bind: California's Battle to End Affirmative Action*. Berkeley: University of California Press.

Chickering, Arthur W., and Zelda F. Gamson. 1991. *Applying the Seven Principles for Good Practice in Undergraduate Education*. San Francisco: Jossey-Bass.

Christie, Nancy G., and Sarah M. Dinham. 1991. "Institutional and External Influences on Social Integration in the Freshman Year." *Journal of Higher Education* 62:412–28.

Clotfelter, Charles T. 1991. "Financial Aid and Public Policy." Pp. 89–123 in Charles T. Glotfelter, Ronald G. Ehrenberg, Malcolm Getz, and John J. Siegfried, eds., *Economic Challenges in Higher Education*. Chicago: University of Chicago Press.

Cofer, James, and Patricia Somers. 1999. An Analytical Approach to Understanding Student Debt Load Response." *Journal of Student Financial Aid* 29:25–54.

College Board. 2005a. *The College Board College Handbook 2006: All-New 43rd Edition*. New York: College Board.

College Board. 2005b. "Tuition Increases Slow at Public Colleges, According to the College Board's 2005 Reports on College Pricing and Financial Aid." Press Release, October 18, 2005. New York: College Board. Accessed on December 31, 2005: http://www.collegeboard.com/press/article/0,,48884,00.html.

Conley, Dalton. 1999. *Being Black, Living in the Red: Race, Wealth, and Social Policy in America*. Berkeley: University of California Press.

Cottell, Philip G. 1996. "A Union of Collaborative Learning and Cooperative Learning: An Overview of this Issue." *Journal on Excellence in College Teaching* 7:1–3.

Crocker, Jennifer, and Brenda Major. 1989. "Social Stigma and Self-esteem: The Self-protective Properties of Stigma." *Psychological Review* 96:608–30.

Crocker, Jennifer, and Diane Quinn. 1998. "Racism and Self-esteem." Pp. 169–87 in Jennifer Eberhardt and Susan T. Fiske, eds., *Confronting Racism: The Problem and the Response*. Thousand Oaks, CA: Sage Publications.

Curry, George. 1996. *The Affirmative Action Debate*. New York: Basic Books.

Davis, Todd M., and Patricia H. Murrell. 1993. "A Structural Model of Perceived Academic, Personal, and Vocational Gains Related to College Student Responsibility." *Research in Higher Education* 34:267–89.

DeSousa, D. Jason, and George D. Kuh. 1996. "Does Institutional Racial Composition Make a Difference in What Black Students Gain from College?" *Journal of College Student Development* 37:257–67.

Devine, Patricia G., and Kristin A. Vasquez. 1998. "The Rocky Road to Positive Intergroup Relations." Pp. 234–62 in Jennifer L. Eberhardt and Susan T. Fiske, eds., *Confronting Racism: The Problem and the Response*. Thousand Oaks, CA: Sage Publications.

Dickens, William T., and Thomas J. Kane. 1999. "Racial Test Score Differences as Evidence of Reverse Discrimination: Less than Meets the Eye." *Industrial Relations* 38:331–63.

Dovidio, John F., K. Kawakami, K. Johnson, C. Johnson, and A. Howard. 1997. "On the Nature of Prejudice: Automatic and Controlled Processes." *Personality and Social Psychology Bulletin* 24:339–53.

Espenshade, Thomas J., Chang Y. Chung, and Joan L. Walling. 2004. "Admission Preferences for Minority Studies, Athletes, and Legacies at Elite Universities." *Social Science Quarterly* 85:1422–46.

Eyler, Janet. 1993. "Comparing the Impact of Two Internship Experiences on Student Learning." *Journal of Comparative Education* 29:41–52.

———. 1994. "Graduates' Assessment of the Impact of a Full-Time College Internship on Their Personal and Professional Lives." *College Student Journal* 29:186–94.

Eyler, Janet, and Dwight E. Giles, Jr. 1999. *Where's the Learning in Service Learning?* San Francisco: Jossey-Bass.

Fantuzzo, John W., Linda A. Dimeff, and Shari L. Fox. 1989. "Reciprocal Peer Tutoring: A Multimodal Assessment of Effectiveness with College Students. *Teaching of Psychology* 16:133–35.

Farley, Reynolds, and William H. Frey. 1994. "Changes in the Segregation of Whites from Blacks during the 1980s: Small Steps toward a More Integrated Society." *American Sociological Review* 59:23–45.

Feagin, Joe R., Hernan Vera, and Nikita O. Imani. 1996. *The Agony of Education: Black Students at White Colleges and Universities*. New Brunswick, NJ: Rutgers University Press.

Fischer, Mary J., and Douglas S. Massey. 2005. "The Effect of Childhood Segregation on Minority Academic Performance at Selective Colleges." *Ethnic and Racial Studies* 29:1–26.

———. 2007. "The Academic Effects of Affirmative Action in Higher Education." *Social Science Research* 36:531–49.

Fiske, Edward B. 2005. *Fiske Guide to Colleges 2006*. New York: Sourcebooks.

Fiske, Susan T. 2003. *Social Beings: A Core Motives Approach to Social Psychology*. New York: Wiley.

Fiske, Susan T., and Shelly E. Taylor. 1991. *Social Cognition*. New York: McGraw Hill.

Fleming, Jacqueline. 2002. "Who Will Succeed in College? When the SAT Predicts Black Students' Performance." *Review of Higher Education* 25:281–96.

Fleming, Jacqueline, and Nancy Garcia. 1998. "Are Standardized Tests Fair to African Americans? Predictive Validity of the SAT in Black and White Colleges. *Journal of Higher Education* 69:471–95.

Flowers, Lamont, Steven J. Osterlind, Ernest T. Pascarella, and Christopher T. Pierson. 2001. "How Much Do Students Learn in College? Cross Sectional Estimates Using the College BASE." *Journal of Higher Education* 72:565–83.

Flowers, Lamont, and Ernest T. Pascarella. 1999. "Cognitive Effects of College Racial Composition on African-American Students after Three Years of College. *Journal of College Student Development* 40:669–77.

Fredrickson, George M. 2002. *Racism: A Short History*. Princeton, NJ: Princeton University Press.

Glazer, Nathan. 1976. *Affirmative Discrimination: Ethnic Inequality and Public Policy*. New York: Basic Books.

Gleason, Philip M. 1993. "College Student Employment, Academic Progress, and Postcollege Labor Market Success." *Journal of Student Financial Aid* 23:5–14.

Golden, Daniel. 2006. *The Price of Admission: How America's Ruling Class Buys Its Way into Elite Colleges—and Who Gets Left Outside the Gates*. New York: Crown Books.

Gould, Elizabeth, P. Tanapat, Bruce S. McEwen, G. Flugge, and E. Fuchs. 1998. "Proliferation of Granule Cell Precursors in the Dentate Gyrus of Adult Monkeys Is Diminished by Stress." *Proceedings of the National Academy of Sciences USA* 95:3168–71.

Gould, Stephen J. 1981. *The Mismeasure of Man*. New York: Norton.

Gratz v. Bollinger. 2003. 123 S. Ct. 2411.

Gray, Maryann J., Sandra Geschwind, Elizabeth H. Ondaatje, Abby Robyn, Stephen P. Klein, and Linda J. Sax. 1996. *Evaluation of Learn and Serve America, Higher Education: First Year Report*. Washington, DC: Rand Corporation.

Grosset, Jane M. 1991. "Patterns of Integration, Commitment, and Student Characteristics and Retention among Younger and Older Students." *Research in Higher Education* 32:159–78.

Grutter v. Bollinger. 2003. 123 S. Ct. 2325.

Hagedorn, Linda S., M. Vali Siadat, Shereen F. Fogel, Ernest T. Pascarella, and Amaury Nora. 1999. "Success in College Mathematics: Comparisons between Remedial and Nonremedial First-Year College Students. *Research in Higher Education* 40:261–84.

Hallinan, Maureen T. 1982. "The Peer Influence Process." *Studies in Educational Evaluation* 7 (3): 285–306.

———. 1983. "Commentary: New Directions for Research on Peer Influences." Pp. 219–31 in Joyce Epstein and Nancy Karweit, eds., *Friends in School*. New York: Academic Press.

Hanushek, Eric A. 1992. "The Trade-off between Child Quantity and Quality." *Journal of Political Economy* 100 (1): 84–117.

Hauser, Robert M., Shu-Ling Tsai, and William H. Sewell. 1983. "A Model of Stratification with Response Error in Social and Psychological Variables." *Sociology of Education* 56:20–46.

Heller, Donald E. 1997. "Student Price Response in Higher Education." *Journal of Higher Education* 68:624–59.

———. 2002. *Condition of Access: Higher Education for Lower Income Students*. New York: Praeger.

———. 2003. *Informing Public Policy: Financial Aid and Student Persistence*. Boulder, CO: Western Interstate Commission for Higher Education.

Herrnstein, Richard, and Charles Murray. 1994. *The Bell Curve: Intelligence and Class Structure in American Life*. New York: Free Press.

Higginbotham, A. Leon, Jr. 1996. *Shades of Freedom: Racial Politics and Presumptions of the American Legal Process*. New York: Oxford University Press.

Hochschild, Jennifer L. 1995. *Facing Up to the American Dream: Race, Class, and the Soul of the Nation*. Princeton, NJ: Princeton University Press.

Holmes, T. H. 1974. "Life Change and Illness Susceptibility." Pp. 45–72 in B. S. Dohrenwend and B. P. Dohrenwend, eds., *Stressful Life Events: Their Nature and Effects*. New York: Wiley.

Holmes, T. H., and M. Masuda. 1974. "Life Changes and Illness Susceptibility." *Journal of Human Stress* 4:3–15

Holmes, T. H., and R. H. Rahe. 1967. "The Social Readjustment Rating Scale." *Journal of Psychosomatic Research* 11:213–18.

Holzer, Harry, and David Neumark. 2000. "Assessing Affirmative Action." *Journal of Economic Literature* 38:483–568.

Horn, Laura J., and Jennifer Berktold. 1998. *Profile of Undergraduates in U.S. Postsecondary Education Institutions: 1995–96, with an Essay on Undergraduates Who Work*. Washington, DC: Office of Educational Research and Improvement, U.S. Department of Education.

Hoxby, Caroline M., ed. 2004. *College Choices: The Economics of Where to Go, When to Go, and How to Pay for It*. Chicago: University of Chicago Press.

Hughes, Everett. 1945. "Dilemmas and Contradictions of Status." *American Journal of Sociology* 50:353–59.

Iceland, John, Daniel H. Weinberg, and Erika Steinmetz. 2002. *Racial and Ethnic Residential Segregation in the United States, 1980–2000*. Washington, DC: U.S. Bureau of the Census.

Iceland, John, and Rima Wilkes. 2006. "Does Socioeconomic Status Matter? Race, Class, and Residential Segregation." *Social Problems* 53:248–73.

Jacobs, Jerry A. 1986. "The Sex Segregation of Fields of Study: Trends during the College Years." *Journal of Higher Education* 57:134–54.

———. 1999. "Gender and the Stratification of Colleges." *Journal of Higher Education* 70:161–87.

Jencks, Christopher. 1972. *Inequality: A Reassessment of Family and Schooling in America*. New York: Basic Books.

Jencks, Christopher, and Meredith Phillips. 1998. *The Black-White Test Score Gap*. Washington, DC: Brookings Institution.

Johnstone, Karla M., Hollis Ashbaugh, and Terry D. Warfield. 2002. "Effects of Repeated Practice and Contextual-Writing Experiences on College Students' Writing Skills." *Journal of Educational Psychology* 94:305–15.

Jones, Elizabeth A., and James L. Ratcliff. 1991. "Which General Education Curriculum Is Better: Core Curriculum or the Distribution Requirement?" *Journal of General Education* 40:69–100.

Kane, Thomas J. 1998. "Racial and Ethnic Preferences in College Admissions." In Christopher Jencks and Meredith Phillips, eds., *The Black-White Test Score Gap*. Washington, DC: Brookings Institution.

Kao, Grace, and Marta Tienda. 1998. "Educational Aspirations of Minority Youth." *American Journal of Education* 106:349–84.

Kasinitz, Philip. 1992. *Caribbean New York: Black Immigrants and the Politics of Race*. Ithaca, NY: Cornell University Press.

Karabel, Jerome. 2005. *The Chosen: The Hidden History of Admission and Exclusion at Harvard, Yale, and Princeton*. New York: Houghton Mifflin.

Keister, Lisa A. 2000. *Wealth in America: Trends in Inequality*. New York: Cambridge University Press.

Kerckhoff, Alan C., and Richard T. Campbell. 1977. "Black-White Differences in the Educational Attainment Process." *Sociology of Education* 50:15–27.

Kern-Foxworth, Marilyn. 1994. *Aunt Jemima, Uncle Ben, and Rastus: Blacks in Advertising Yesterday, Today, and Tomorrow*. New York: Praeger.

King, Jacqueline E. 2002. *Crucial Choices: How Students' Financial Decisions Affect Their Academic Success*. Washington, DC: Center for Policy Analysis, American Council on Education.

Kohn, Melvin. 1985. *Class and Conformity: A Study in Values*. 2nd edition. Chicago: University of Chicago Press.

Kozol, Jonathan. 1991. *Savage Inequalities: Children in America's Schools*. New York: Crown Publishers.

———. 2005. *The Shame of the Nation: The Restoration of Apartheid Schooling in America*. New York: Crown Publishers.

Kuh, George D. 1993. "In Their Own Words: What Students Learn Outside the Classroom." *American Educational Research Journal* 30:277–304.

Kuh, George D., and Shouping Hu. 2001. "The Effects of Student-Faculty Interaction in the 1990s. *Review of Higher Education* 24:309–32.

Kuh, George D., Jullian Kinzie, John H. Schuh, and Elizabeth J. Whitt. 2005. *Student Success in College: Creating Conditions That Matter*. San Francisco: Jossey-Bass.

Kuh, George D., Elizabeth J. Whitt, Rosalind E. Andreas, James W. Lyons, and C. Carney Strange. 1991. *Involving Colleges: Successful Approaches to Fostering Student Learning and Personal Development Outside the Classroom*. San Francisco: Jossey-Bass.

Labov, William. 1972. *Language in the Inner City: Studies in the Black English Vernacular*. Philadelphia: University of Pennsylvania Press.

Labov, William, and Wendell A. Harris. 1986. "De Facto Segregation of Black and White Vernaculars." Pp. 1–24 in David Sankoff, ed., *Current Issues in Linguistic Theory 53: Diversity and Diachrony*. Amsterdam: John Benjamins Publishing.

Lareau, Annette. 2000. *Home Advantage: Social Class and Parental Intervention in Elementary Education*. 2nd edition. Lanham, MD: Rowan and Littlefield.

———. 2003. *Unequal Childhoods: Class, Race, and Family Life*. Berkeley: University of California Press.

Lehman, Darrin R., and Richard E. Nisbett. 1990. "A Longitudinal Study of the Effects of Undergraduate Training on Reasoning." *Developmental Psychology* 26:952–60.

Lemann, Nicholas. 1999. *The Big Test: The Secret History of the American Meritocracy*. New York: Farrar Straus Giroux.

Leppel, Karen. 2002. "Similarities and Differences in the College Persistence of Men and Women." *Review of Higher Education* 25:433–50.

Lokos, Lionel. 1971. *The New Racism: Reverse Discrimination in America*. New York: Arlington House Publishers.

Lounsbury, John W., and Daniel L. DeNeui. 1995. "Psychological Sense of Community on Campus." *College Student Journal* 29:170–77.

Manning, M. M. 1998. *Slave in a Box: The Strange Career of Aunt Jemima*. Charlottesville: University Press of Virginia.

Markus, Gregory B., Jeffrey P. Howard, and David C. King. 1993. "Integrating Community Service and Classroom Instruction Enhances Learning: Results from an Experiment." *Educational Evaluation and Policy Analysis* 15:410–19.

Massey, Douglas S. 1990. "American Apartheid: Segregation and the Making of the Underclass." *American Journal of Sociology* 95:1153–88.

———. 2001. "Segregation and Violent Crime in Urban America." Pp. 317–46 in Elijah Anderson and Douglas S. Massey, eds., *Problem of the Century: Racial Stratification in the United States*. New York: Russell Sage Foundation.

———. 2004. "Segregation and Stratification: A Biosocial Perspective." *DuBois Review: Social Science Research on Race* 2:7–26.

———. 2006. "Social Background and Academic Performance Differentials: White and Minority Students at Selective Colleges." *American Law and Economics Review* 8 (2): 1–20.

Massey, Douglas S., Camille Z. Charles, Garvey F. Lundy, and Mary J. Fischer. 2003. *The Source of the River: The Social Origins of Freshmen at America's Selective Colleges and Universities*. Princeton, NJ: Princeton University Press.

Massey, Douglas S., Camille Z. Charles, Margarita Mooney, and Kimberly Torres. 2007. "Black Immigrants and Black Natives Attending Selective Colleges and Universities in the United States." *American Journal of Education* 113:243–71.

Massey, Douglas S., and Nancy A. Denton. 1989. "Hypersegregation in U.S. Metropolitan Areas: Black and Hispanic Segregation along Five Dimensions." *Demography* 26:373–93.

———. 1993. *American Apartheid: Segregation and the Making of the Underclass*. Cambridge, MA: Harvard University Press.

Massey, Douglas S., and Mary J. Fischer. 1999. "Does Rising Income Bring Integration? New Results for Blacks, Hispanics, and Asians in 1990." *Social Science Research* 28:316–26.

———. 2000. "How Segregation Concentrates Poverty." *Ethnic and Racial Studies* 23:670–91.

———. 2005. "Stereotype Threat and Academic Performance: New Data from the National Longitudinal Survey of Freshmen." *The DuBois Review: Social Science Research on Race* 2:45–68.

Massey, Douglas S., and Margarita Mooney. 2006. "Factors Affecting School Choice among Students at Selective Colleges." Working Paper, Office of Population Research, Princeton University.

———. 2007. "The Effects of America's Three Affirmative Action Programs on Academic Performance." *Social Problems* 54:99–117.

McDonough, Patricia M. 1997. *Choosing Colleges: How Social Class and Schools Structure Opportunity*. Albany: State University of New York Press.

McEwen, Bruce, and Elizabeth N. Lasley. 2002. *The End of Stress as We Know It*. Washington, DC: Joseph Henry Press.

McWhorter, John. 2000. *Losing the Race: Self-sabotage in Black America*. New York: Free Press.

Meltzer, Tom, Christopher Maier, Carson Brown, Julie Doherty, Andrew Friedman, and Robert Franek. 2005. *Best 361 Colleges, 2006*. Princeton, NJ: Princeton Review.

Michelson, William. 2005. *Time Use: Expanding the Explanatory Power of the Social Sciences*. Boulder, CO: Paradigm Publishers.

Morgan, Stephen L. 2005. *On the Edge of Commitment: Educational Attainment and Race in the United States*. Stanford, CA: Stanford University Press.

Mruk, Christopher J. 1999. *Self-esteem: Research, Theory, and Practice*. New York: Springer.

Nora, Amaury, Alberto F. Cabrera, Linda S. Hagedorn, and Ernest T. Pascarella. 1996. "Differential Impacts of Academic and Social Experiences on College-Related Behavioral Outcomes across Different Ethnic and Gender Groups at Four-Year Institutions." *Research in Higher Education* 37:427–51.

Ogbu, John U. 1977. *Minority Education and Caste: The American System in Cross-cultural Perspective*. New York: Academic Press.

———. 1981. "Education, Clientage, and Social Mobility: Caste and Social Change in the United States and Nigeria." In Gerald D. Berreman, ed., *Social Inequality: Comparative and Developmental Approaches*. New York: Academic Press.

———. 1991. "Minority Responses and School Experiences." *Journal of Psychohistory* 18:433–56.

Oliver, Melvin L., and Thomas M. Shapiro. 1997. *Black Wealth, White Wealth: A New Perspective on Racial Inequality*. New York: Routledge.

Orfield, Gary. 2001. *Schools More Separate: Consequences of a Decade of Resegregation*. Cambridge, MA: Harvard Civil Rights Project.

Osterlind, Steven J. 1996. "Collegians' Scholastic Achievement in General Education: A National Look." Paper presented at the Annual Meetings of the American Educational Research Association, New York, April.

———. 1997. *Collegian Achievement in General Education: A National Look*. Washington, DC: George Washington University.

Owen, David. 1999. *None of the Above, Revised: The Truth behind the SATs*. Lanham, MD: Rowan and Littlefield.

Oyserman, Daphna, Markus Kemmelmeier, Stephanie Fryberg, Herzi Brosh, and Gamera Hart-Johnson. 2003. "Racial and Ethnic Schemas." *Social Psychology Quarterly* 66:333–47.

Pascarella, Ernest T., Louise Bohr, Amaury Nora, Mary Desler, and Barbara J. Zusman. 1994. "Impacts of On-Campus and Off-Campus Work on First-Year Cognitive Outcomes." *Journal of College Student Development* 35:364–70.

Pascarella, Ernest T., Louise Bohr, Amaury Nora, and Patrick T. Terenzini. 1995. "Intercollegiate Athletic Participation and Freshman-Year Cognitive Outcomes." *Journal of Higher Education* 66:369–87.

Pascarella, Ernest T., Louise Bohr, Amaury Nora, Barbara J. Zusman, Patricia Inman, and Mary Desler. 1993. "Cognitive Impacts of Living on Campus versus Commuting to College." *Journal of College Student Development* 34:216–20.

Pascarella, Ernest T., Marcia I. Edison, Amaury Nora, Linda S. Hagedorn, and Patrick T. Terenzini. 1998. "Does Work Inhibit Cognitive Development during College?" *Educational Evaluation and Policy Analysis* 20:75–93.

Pascarella, Ernest T., Marcia I. Edison, Elizabeth J. Whitt, Amaury Nora, Linda S. Hagedorn, and Patrick T. Terenzini. 1996. "Cognitive Effects of Greek Affiliation during the First Year of College." *National Association of Student Personnel Administrators Journal* 33:242–59.

Pascarella, Ernest T., Lamont Flowers, and Elizabeth J. Whitt. 2001. "Cognitive Effects of Greek Affiliation in College: Additional Evidence. *National Association of Student Personnel Administrators Journal* 38:280–301.

Pascarella, Ernest T., and Patrick T. Terenzini. 2005. *How College Affects Students: A Third Decade of Research*. San Francisco: Jossey-Bass.

Pascarella, Ernest T., Rachel Truckenmiller, Amaury Nora, Patrick T. Terenzini, Marcia Edison, Linda Serra Hagedorn. 1999. "Cognitive Impacts of Intercollegiate Athletic Participation." *Journal of Higher Education* 70:1–26.

Perry, Theresa, Claude Steele, and Asa Hilliard III. 2004. *Young, Gifted, and Black: Promoting High Achievement among African American Students*. Boston: Beacon Press.

Pettigrew, Thomas F. 1998. Prejudice and Discrimination on the College Campus." Pp. 263–79 in Jennifer Eberhardt and Susan T. Fiske, eds., *Confronting Racism: The Problem and the Response*. Thousand Oaks, CA: Sage Publications.

Phillips, Meredith, Jeanne Brooks-Gunn, Greg J. Duncan, Pamela Klebanov, and Jonathan Crane. 1998. "Family Background, Parenting Practices, and the Black-White Test Score Gap." Pp. 103–49 in Christopher Jencks and Meredith Phillips, eds., *The Black-White Test Score Gap*. Washington, DC: Brookings Institution Press.

Pike, Gary R. 1991. "Using Structural Equation Models with Latent Variables to Study Student Growth and Development." *Research in Higher Education* 32:499–524.

———. 1992. "The Components of Construct Validity: A Comparison of Two Measures of General Education." *Journal of General Education* 41:130–59.

Pike, Gary R., and Jerry W. Askew. 1990. "The Impact of Fraternity or Sorority Membership on Academic Involvement and Learning Outcomes." *National Association of Student Personnel Administrators Journal* 28:13–19.

Portes, Alejandro, and Kenneth L. Wilson. 1976. "Black-White Differences in Educational Attainment." *American Sociological Review* 41:414–31.

Ratcliff, James L., and Elizabeth A. Jones. 1993. "Coursework Cluster Analysis." Pp. 256–59 in Trudy W. Banta, ed., *Making a Difference: Outcomes of a Decade of Assessment in Higher Education*. San Francisco: Jossey-Bass.

Riggio, Ronald E., John W. Fantuzzo, Sharon Connelly, and Linda A. Dimeff. 1991. "Reciprocal Peer Tutoring: A Classroom Strategy for Promoting Academic and Social Integration in Undergraduate Students." *Journal of Social Behavior and Personality* 6:387–96.

Rockquemore, Kerry Ann, and David L. Brunsma. 2002. *Beyond Black: Biracial Identity in America*. Thousand Oaks, CA: Sage Publications.

Rosenberg, Morris, and Roberta G. Simmons. 1971. *Black and White Self-esteem: The Urban School Child*. Washington, DC: American Sociological Association.

Rosenzweig, Mark R. and Kenneth I. Wolpin. 1980. "Testing the Quantity-Quality Fertility Model: The Use of Twins as a Natural Experiment." *Econometrica* 48 (1): 227–40.

Rothstein, Richard. 2004. *Class and Schools: Using Social, Economic, and Educational Reform to Close the Black-White Achievement Gap*. New York: Teachers College Press, Columbia University.

Rushton, J. Philippe. 2000. *Race, Evolution, and Behavior: A Life History Perspective.* Port Huron, MI: Charles Darwin Research Institute Press.

Sampson, Robert J., Jeffrey D. Morenoff, and Thomas Gannon-Rowley. 2002. "Assessing Neighborhood Effects: Social Processes and New Directions in Research." *Annual Review of Sociology* 28:443–78.

Schmidt, Peter. 2007. *Color and Money: How Rich White Kids Are Winning the War over College Affirmative Action.* New York: Palgrave Macmillan.

Schuman, Howard, Charlotte Steeh, Lawrence Bobo, and Maria Kryusan. 1997. *Racial Attitudes in American: Trends and Interpretations.* Revised edition. Cambridge, MA: Harvard University Press.

Sellin, Thorsten, and Marvin E. Wolfgang. 1964. *The Measurement of Delinquency.* New York: Wiley.

Sewell, William H., and Robert M. Hauser. 1980. "The Wisconsin Longitudinal Study of Social and Psychological Factors in Aspirations and Achievements." *Research in Sociology of Education and Socialization* 1:59–99.

Shulman, James L., and William G. Bowen. 2001. *The Game of Life: College Sports and Educational Values.* Princeton, NJ: Princeton University Press.

Smith, Sandra, and Mignon Moore. 2000. "Intraracial Diversity and Relations among African Americans: Closeness among Black Students at a Predominantly White University." *American Journal of Sociology* 106:1–39.

Somers, Patricia. 1995. "A Comprehensive Model for Examining the Impact of Financial Aid on Enrollment and Persistence." *Journal of Student Financial Aid* 25:13–27.

Sowell, Thomas. 2004. *Affirmative Action around the World: An Empirical Study.* New Haven, CT: Yale University Press.

Spencer, Jon M. 1997. *The New Colored People: The Mixed Race Movement in America.* New York: New York University Press.

Springer, Sally P., and Marion R. Franck. 2005. *Admission Matters: What Students and Parents Need to Know about Getting into College.* San Francisco: Jossey-Bass.

St. John, Edward P. 1990. "Price Response in Persistence Decisions: An Analysis of the High School and Beyond Senior Cohort." *Research in Higher Education* 31:387–403.

———. 1991. "The Impact of Student Financial Aid: A Review of Recent Research." *Journal of Student Financial Aid* 21:18–32.

St. John, Edward P., and C. Masten. 1990. "Return on the Federal Investment in Student Financial Aid: An Assessment for the High School Class of 1972." *Journal of Student Financial Aid* 20:4–23.

Stage, Frances K., and Palisa Williams Rushin. 1993. "A Combined Model of Student Predisposition to College and Persistence in College." *Journal of College Student Development* 34:276–82.

Steele, Claude M. 1988. "The Psychology of Self-affirmation: Sustaining the Integrity of the Self." Pp. 261–302 in Leonard Berkowitz, ed., *Advances in Experimental Social Psychology*. New York: Academic Press.

———. 1992. "Race and the Schooling of Black Americans." *Atlantic Monthly* 269 (4): 68–78.

———. 1997. "A Threat in the Air: How Stereotypes Shape Intellectual Identity and Performance." *American Psychologist* 52:613–29.

———. 1998. "A Threat in the Air: How Stereotypes Shape Intellectual Identity and Performance." Pp. 234–62 in Jennifer L. Eberhardt and Susan T. Fiske, eds., *Confronting Racism: The Problem and the Response*. Thousand Oaks, CA: Sage Publications.

———. 1999. "Thin Ice: 'Stereotype Threat' and Black College Students." *Atlantic Monthly* 284 (2): 44–47, 50–54.

Steele, Claude M., and Joshua Aronson. 1995. "Stereotype Treat and the Intellectual Test Performance of African Americans." *Journal of Personality and Social Psychology* 69:797–811.

Steele, Claude M., Steven Spencer, Robert Nisbett, M. Hummell, K. Harber, and D. Schoem. 2009. "African American College Achievement: A 'Wise' Intervention." *Harvard Educational Review*, forthcoming.

Steinberg, Jacques. 2002. *The Gatekeepers: Inside the Admissions Process of a Premier College*. New York: Viking.

Sterling, P., and J. Ayer. 1988. "Allostatis: A New Paradigm to Explain Arousal Pathology." Pp. 629–49 in S. Fischer and J. Reason, eds., *Handbook of Life Stress, Cognition, and Health*. New York: Wiley.

Sweet, Frank W. 2000. *A History of the Minstrel Show*. Palm Coast, FL: Backintyme Publications.

———. 2005. *Legal History of the Color Line: The Rise and Triumph of the One-Drop Rule*. Palm Coast, FL: Backintyme Publications.

Taylor, Howard F. 1980. *The IQ Game: A Methodological Inquiry into the Heredity-Environment Controversy*. New Brunswick, NJ: Rutgers University Press.

Terenzini, P. T., L. I. Rendon, M. L. Upcraft, S. B. Millar, K. W. Allison, P. L. Gregg et al. 1994. "The Transition to College: Diverse Students, Diverse Stories." *Research in Higher Education* 35:57–73.

Thernstrom, Stephen, and Abigail Thernstrom. 1999. "Reflections on the Shape of the River." *UCLA Law Review* 46:1583–1631.

———. 2003. *No Excuses: Closing the Racial Gap in Learning*. New York: Simon and Schuster.

Thomas, William I., and Dorothy S. Thomas. 1929. *The Child in America*. 2nd edition. New York: Alfred Knopf.

Tinto, Vincent. 1993. *Leaving College: Rethinking the Causes and Cures of Student Attrition*. 2nd edition. Chicago: University of Chicago Press.

Topping, Keith J. 1996. "The Effectiveness of Peer Tutoring in Further and Higher Education: A Typology and Review of the Literature." *Higher Education* 32:321–45.

Torres, Kimberly C. 2008. "'Culture Shock': Black Students Account for Their Distinctiveness at an Elite College." *Ethnic and Racial Studies* 31:1–23.

Torres, Kimberly C., and Camille Z. Charles. 2004. "Metastereotypes and the Black-White Divide: A Qualitative View of Race on an Elite College Campus." *DuBois Review: Social Science Research on Race* 1:115–49.

Tucker, William H. 2002. *The Funding of Scientific Racism: Wickliffe Draper and the Pioneer Fund*. Urbana: University of Illinois Press.

U.S. General Accounting Office. 1995. "Higher Education: Restructuring Student Aid Could Reduce Low-Income Student Dropout Rate." Research Report 95-48, U.S. General Accounting Office, Washington, DC.

U.S. News and World Report. 2005. *US News Ultimate College Guide 2006*. New York: Sourcebook.

Waters, Mary C. 1999. *Black Identities: West Indian Immigrant Dreams and American Realities*. Cambridge, MA: Harvard University Press.

Watson, Lemuel W., and George D. Kuh. 1996. "The Influence of Dominant Race Environments on Student Involvement, Perceptions, and Educational Gains: A Look at Historically Black and Predominantly White Liberal Arts Institutions." *Journal of College Student Development* 27:415–24.

White, Michael J., Ann H. Kim, and Jennifer E. Glick. 2005. "Mapping Social Distance: Ethnic Residential Segregation in a Multiethnic Metro." *Sociological Methods & Research* 34: 173–203.

Whitt, Elizabeth J., Marcia I. Edison, Ernest T. Pascarella, Amaury Nora, and Patrick T. Terenzini. 1999. "Women's Perception of a 'Chilly Climate' on Cognitive Outcomes in College: Additional Evidence." *Journal of College Student Development* 40:61–78.

Wilkes, Rima, and John Iceland. 2004. "Hypersegregation in the Twenty-first Century." *Demography* 41:23–36.

Wilkie, Carolyn, and Marquita Jones. 1994. "Academic Benefits of On-Campus Employment to First-Year Developmental Education Students." *Journal of the Freshman Year Experience* 6:37–56.

Willis, Robert J. 1973. "A New Approach to the Economic Theory of Fertility Behavior." *Journal of Political Economy* 81:S14–S64.

Wilson, John K. 1995. *The Myth of Political Correctness: The Conservative Attack on Higher Education*. Durham, NC: Duke University Press.

Wolfgang, Marvin E., Robert M. Figlio, Paul E. Tracy, and Simon I. Singer. 1985. *The National Survey of Crime Severity*. Washington, DC.: U.S. Government Printing Office.

Wolfle, Lee M. 1983. "The Effects of Higher Education on Achievement for Blacks and Whites." *Research in Higher Education* 19:3–9.

Yale Daily News. 2005. *The Insider's Guide to the Colleges, 2006: 32nd Edition*. New York: St. Martin's.

Zwick, Rebecca. 2002. *Fair Game? The Use of Standardized Admissions Tests in Higher Education*. New York: Routledge.

Index

The letters *f* and *t* refer to figures and tables on the pages indicated.